D0389170

NEVER TOO YOUNG TO DIE

Also by Lewis Cole

Dream Team

A Loose Game

NEVER TOO YOUNG TO DIE

The Death of Len Bias

LEWIS COLE

Pantheon Books New York

 Published in the United States by Pantheon Books, a division of Random House, Inc., New York, and simultaneously in Canada by Random House of Canada Limited, Toronto.

Portions of this book have appeared previously in a somewhat different form in *Rolling Stone* and *Washingtonian*.

Library of Congress Cataloging-in-Publication Data

Cole, Lewis.
Never too young to die : the death of Len Bias / Lewis Cole.
p. cm.
Summary: A biography of the Maryland basketball superstar with emphasis on the events that led to his death from cocaine.
ISBN 0-394-56440-5
1. Bias, Len, 1963–1986. 2. Basketball players—United States—Biography. 3. Athletes—United States—Drug use. [1. Bias, Len, 1963–1986. 2. Basketball players. 3. Athletes—Drug use.]
I. Title.
GV884.B53C65 1989
362.29′8′092—dc20 88-43128
[B]

Book Design by Anne Scatto

Manufactured in the United States of America

First Edition

CONTENTS

For Aaron
"Anno"
born June 17, 1986

ACKNOWLEDGMENTS

This is the tale of two young black men and their encounter with three institutions of black American life: sports, drugs, and the law. As much as possible, I have tried to let the principals speak for themselves. The quotes dated 1986 are taken from newspapers, magazines, and television interviews and are identified in the text. The witness statements quoted in chapter 3 ("Investigation") are from the police interrogation records. All other quoted material is from interviews I conducted between spring 1987 and spring 1988; I have dated these statements with the handy designation "today."

I thank all those who spoke to me. Several were of especial help, and I should like to thank them individually: Robert Bonsib, Wayne Curry, Molly Dunham, the Reverend G. L. Edmund, Neal Eskin, Alan Goldstein, Neff Hudson, Tom Keyser, Peggy Liss, Thomas Morrow, Loretta Tribble, Richard Watkins, Bob Wagner, Sue Weil, and the Reverend Levi Woods.

Lester Grinspoon and James B. Bakalar's *Cocaine, A Drug and Its Social Evolution* and the hearings of the House Select Committee on Drug Abuse were invaluable guides to the chemistry and history of cocaine. Edgar Adams of the National Institute of Drug Abuse, Paul Chevigny, Lester Grinspoon, Bryan Harris and the staff at the Sasha Bruce Youth House, "Mrs. Lacey," Christine Rose, Lynn Chapman Stern, Oliver Sacks, Susan Weiss and Robert M. Post of the National Institutes of Health, and the staff of the House Select Committee provided essential aid in my understanding of the crack-cocaine plague.

I thank Andrea Miller and Laura Nixon, who ably and expeditiously transcribed the interviews.

Finally, my gratitude to those who offered encouragement, inspiration, support: David Black; Deborah Black; Susan Murcko; Doug Stern; Bob Wallace; Dale Walker; Helen Yglesias; Rafael Yglesias; my editor Wendy Wolf and her colleague Ed Cohen; my agent Peter Matson; my wife, Cathy Wein, and my son, Aaron.

"You're never too young to die. You have to live life to the fullest."

—Bernard Smith, 15 years old, on a Washington, D.C., basketball court after the death of Len Bias (quoted in the Washington Post*)*

PROLOGUE

The youth and his father arrived home a little before ten that night. Later the father testified he had never seen his son so happy. In the last two days the twenty-two-year-old had fulfilled the dream of a lifetime. He had become a professional basketball player. And not simply a player, but a star. At the National Basketball Association's annual draft, he had been chosen second by the most prestigious team in the league. The Boston Celtics, the commissioner had announced, pick . . . Leonard Bias! Confident, elegant—style meant a lot to him—Leonard had stood up and the fans in New York's Felt Forum had erupted, yelling his name, their crescendo of chants and cheers announcing one thing: the future belonged to him.

For the next half hour he answered the reporters' predictable questions. "He's a pretty cool guy," his father, who was to accompany him through the thirty-six-hour whirlwind, told one reporter. "It's hard to know what he's thinking." Not that afternoon. Leonard was effusive and poetic. Yes, he was going to buy a Mercedes with his new contract. Yes, he was eager to join a squad that featured other stars. Yes, he was looking forward to winning a championship with his new team. Yes, this was a dream come true—a dream to play in the NBA, a dream to play for the Celtics, a dream within a dream.

Then his professional responsibilities—already!—called. A flight to his new home was waiting: the Celtics wanted him to appear on the local six o'clock news.

Leonard, his father James, and a vice-president from the sports representation firm Leonard had hired to handle all legal and financial matters—he wasn't only a player, but a property, something of value—flew to Boston. There the royal treatment continued: a press conference; luxury hotel accommodations; lavish praise from Red Auerbach, the legendary Celtics president, who said no rookie in the team's storied history—not even Bob Cousy, not even Bill Russell—had ever excited keener anticipation or quicker acceptance from the fans. "He's the guy we wanted," Auerbach told the press. "He's a great kid."

The next morning Leonard began to reap the material rewards of his success. A limousine drove him and James Bias—Big James, Leonard sometimes called him—to the Reebok offices. While his agent worked out the final terms of the endorsement deal, company executives gave Leonard and Mr. Bias a tour of the plant. When they were finished the agent announced they had come to terms: one million dollars for five years, a mutually beneficial pact that in one stroke, the agent claimed, assured Leonard of lifelong financial security. Celebrating the agreement, the executives took Leonard and Mr. Bias to a promotional party. There he met some members of the Celtics and was introduced by the president of Reebok as the firm's newest "family member," before leaving with his father for the last shuttle home.

Now, finally, the plane was landing; in moments he would be safe, out from under the lights, free from questions, home.

In the airport parking lot, Leonard and Mr. Bias got into Leonard's new cobalt-blue Nissan X-Z. As soon as he had signed with his agent, Leonard had secured a fifteen-thousand-dollar loan. In school he had never seemed to have enough money and would work any job, even helping his friend Brian Tribble clean government offices, to get some cash. The car was the first thing he had acquired with his borrowed riches, arranging a lease and saying a happy goodbye to the broken-down Cutlass he had endured during his four years in college. Cars meant a lot to him; they were one of your personal signatures in the world, a measure of achievement.

They cruised past Northeast Washington and the galaxy of suburbs surrounding the capital city: Anacostia, Seat Pleasant, Landover Hills. The whole area was one world, a de facto black city that included the slums of H Street, the mansions of Kenilworth Gardens, the suburban tracts of Maryland. Here he was already a legend: Len Bias, the player who came from the street and made good, the born-again Christian who sported a thick gold chain around his neck, the boy-next-door who was a millionaire, the brother off the block who could bring the crowd to their feet with basket-rattling dunks.

The family home was in Landover. The house was a comfortably sized brown suburban ranch set on a street of tidy lawns, generous backyards, two-car garages. Though only minutes from both modern malls and desolate housing projects, the street had a fifties' feel about it, a place where teenage boys would spend their Saturday afternoons washing their fathers' sedans. That afternoon his mother had spoken about her son's fortune in the naive tone of an Andy Hardy mom. "I'm thrilled that Len was picked by the Number One team in the country," she said. "We'll celebrate as soon as he and his dad get back. I think that everything has worked out perfectly for Len in his basketball career. He played three years in high school and carried his team. He played four years in college and carried the team his last two years, and now he's going on to a team where he'll have a year or so to prepare himself to start."

When the two men reached the house, she hadn't yet returned from her church meeting. Later she said she had felt low all day, not "hurt or pain, but just a lowness I couldn't describe." Leonard waited a while, unloading free sneakers he had brought back for his family. Then, worried about other gifts left unattended in his open car, he told his father he would come back tomorrow, and took off.

It was less than ten miles from his house to the University of Maryland's College Park campus. He roomed in Washington Hall with Jeff Baxter, another hometown star. The two of them shared a three-bedroom suite with three other players from the basketball team. The sprawling university was the players' turf, where they were pampered and protected by their coach, the nationally famous Lefty Driesell. Leonard had arrived here four years earlier as a local star of still questionable ability and had emerged as an All-American, the team's adored, envied leader, arguably the most popular, best-known man on campus. A shot of him slamming the ball over his head backward into the basket adorned the cover of that season's yearbook, while the next two pages were filled with stats and awards and color shots of him at *Playboy*'s All-American Team Weekend. For his teammates and buddies Leonard was more than simply a friend. He was a natural resource. His stardom rewarded everyone he was close to: for his coaches, new respect; for a teammate, perhaps an entrance through the back door into the NBA; for his friends, the thrill of leading the life of a celebrity.

Some of his teammates were there when he arrived; they joked and congratulated him. He dumped his bags—the Celtics and Reebok had loaded him down with freebies—and called one of his many girlfriends.

The young woman came to visit for a short time. When she left, he told the other guys he was going out. Shortly past twelve he showed up at the home of his friend Brian Tribble, an ex-student who shared an apartment in the university area. Around one o'clock he was stopped on campus by a college cop who congratulated him on his success. After that he went into a College Park liquor store and bought a six-pack of Private Stock beer and a bottle of cognac, then autographed a picture for the star-struck store manager.

No one knows where he went after that—or if they do, they have not yet said. But when he reappeared at the dorm two hours later with Tribble, he wanted to have some fun. They roused two teammates, an easygoing center named Terry Long and a tall, thin sophomore forward named David Gregg. It was between two and three in the morning, the end of Leonard's long day. In the room were the six-pack, the cognac, and approximately an ounce of 88 percent pure cocaine. The boys shut the door and began to party.

DEATH

Loretta Tribble, Brian's mother, wakes early that Thursday morning. Careful not to rouse Priscilla—their appointment isn't for several hours—she rises and wanders into the living room. Outside Vista Street rests, sleepy as a Southern town, neat as a New England village, a cul-de-sac of modest one-family homes not very changed from when she first came here twenty-six years ago. The morning is still cool, the summer heat—the swampy Washington summer airlessness she has never gotten used to—has yet to hit. She sits in her chair, gathering strength for the day. Short, plump, she is the picture of an angelic grandmother, fleecy puffs of graying hair framing her even softer-looking café-au-lait skin.

She checks the clock. At nine she has to take Priscilla to the social worker. When she was two Priscilla contracted spinal meningitis; the disease left her epileptic and retarded. For the last ten years Mrs. Tribble has tended to the girl herself, maintaining her on medication. Now she is afraid Priscilla has been overmedicated. A new doctor has suggested an experimental protocol, but won't start treatment without a series of diagnostic workups. Today they are getting the results of the tests; if everything reads well there will be hope once again.

Priscilla is her oldest daughter; there are three more children, Gloria, Thomas ("Junior"), and Brian. Raising them hasn't been easy. Loretta and Tommy married young and without parental approval. Tommy was a jazz drummer and their first years were spent on the road. Then, after Priscilla was born, Mrs. Tribble suffered a heart attack; two years later, Priscilla got sick. They were in Washington at the time, far from Mrs. Tribble's hometown of Fall River, Massachusetts. Tommy decided to give up the road and learn a new trade. The two of them became upholsterers. They converted the basement into a workshop, spreading material over wooden sawhorses and plywood tables; Tommy cut the goods while Mrs. Tribble hemmed yards of fabric by hand. Their work was impeccable, and after a while they could count on a steady clientele.

As she matured, Priscilla's condition deteriorated. After the girl graduated from a special high school, she had no place to go. The Tribbles tried putting her in a home, but Loretta couldn't stand the separation and brought her back home. Brian was the one who had grown up with her, having to deal daily with his sister's affliction. Once he held her while she was racked by sixteen consecutive seizures. Mrs. Tribble remembered the boy struggling and crying as he pinioned his sister.

But now, finally, all the kids were settled down. Gloria and Junior were doing fine in their jobs. Brian was coming into his own. He had suffered his disappointments, wanting to be a basketball player, quitting school, floating around for something to do. But recently he had decided to go into the cleaning and drapery business and had just gotten a five-thousand-dollar bid for a contract. He had moved in with his friend, Mark Fobbs, to an apartment near the campus, living on his own for the first time since his abortive stay at the university. Sure, he still made mistakes. When he won the ten-thousand-dollar settlement from his motorcycle accident she hoped the money would go for a down payment on a house—that he would be the first of her kids to own some real estate. Instead he had traded in his Volvo and used the money for the first payment on a Mercedes. But it was his money, after all. She just knew Brian was going to be fine. Now, once she got Priscilla right, life could finally proceed into the satisfying calm promised as the reward for hard work and good living. Priscilla deserved this last chance. Her endurance had taught Mrs. Tribble something: your devotion to your children enabled them to survive.

The phone rings, breaking the early-morning stillness. It's Brian.

"What's the matter?" she says.

"It's Len, Momma."

His friend, Len Bias. She had seen the television news clips the day before of Leonard at the draft. He had appeared in a stylish suit he had bought in Georgetown several weeks before. At first he looked glum and deadpan. Then he smiled. She had often thought Leonard's grin transformed him—his eyes lit up, the dimple on his chin got deeper and deeper, as though he were relishing his delight in living. Afterward, Brian had called. Bias had telephoned him from his hotel room in Boston saying he was bringing home some free sneakers for Brian—Brian loved sneakers. "You believe this guy?" her son had asked her. Here he is getting drafted and he's taking the time to call and tell me he's gotten a pair of sneakers for me.

Now Brian sounds scared, out of breath.

"He's having a seizure, Momma," he says.

"What? That's crazy, Brian."

"He's not breathing."

Mrs. Tribble tells him to put Len on his side—a technique she uses with Priscilla—and hangs up. She tries to make sense of the situation. What Brian has told her *is* crazy. Bias is a perfect physical specimen. He and Brian spend hours lifting weights in the basement; he has the appetite of a horse. He loves her brownies. "Hey, shorty!" he'll tell her, while he and Brian watch television, Bias's stretched-out legs spanning her living room, "make me some of those brownies!" She finally put her foot down, telling him they weren't a rich family and she was drawing the line: from now on, he was going to have to supply his own milk.

Nine-one-one, she thinks, realizing she forgot to tell Brian to call the emergency unit.

She dials him at home. "Brian," she tells the sleepy voice on the other end of the line, "call a paramedic."

"No," says the voice.

"Where's Brian?" she asks.

Brian isn't home, the speaker says, and identifies himself as Mark's brother, Gideon.

Almost as soon as she hangs up the phone it rings again. Brian once more.

She starts to tell him to call 911, but he interrupts. Her son—smart boy—has already dialed the emergency crew on his own. The paramedics are now there, administering CPR, preparing to take Bias to the hospital.

"They can't find a heartbeat," he tells her. "This can't be, Momma. They can't find a beat."

~~~

At about the same time Mrs. Tribble is trying to reach Brian, Jeff Baxter, Bias's roommate, opens his eyes. A heavy sleeper, Baxter is groggy after last night's partying, but he senses someone in the room. The long, austere face of David Gregg with its hollow, sculpted cheeks and almond-shaped, cautious eyes looms above him.

"Get up, man," David says, "Lenny's on the floor! He's dying! He can't get up!"

Baxter rouses himself from the last hold of sleep. He is sure David is fooling. "Stop playing," he says. "It's too early in the morning."

Gregg says he isn't kidding.

Baxter gets out of bed. He's exhausted. The night before, he didn't get home from his girlfriend's until two. He entered his room and found the spoils of professional basketballdom—spanking new gym clothes, pairs of sneakers, socks, and a large gym bag emblazoned with the Boston Celtics emblem—scattered on the floor and strewn over the bed. Baxter was awed. He knelt down and rifled through the bag, surveying the treasures, thinking, Lenny is going to the Celtics! He's getting paid to play ball!

Hearing some noise from Terry Long's room, Baxter had knocked on the locked door. Maybe Lenny was there.

"Who it is?" someone asked.

"Bax," he answered.

"Guido, the killer pimp," someone joked through the door, a kidding reference to the Tom Cruise character in the movie *Risky Business*.

After a little while the door opened. Baxter greeted Terry Long, David Gregg, and Brian Tribble, whom Baxter knew from his high-school basketball days. In the last two years Tribble and Leonard had spent a lot of time together, going to clubs, hanging out. Baxter rarely joined them.
~~~

Lenny and he exchanged a high five. Lenny was excited—just like a kid with his first pair of Dr. J's, Baxter recalled later.

While the others drank beer, listened, and talked among themselves, Bias told Baxter the story of the draft. Before the picks began, Bias had been waiting up front with other invited players. A guy had come up to him and told him to pack his bags. Where am I going? Lenny had asked. Where do you think? the guy answered, the Boston Celtics. The Celtics were high on him. Larry Bird himself had said that he was going to come to training camp early that year to show him certain moves. He had already met Danny Ainge and DJ at a Reebok's reception . . .

For an hour Bias went on. Baxter listened, sipping at a bottle of Private Stock beer. No boozer—he limited himself to such refinements as strawberry daiquiris and other "girl drinks"—he had become tired almost with his first sip and finally excused himself, saying he had a class the next morning. For a moment he wondered whether or not he should tell Lenny to come to bed. Sometimes he felt Lenny was pushing himself too hard and he would tell him to get some rest. But the late hour and the presence of the other teammates and Tribble—acquaintances of Baxter, but not the crowd he hung with—silenced him. He said good night, stashed the half-empty bottle in the dorm refrigerator, and went to sleep.

Now in the flush of morning light he picks his way past the scattered trophies of Leonard's just beginning professional career. Still wondering what the hell is happening, he enters Terry Long's room.

In the familiar room, Leonard lies on the floor, eyes half open, his thick braided gold chain hanging heavily around his neck. A wisp of a white man, a paramedic, Baxter realizes, leans over the inert body attaching an oxygen mask to Leonard's face, trying to breathe life into the motionless giant.

Leonard Bias was a native son of Washington. But not the Washington of guidebooks and presidential inaugurals. Leonard's hometown was different from the nation's capital. His city even has its own name. It's called "D.C." or "the District," and ranks as a rarity among American metropolises: its ghetto is white. Drive around it—its borders are roughly a half moon sweeping into Maryland from either end of Connecticut Avenue—and you could be in a foreign country: D.C. is a virtually all-black land, an African-American city.

"City," not "ghetto." D.C. is different from other concentrations of black populations in the Northeast. First of all, official Washington is smaller and more civil than its Northern cousins. D.C., like official Washington, shares this trait. The city has a human scale. You don't find vast, frightening tracts of government housing; here even the most institutional salmon-brick federal housing projects stand no higher than three stories, the most notorious drug hangouts, frequently described after Bias's death as nightmarish war zones, turn out to be tree-lined streets where at least one substantial church exercises a civilizing influence from a corner perch. There is none of the terrifying claustrophobia of unrelieved squalor. The streets defy the monochromatic landscape of poverty and disillusion common to most Northeastern Sowetos. Instead, the corners of black Washington present a heterogeneous mix of professionals, working people, and unemployed, a whole society rather than a ravaged one—for once the sociologist's term comes true: the black *community*.

And the people in this community are different. For one, they are friendly; they display an ironic sense of humor that combines a Northerner's tough sensibility with a Southerner's grace of judgment. They are also—and ultimately this is more important—in a different relation to whites than blacks in other American cities. Here they rule. Freed from the humiliation and powerlessness that accompanies being a minority population, they behave with a relaxed expansiveness foreign to ghetto dwellers. The edge of suspicion and hostility that marks even the briefest social transactions between black and white strangers in New York is absent. Unconfined, black Americans in the District emerge as a people, possessing their own standards of beauty, social behavior, and culture, an integral, cohesive, irreducibly distinct unit of humanity.

Yet paradoxically this freedom also shows, in more dramatic relief than other places, the strict limits of black autonomy in our society. A sense of isolation and irrelevance accompanies the triumphant independence. The District is a representative part of privileged, Reaganite America; it boasts its own BMW's and Mercedes, expensive nightclubs where the drinks of choice are $125 bottles of champagne, and young professionals who possess the cool self-assurance (bolstered by a blithe historical ignorance) of the slick players of *L.A. Law*. Yet the community remains as segregated from white life as any slave quarters on a plantation, parallel to, rather than integrated into, the society. It's a fish bowl—a busy fish bowl, with sometimes well-fed, gorgeous denizens, but a fish bowl nonetheless.

One of the community's shrines is also one of its quintessential images. Cedar Hill, the home of Frederick Douglass, the black abolitionist, is an impressively bourgeois twenty-room brick-and-stucco mansion that crowns the highest point in Anacostia, the once swampy ground across the river from the Capitol. Cedar Hill was bought by Douglass in 1877, when he was seventy-one years old. The purchase was an act of spirited defiance: Douglass's all-white neighbors were unaware that the new "king of the mountain" was black, knowing him only as a bank president; Douglass reminded them daily of their arrogant ignorance as he trod the seventy-two steps leading to his castle.

Now the place is a museum kept immaculately by the government. But the memorial cools the revolutionary heat of Douglass's example. His superb defiance of local geography has been made moot. The once white suburb is now one of the poorest sections of D.C., an isolated area famous for dope deals and murders. The radical import of Douglass's legacy is dulled. Douglass's call for emancipation challenged and continues to confront the fundamental structures of our society. But in the museum Douglass is presented as just another entry in the pantheon of America's ethnic heroes—a sort of black Lafayette, or Kosiuscko, fighting for his people—rather than as a revolutionary, a latter-day Tom Paine who spoke to the whole society, white as well as black. "Oh," one Negro teacher who was escorting her class around the house remarked to a visiting white, "*you're* interested in black history?" Standing on Douglass's porch you feel the house isn't a triumphant palace but a place of permanent exile, separated by the river from the power represented by the Capitol dome.

Autonomy without power, recognition without relevance—

Douglass's fate is D.C.'s. For all of the District's spirited independence, the community doesn't seem to have escaped what the WPA guidebook in 1942 brilliantly called "a specious self-sufficiency." To be sure, the ways in which this oppression works are subtle, in a 1980's style. What you find here is the debasement—not the realization—of the goals of the movement of the sixties for equality and social justice. The calls for economic justice have diminished to a vapid, avid materialism in which kids vie for the fanciest clothes and thickest gold chains, the demands for political equality reduced to a black administration still utterly dependent on white acceptance, the history of unparalleled struggle (*recent* struggle; Len Bias was five when Martin Luther King was murdered) diluted into meaningless ritual celebrations of racial pride, promises of citizenship cheapened into the condescending hero worship of black entertainers.

The city doesn't represent freedom but another incarnation of the color line, that part of our history which, like some science fiction monster, always finds a new form to inhabit so it may continue its ravaging existence. About this both completely apparent and utterly denied truth of our society, W.E.B. Du Bois, another hero of black American life and a prodigy of rational intellect, once wrote, the "fact of racial distinction based on color was the greatest thing in my life and absolutely determined it, because this surrounding group was settled and determined upon the fact that I was and must be a thing apart. It was impossible to gainsay this. It was impossible for any time and to any distance to withdraw myself and look down upon these absurd assumptions with philosophical calm and humorous self-control. If, as happened to a friend of mine, a lady in a pullman ordered me to bring her a glass of water, mistaking me for a porter, the incident in its essence was a joke to be chuckled over; but in its hard, cruel significance and its unending inescapable sign of slavery, it was something to drive a man mad."

In the closed society of D.C., ball players like Bias are crown princes. Even if they are poor, they lead privileged lives, adored and admired by everyone, embodying—for professional government employees as well as street people hanging out at the local cash-and-carry store—the community's hopes for success.

Ball players acquire this status partly because of the sheer wealth that goes with playing in the NBA. The average black family earns approximately sixteen thousand dollars a year. Most NBA rookies start at salaries five times that amount, while the average annual pay in the league is over $200,000. Aspiring athletes know the stories of fabled superstars like Moses Malone or Patrick Ewing who left their working-class homes to sign contracts worth over $2 million a year. Players like Bias, first-round choices, can expect to receive over a half a million with their first contract—not only vastly more money than they would get as, say, starting teachers or research scientists, but also significantly more than beginning football or baseball players.

But the promise of the good life is not the only reason basketball players claim a special importance in the black community. These young players represent an artistic—even spiritual—accomplishment. More than any other sport, basketball is identified with blacks in the popular mind; in the realm of popular culture, the game is an Afro-American fiefdom. With few exceptions, Negro athletes set the standards and introduce the innovations that are emulated and imitated on the playgrounds where white kids spend hours trying to be Michael Jordan or Dominique Wilkens. Basketball has become a source of social power; in succeeding at the game, a player becomes a citizen, for once not by appropriating white behavior, but rather by performing in such an individual fashion that whites want to be like you. The young black kids working out in the playgrounds and dominating the high-school and police leagues are the future of this tradition.

Because of the peculiar nature of their hometown the young ball players of Washington are treated a special way. Basketball has two distinct strains. One is pastoral, the heritage of Dr. James Naismith, the seminarian who invented the game as an exercise to replace winter calisthenics classes. The other is urban, the "city game," the tough entertainment of ensemble and ego fashioned by succeeding generations of immigrant kids and ruled by deals, tough accents, and crassly commercial considerations. In the capital city, these two traditions merge. Power radiates from the white, professional ghetto of downtown. Meanwhile, D.C., the District, remains a sleepy, swampy, provincial Southern city. The young basketball player enjoys the best of both worlds: he is wined and dined in fancy Georgetown restaurants by agents while on the streets of the District the heroic events of his career—first notice in junior high school, emergence as a high-school star, college recruit courted by over one hundred schools—are recounted with a small-town air of pride and familiarity.

In Terry Long's room, Baxter turns to Keith Gatlin. Another guard, Gatlin is lanky, with a mischievous, crinkled smile. When Driesell had recruited Baxter the coach had sworn he wouldn't sign any more backcourt players, but Gatlin had come in the next year and established himself as a starter. In one game against North Carolina, traditional rivals of the Terrapins, he had enjoyed a moment of unalloyed showmanship. In the overtime he had gone to the line and made two clutch free throws, giving his team a three-point lead. Then—icing on the cake—he bounced the ball off a North Carolina player's unsuspecting back, grabbing his own pass and instantly scoring a lay-up, a playground stunt he explained to the press afterward by saying that he had always told them he was a nut.

"What happened?" Baxter asks him.

"They were doing that shit," Gatlin says.

"Doing *what*?" Baxter asks again.

Gatlin's voice is straightforward, somber. No playground antics now. "Doing that shit," he repeats.

"Doing herb?" Baxter says. Baxter has never touched marijuana. Drugs scare him. In the early seventies he saw hippies smoking dope and (he imagined) shooting heroin during a demonstration in downtown Washington; for weeks later he was terrified of going out, insisting his brother accompany him to school. He knows of course that other players smoke—rumor has it that Gregg and Long do a lot of dope—marijuana—but he has never known Lenny to be associated with it. "Doing reefer?"

"I don't know," Gatlin says. "He was doing something."

Wanting an answer, Baxter turns and grabs Gregg. Pushing the taller, younger man into the bathroom, Baxter shuts the door, sticking his elbow under Gregg's chin. "What happened?" he demands.

David fends him off. "Nothing, man," he says. "He was drinking and he fell out."

Knowing he won't get more from Gregg, Baxter walks out into the common room. The other members of the team and Tribble are moving about. Lenny lies on the floor. The paramedics have tried shocking the heart with electrical paddles; they hope that if they can revive the strong engine of his heart and supply oxygen to the brain permanent damage will be minimized. But Bias still has no pulse—in the language of the paramedic, "no electrical activity in the heart of any kind." Now the paramedics are getting ready to strap the body to the stretcher.

Baxter stares at the immobile body. His reaction parallels that of virtually all who find out about the tragedy, a response that explains much of the shock and incredulity that greet the event: he doesn't believe what he sees. Leonard still appears warm and strong, the strongest body Baxter has ever known. He looks at the sculpted muscles etched with power and doesn't comprehend the sight. What seems impossible to him isn't that Bias is prone or unconscious, but that he is *helpless*. Leonard helpless is a contradiction in terms. Leonard is the leader, the spark, the energy. The sight of Len without expression, motionless, defies everything Baxter knows of nature, of life. To Baxter it's a vision that can mean only one thing: the world has gone totally insane.

Of all D.C.'s basketball heroes, none excited more pride and delight than Leonard Bias. People in the community identified with him; he was a representative man, working-class, religious, sharing with his less-talented homeboys a taste for fashion and a fascination with style. Even more importantly, they identified with his "game"—the basketball expression for the quality of a player's performance. Bias's "game" mixed power and finesse, force and style. "He had the body of a god," says Sally Jenkins, the *Washington Post* reporter who covered the Terrapins during Bias's last year, "and he played like a god."

He was a staggeringly acrobatic player, gathering himself to jump in an instant, displaying a Baryshnikov-like force and ease in his leaps. At the same time, he never backed away from physical contact; indeed, he liked payback, and gained a reputation for scrapping. He was a scorer, delivering his often intimidating, powerful slam-dunks, with the immodest panache of a youthfully exuberant Cyrano. But he also commanded a shooter's touch—the smooth, snapping release usually displayed by guards that sends the ball arching through the basket, one of the gorgeous wonders of the game—and like those guards, Bias was a threat from long distance. One way to think of basketball is as a game of possibility. Can a player shoot with his left hand as well as his right? Does he lose the ball after two dribbles or can he drive to the basket? Can he pass if his opportunity to score is denied? The greater the combination of prowess, invention, and determination, the more thrilling the player, the more thrilling the game. Bias provided such excitement.

His most famous and revelatory performance came in a game at North Carolina during his senior year. Underdogs, the Terps were playing in North Carolina's new, swank gym where the home team boasted an undefeated record. With three minutes to go, North Carolina was ahead by eight, in college ball a substantial enough lead to assure a victory. But Bias simply seized control of the game. He hit an outside jumper, then stole a North Carolina in-bounds pass and scored with a powerful dunk. Inspired by his play, a teammate named Speedy Jones stole another pass and Jeff Baxter hit a lay-up. Maryland was now down by only three. Of the Terps' sixty-five points Bias had scored thirty-one. He blocked a shot, stopped another basket, got another rebound, and scored, setting up the final basket by Jeff Baxter, which tied the game and sent it into overtime. Bias's team eventually won. The performance was so fiercely aggressive that it remains compelling even on tape, when you know the outcome. Those three minutes display Bias's game at its best: the sheer defiance and ego of in-your-face playground one-on-one performed with a professional's skill and grace.

But Bias's development as a player was as significant as his style of play.

"He didn't have a great senior year," Lefty Driesell, Maryland's coach, told the press during Bias's junior season. "His potential was always there; you could see that the minute he stepped on the court. But you didn't know if he was going to be one of those raw talents that worked out or one that flopped. It was only after he got to Maryland and I realized how hard he was willing to work that I began to believe he could be a great player."

How hard he worked—the words were fundamental to the fable of Bias's success. At each level of competition he had displayed the tenacity, intelligence, and talent to make the right choice and overcome his failings. He had gone from the gawky junior-high-school player to the powerful high-school star who displayed a bad attitude to the well-rounded, complete leader of his college team.

This aspect of his development resulted in the public persona of an all-American boy. Bias helped cultivate this image. He presented himself as a diligent student: "One thing I really want is my degree," he told Sally Jenkins in February of his senior year. "I didn't used to want it that much. But now I do, badly." He showed himself a devoted son—he told the press he was going to take care of his parents with his expected new wealth—and a private individual with a penchant for drawing and a boyish love of cars.

"He's a very private person," his mother informed an interviewer that year, confirming this view of Bias. "He loves to draw, and writes very well and loves poetry. He enjoys music, mostly contemporary jazz artists like Al Jarreau, and gospel music. We are born-again Christians. It's as if he lives in two separate worlds. When he's playing ball, everyone can see his talent, his macho image. Off the floor, he loves the privateness and peacefulness."

But for his peers Bias's success meant something different than a triumph of American individual enterprise; his achievement was a political, social, even spiritual triumph. For them, as black Americans, life is an existence at war. They inhabit a landscape under fire where personal destruction is a constant threat. Especially for children daily experience is a siege of evil as unremitting and unpredictable as violence on a battlefield. The deadliest, most immediate and ubiquitous danger comes of course from drugs. But drugs are only the most apparent threat. An arsenal of oppression confronts them: crime, unemployment, and the continuous neglect and abuse they suffer from social institutions such as the police, hospitals, and schools that are supposed to benefit them. So Bias's triumph was not simply that he was going to be rich. His acclaim and promised wealth was a victory for life—for the values of his family and his own perseverance and personal courage, a symbol of personal achievement: a Cedar Hill he had conquered on his own. In the words of the street, he had "gotten over." In the poetry of the social anthem of the movement that was at its height when he was an infant, he had "overcome." Like Muhammad Ali or Richard Pryor or Malcolm X, he was that most genuine and rare of heroes: a nigger who won.

By seven o'clock the paramedics are taking Leonard to Leland Memorial Hospital. On campus the word is already spreading about what has happened. Outside Washington Hall, some students gather in the clement morning. The site is an incongruous setting for the unfolding drama. Built in the university's neocolonial style, the dorms are mock manor houses, three-story buildings connected by little cottages and fronted with three-columned porticos. Stately oaks line the red-brick avenue hemming the quad. Underneath the newly budded branches are barbecue grills, a suburban touch; the center of the quad is a recreational area with several basketball hoops where members of the team, Lenny included, often play pickup games. Across from the dorms rises the white steeple of the university's memorial chapel; behind them lies a large parking lot dotted with huge dumpsters the students use for garbage cans. The whole looks like the setting for an expensive summer camp—a pristine, privileged, idyllic sanctuary.

Inside the dorm, Baxter is searching unsuccessfully for his car keys.

"Ride with me," Tribble tells him.

Baxter goes outside. Tribble sits in the passenger seat of Lenny's new car. Tribble gives Baxter the keys and they drive through the campus to the hospital, which is less than five minutes away. Neither speaks. Tribble can of course tell Baxter what happened. But since the confrontation with David Gregg, Baxter hasn't asked any of the men who were in the room with Lenny what took place. He doesn't want to. Dazed by the events, he remains sure—and wants to remain sure—of only one thing: Lenny isn't dead and he isn't going to die.

. . .

Baxter had known Bias for five years. He considered himself the star's closest friend on the team, sharing Bias's three passions: women, clothes, and basketball. Starting at the same point, their careers at Maryland had diverged dramatically. Bias had advanced to superstar status. Baxter had become a sub.

They had met as high-school juniors at Howard Garfinkle's Five Star Basketball Camp. The camp is a showcase for promising young talents and willing-to-pay hopefuls. Invited guests, Bias and Baxter had roomed and played together. The experience had left Baxter with mixed impressions.

"At that point," Baxter remembers today, "as far as I knew him, he was a person who was very likable, but he had a selfish air about him, an attitude. . . . On the court he would shoot the ball each time he got it. He would cry. Not *cry* literally, but like, 'Why don't you all give me the ball?' Sometimes he would just put his head down, sulking, and the coach would look at him and say, 'Well, I guess we got to give Lenny the ball.' It was that type of subtle but showy thing."

What was particularly annoying about Bias's selfishness was that he had not yet proved himself as a player.

"He had a talent that he did not know he had. It was just hidden. It was like a spurt—a surprise. It would pop up. He would make a move, and he would not realize he had made it until after the game. 'I made that move,' he'd say, 'can you believe it?' I'd say, 'Yeah, I believe it. I saw it.' "

After the camp, Baxter rarely saw Bias. The two players lived in different parts of the city and there was no reason for them to befriend each other. Instead, each lived through the fantasies, extravagances, pressures, and perils of recruitment for college, both eventually ending, independently, at Maryland.

How Baxter arrived there reveals something of the pressures experienced by high-school athletes as they consider their college careers.

A recognized player, although no All-American, Baxter was recruited by close to a hundred schools, the usual number for a player of his caliber. Following the advice of his brothers and mother, a nurse who had raised her five children alone, often holding two full-time jobs, he narrowed his selection to four schools: Brown, Syracuse, North Carolina, and Maryland.

Attending the first—Brown—was a fantasy. Baxter loved the school, but his hopes, however faint, for a professional career rested on his reputation as a college player. He could hardly chance performing in an Ivy League athletic program that received little publicity because it wasn't "big-time," as they call universities with major investments in their teams. North Carolina—Maryland's historic rival in the Atlantic Coast Conference, one of the four North Carolina universities commonly referred to as Tobacco Row which frequently recruit from the District—had promised him a scholarship only if another guard refused to sign. That left Syracuse and Maryland. Baxter was unequivocal in his choice. "Syracuse was the ultimate, in my mind," he says. "I liked the people, the surroundings, the coach." Especially the coach. He promised to play Baxter immediately, showing a candor and commitment rare among college coaches who often enforce competition between players by keeping the athletes worried about their team status.

Instead he ended up at Maryland.

Partly this decision was his family's. Several players from the District had gotten into serious criminal trouble while attending schools away from home. Baxter's mother didn't want her son falling under bad influences, no matter how passionately he argued that going away was an important step in his growing up. But the key factor in the decision wasn't a relative, but a stranger, Lefty Driesell.

Coach Driesell was the public face of Maryland basketball and, probably, the man most popularly associated with the school as a whole. Fiercely competitive, demonstrative, self-assured, pious—he frequently announces he's a "born-again Christian"—he was a coach for the Reagan era, an embodiment of the simple virtues of rugged individualism. The Terp coach for the last seventeen years, he was the dominant, constant personality of the team, the true star of every contest, revving the crowd, baiting the refs, exhorting his players. During his tenure he had revived a practically moribund program to national standing and financial profit: one estimate claims Maryland earned approximately two million a year from its basketball program, of which over half went into the university's coffers. Driesell had capitalized personally on this athletic success. Like Bear Bryant in Alabama or Woody Hayes in Ohio or Dean Smith in North Carolina, he had become a darling of the state. As a coach he enjoyed the personal influence of a politician, the charisma of an entertainment star, and the moral authority of a religious leader. The only condition he had to meet to continue receiving this privileged treatment was to make sure his teams scored more points than their opponents. He performed this task well: at the time he recruited Baxter and Bias, he boasted twenty-two straight years of victorious college teams, thirteen of them nationally ranked, and his winning percentage was among the highest of all coaches.

Tall, balding, carrying himself with a marshal's ramrod posture but featuring an almost goofy smile and speaking in an unhurried Tidewater accent that suggests down-home modesty and native wit, Driesell is a notorious recruiter. Recruitment—convincing players to attend your school—is perhaps the single most important task of a college coach. Requiring few players and almost no equipment, college basketball is the penny stock in amateur athletics: one key player can turn a mediocre squad into a national title contender and attract considerable media attention and new sources of financial support. Consequently, the competition for players is fierce, a struggle between opposing coaches that sometimes plays itself out throughout an athlete's entire high-school career. Driesell, said to have honed his talents of persuasion as a car salesman, is considered a master of the game: indefatigable, imaginative, shameless.

Baxter's experience proves the success of Driesell's tactics. Even five years later, Baxter remains amazed at the way Driesell assured Baxter's family that Maryland was going to be the best environment in which Jeff could grow as a player and student.

"You can call it smooth talking. You can call it recruiting tactics. You can call it just doing your job. But whatever you call it, he did what he had to do to sell my parents. He just totally manipulated and transferred my family's thought to the University of Maryland, even when I was telling them that I didn't care what they all say, there was just something about this guy I did not like."

Baxter's reservations about Driesell stemmed from the coach's history with guards, Baxter's position. Driesell is known as a "big-man's" coach, specializing and favoring frontcourt players. Of the famous guards he had coached, several had proceeded from Maryland into disappointing and troubled professional careers. The most notorious case was John Lucas. An effervescent, exciting athlete with a love for sport, Lucas was honored as the Number One NBA pick the year he graduated. But after several years in the pros Lucas confessed he was a cocaine addict. The latter part of his playing life was spent shuttling between teams, press conferences in which he announced his chagrin at betraying his fans and teammates and his determination to go straight, and yet another stay at another detox center. And Lucas was not alone. Around the time Baxter was thinking of attending Maryland there were several other players whose experience mirrored Lucas's.

"There was something about him [Driesell] I never liked. It was just an air that he carried about him. . . . I think it may have been that I saw so many guards go there that I thought he had messed up. . . . [Maybe] it was other things I did not know about then [but] I would be looking at the TV and I would be, like, how can Jo Jo Hunter not be doing well? How can Billy Bryant not be doing well? How can Turk Tillman? So I just thought he was not a good coach."

At the hospital, the players take turns at the telephone booths calling family and friends. Outside a steady line of cars pulls up. Bias has only been in the emergency room for a few minutes, but already all the central characters of his life have heard the news.

Inside the emergency room the medical team continues trying to revive his heartbeat. The doctors administer the drugs used to resuscitate cardiac-arrest victims: sodium epinephrine to stimulate the heartbeat, sodium bicarbonate to normalize the acidity in the bloodstream, lidocaine to control an irregular heartbeat, calcium to stimulate the heart muscle, and bretyline. Nothing works. The unit calls a specialist in Virginia to rush over and implant a pacemaker in the heart muscle. Now the hope that Bias will escape serious damage—even if they can resurrect a self-generated heartbeat—is disappearing. The doctors are just fighting for his life. One of them asks the people outside if Bias has taken any alcohol or drugs recently. No, he's told, Bias was only drinking a couple of beers.

But among the boys the rumor that Leonard has taken cocaine is already spreading. In a corner, Speedy Jones, a stocky forward who has been a friend of Bias's, grabs Terry Long.

"What were you doing?" Jones demands, pressing up against the large center. "What were you doing?"

The easygoing Long defends himself. "We weren't doing anything." Jones lets Long go, and Long walks away, his head in his hands.

A doctor and nurse come out of the emergency room. They say Leonard is going to be all right.

Worried and relieved, Baxter goes to call his mother. She tells him to stay at the hospital—overruling him again, since Baxter desperately wants to go back to campus, away from the predictable media blitz and the difficult questions that are certain to be asked.

He walks down the corridor. When he turns the corner he meets David Gregg, the first time he has found himself alone with the player since their confrontation in the dorm room.

"What were you doing, man?" Baxter demands.

But Gregg refuses to answer.

"Was it reefer?" Baxter asks, no longer accepting the story about Bias's falling out after some beer.

Gregg's reply is to start crying.

"Was it cocaine?" Baxter continues.

Gregg cries harder now—"furiously," Baxter says, remembering the moment. "He just started crying furiously. And that was when I knew. That's when I knew that's what it was."

For Baxter the one attraction Maryland had was Bias.

"Lenny hadn't flowered that much as a player, but I was excited because I was going to be with a nut and I was going to be having some fun. I was like, I'm going to be with Lenny, I know we're going to be as silly as I don't know what! Which we were. We had a ball my freshman year."

As players, they became campus royalty, members of a fraternity ruled by the unquestioned authority of Lefty Driesell. They roomed in a separate dorm, ate special meals, the chefs preparing filet mignon, lasagna, or shrimp per individual request, and enjoyed the personal attention of an academic advisor who monitored their scholastic progress. Driesell treated them with the kindly paternalism of a benign autocrat. When a female student filed charges against a player named Herman Veal for attempted rape, Driesell called the young woman, unsuccessfully attempting to convince her to drop the complaint. Upon hearing that the Women's Center, the campus feminist organization, objected to his interference, Driesell replied that he was the Men's Center and didn't care what they thought.

The players paid a price for this privileged treatment. They followed a schedule as rigorous as a pro's: they had to attend full, double practices on the weekend in the pre-season, 2½-hour daily practice from October on, and play approximately thirty games a year, at least half off campus and many in places as far away as Hawaii, while keeping their grades at a C average. Driesell only pampered them as students; as players they were already considered pros.

"Lefty is the kind of coach who doesn't wait for you to blossom," explains Baxter. "You're supposed to be able to play once you get there. And if you can't play, you'd just have to sit, you'd just have to wait until he felt he needed you, until he felt you were ready to take over."

As freshmen, Baxter and Bias both sat a lot. They would goof on the court antics of the players, making fun especially of Adrian Branch, the team's top scorer, a tricky forward whom they sometimes called Tragic Magic since he often failed in his attempts to imitate the famous feats of the nonpareil Magic Johnson. The rest of the time they would simply bitch, "just sit on the bench, paying attention to nothing. 'Man, I'm transferring,' Lenny would say to me. 'Me too,' I'd say, 'let's leave tonight.' "

But after the freshman season, Baxter's and Bias's careers diverged. Unlike the Syracuse coach, Driesell withheld assurances from his players, encouraging them to compete for their places on the team, hoping the battles between the athletes during practice would separate the exceptional from the mediocre talents.

Bias responded on cue to this challenge. After his faltering start, Leonard emerged as the team's dominant player. At the end of his freshman year he won a crucial game with a daring, last-second shot. In his next season, he challenged Adrian Branch as the team's hero, clinching the role when he led the Terps to victory in that year's Atlantic Coast Conference (ACC) tournament—the first time Driesell had ever won that championship.

"He really could shoot. . . . I remember one game when Red Auerbach was there. Lenny went up with his right hand and John Salley began to block him. Lenny switched over to his left hand for the jump shot. Red Auerbach just took off his hat and threw it to the ground. He was amazed, just like everyone else was. Going out to play with him every game was a joy. Some players when you play with them for a long time you become . . . Yeah, I know his game, he can't do this, he can't do that. But there was nothing Lenny couldn't do."

At the same time Baxter saw his own hopes for a professional future disappear. Playing out of position—as a point guard he was responsible for making plays, rather than scoring, which was his natural talent and inclination—he squabbled with Driesell. "I told him, 'I know I can play and basketball really doesn't mean that much. If you try to bring me down, that's not the move. You're sitting me because you've got an attitude with me, a personal attitude, and that's not the right thing. . . . You can have a personal attitude toward me, but not on the floor.' Driesell retaliated with something like 'Stay in line, I'm the coach, I've been the coach for eighteen years and I know basketball,' and all this other bull. With Coach Driesell you have to talk to him like it's man to man, even though it's boy to man, because if you don't he will feel more powerful than he already is. . . . If you're not tough you can just lose it. I can remember a number of players crying, getting totally upset at the fact that he wasn't playing them, [and when they would talk to him] they had their head down, and you couldn't do that because it was giving him the upper hand, it was like he was saying, 'I got you.' "

By his senior year Bias was the campus star. He had become a valuable commodity, what the entertainment industry calls a crossover, a black who, like Michael Jackson or Bill Cosby, attracts an integrated following. Before games, the Cole Field House concession stands sold full-sized paper cutouts of Bias, which adoring fans taped to their bodies; if Bias looked up he saw a weird motley of doubles cheering him on. He led a charmed life. He seemed to enjoy lots of cash—none of his friends knew where the money came from—and prodigious love affairs, some fairly serious, with a startlingly varied array of women, including fans, "season girls," and off-campus admirers.

"He had so many different women. Twenty, thirty. You never knew. They would come to the dorm room. He would go get them. He was 'the Man.' . . . One night he came in about five-thirty or six [in the morning]. He woke me up. I was like, what's going on? Then I said, 'Man, you need to lay down. You need to cool out for a while. That running around is going to knock you out. As a matter of fact, it's going to kill you.' And he said, 'I know—and I'm tired too.' And he slept. He slept right on the floor. He slept all day."

Bias's celebrity status revived the old popular impression of him as spoiled and bossy.

"People saw an air about him. There were a lot of women who would drop at his feet, and if they did, then what was he supposed to do? Say no? Leave me alone? He couldn't because there were so many coming at him. And then, some of the people who said he acted like a king were jealous."

But to Baxter, Leonard wasn't vainglorious, but childlike, shy, spontaneous, pleasure-loving.

"Lenny was just so warm. He would do anything for you, anything. He never thought he was too big. He never realized how much he was in the spotlight—to this day I will say that. He had excellent taste in clothes. When I got to Maryland, I started taking him shopping with me. I'd say, 'Get that, that'll look nice.' He'd get the clothing and come up to me and say, 'You like this, man?' I'd say, 'Yeah, yeah, that's large, I can wear that'—because, you know, at the time the large style was in. . . . We had a fun time when we shopped. We used to do anything. I remember one time I was walking in the store to buy some clothes and Lenny just grabbed me by my legs and pulled me down on the floor—just *threw* me down and jumped back up. And the store lady came out. 'What happened?' she said. And he said, 'He hit me! He hit me! I had to hit him back!' Like he was a little kid. As for personality—good God! And talent! He had so many artistic talents it wasn't even funny! He could paint—he never pursued it, but good God he could draw! And he had the most beautiful penmanship I ever saw. I used to have him sign stuff for me all the time. 'They're going to know it's not you,' he would say. I'd say,

'Shut up, man, they're not going to know it's not me, just sign it.' "

For Baxter, Bias was living out, on a more heroic, more glamourous scale than Baxter had ever allowed himself to imagine, his own now hopelessly crippled dream career. Whatever envy, anger, or resentment he felt for Bias's success competed with a sense of wonder—and, inevitably, a teammate's shared pride.

"He bought his suit in a store in Georgetown. Very good-looking. An ugly tie by my estimation. I told him, 'You need to get a new tie.' But he had to leave the next morning so he said forget it. Anyway he had nice shoes. He was set. He was ridiculously excited. He was like, 'I'm going to New York, shorty, I'm going there! We're going to be all right, we're going to be all right!' "

At 7:15 that morning, as the doctors work on Bias, two young women are leaving their apartment on Annapolis Road in Bladensburg, a Beltway suburb close to the university. Their names are Julie Walker and Gail Diamond. Both are in their midtwenties, students holding down full-time jobs. This morning they happen to be starting their long day earlier than usual. Julie and Brian Tribble have been close friends—not lovers, both are quick to point out—since childhood. To Brian, Julie is like a sister. With Gail's approval, Julie has given Brian keys to the apartment and recently she has agreed he can leave a portable safe in her closet.

As Julie turns the lock and opens the apartment door, two men push her back inside. Both are slim and wear two-piece sweat suits, white Reebok tennis shoes, and blue cloths over the lower half of their faces. In their hands they hold two small, silver-colored flat handguns.

Julie screams.

One mugger—the other is mute throughout the episode—threatens to kill her if she makes another sound.

Brandishing the guns, the two men, both shorter than the women—Diamond in particular being a big-boned six feet—push the unresisting girls onto the floor. The talker orders them to keep their heads down. He leads Julie down the hall to her room. When Diamond looks up—she is afraid something terrible is going to happen to her disappearing roommate—the mute one shoves her head back down roughly.

After a moment the talker returns. He ties Diamond's hands behind her back; then she feels his fingers at her neck.

"Don't," she says, terrified he is about to rape her. "Please don't touch me."

"I ain't about all that, baby," he answers. "I ain't about all that."

The talker binds her ankles and hands with shoestrings. Then he hustles her into the master bedroom. There her roommate lies on the floor, similarly trussed, a blanket over her head. Depositing Diamond on the bed, the talker throws another blanket over her and starts to gag her.

Diamond complains she can't breathe.

"You want me to shoot you," the talker threatens, "then you won't have to breathe."

Diamond doesn't say a word and the talker cools down, telling her if she's quiet she won't get hurt.

For the next fifteen minutes or so the girls lie helpless as the men go about their seemingly aimless business. At one point the talker comes in, demanding to know where the money is, then leaves before getting an answer. Blinded by the blanket, Diamond traces the progress of the robbers through aural cues: the tinkling of a bead curtain as the men move into the living room, a toilet being flushed, drawers being opened, the robbers removing the curtain, the telephone cord being cut, her watch going off at eight o'clock.

Then silence. Neither woman has actually heard the apartment door close. Maybe the muggers are only pretending to be gone, waiting for the girls to come out?

Diamond is afraid to speak or move.

Finally Julie asks if she's all right.

"Yeah," she answers. "I don't hear anything."

Julie tells her they should try to untie themselves. Diamond throws her legs over the bed and leans over to untie Walker's hands. The young women free each other and creep down the hall, still afraid the thieves plan to surprise them. The door stands ajar—the robbers didn't want them to know they were gone. The young women bolt down the hallway to their neighbor's and call the police.

The first thing one notices about Bias's friend Brian Tribble is his extraordinary good looks. The natural gift of his features defines him in the world: he is handsome as women are beautiful. A mask of severe angles, shaded by passionate, somber, steady brown eyes and thick flat eyebrows that arch and slant with disbelief and defiance, his mahogany face—when he was growing up he was called a "red nigger"—has a Latin-loverish, movie-star intensity. Like an actor, he is charged with a nervous energy that, coupled with his compact, muscular stature, makes him seem pent up, explosive, dangerous, a quality that adds to his allure.

But good looks, unfortunately, were not the gift Tribble—Brian Lee Tribble the papers called him later, making him sound like a gunfighter, or "Trib," as Baxter and other playground players named him—wanted from life. His desire—from childhood on—was to be a ball player. Tribble loves basketball. He can talk about it for hours, comparing players, remembering plays, trading stories, recalling a narrow-minded prediction about an athlete, discussing in the most minute detail a coach's wrong strategic choice or a rookie's surprise performance, reviewing an endless mental photo album of treasured moments. His relationship to the game—and in this respect, Tribble is not different from most of the other significant men who entered Bias's life—is not that of a casual fan toward a sport, but of a devotee toward an art form. For him, basketball reflects and illuminates the world. It transforms the everyday into revelatory drama, presents moments when the transcendent meets the mundane. It is an arena in which great stories are played out by athletes whose careers, like the stories of classical heroes, trace arcs of triumph or despair, and present moral tales of fortitude or compromise. The games are contests of style and courage, summoning from the audience admiration, awe, compassion. It is the grand world, a theater for glory, like the heroic salt seas of Scottish folk songs, or—for today's young middle class—stock-brokerage trading rooms.

Tribble was a particular kind of player: a shooter. Shooting is the moment of individual artistry in the game that (like the home-run ball or the touchdown pass) excites everyone's imagination.

"For me," Tribble explains today, "basketball was an outlet." His husky voice has a menacing, almost thuggish, throatiness, at odds with the finely tuned emotion visible in his face, his intonation and vocabulary seeming to have been schooled in the streets. "I was big and strong and wanted to play football, but I liked to shoot. The thing with me was players would say, 'Trib can shoot.' "

As a kid he played center in the neighborhood police leagues. But then—this happens to a lot of ball players—nature tricked him. Other boys matched his growth. He found himself a guard or forward at best. At the same time he became difficult to coach.

"As I got older, I got an attitude. I'd call a timeout by myself and the coach would say, 'You don't call a timeout.' There was one junior-high-school game when the coach benched me. I was ready that day. I had my game down, I was ready to play. And he didn't call me. Then at the end of the game he said, 'Trib, you want to shoot the last shot?' I said, 'Let your other boy do it.' "

Other bad choices followed. He picked the wrong high school to attend, the coach not playing Tribble as much as the youngster thought he deserved. "They were using other guys instead of me. That would tear me up." And the game itself kept getting harder, more physically demanding, less satisfying.

By his senior year, Tribble had no prospect for a basketball scholarship. His only possibility was to attend American University, hope to make it as a "walk-on," a nonscholarship player selected from a general tryout, and receive a "partial."

That summer he entered a University of Maryland college preparatory program. Tutored in math, reading, and English—his reading award still crowns a shelf of family accomplishments in his parents' house—Tribble earned seven credits, and was accepted at the state school. That fall he signed up for eighteen credits; he worked part time as a night package handler at UPS, and later clerked at Howard University Hospital two days a week and every other weekend.

But Maryland also disappointed him.

His troubles with basketball continued. He played junior varsity, under a coach named Mel Cartwright.

"Lefty came up one day and started correcting me. I answered him instead of just going to my room or something. Man, I was only JV, and Mel Cartwright is behind Lefty waving his hands, saying no, but I didn't care. And there was something else. I kept on thinking that the college players would be much better than me. But they weren't shit. I'd score off of them in pickup games."

And the campus social atmosphere also bothered him.

"White kids are crazy, man. They play the radio loud—Led Zeppelin—never want to work. Acting like they were little kids. And I was playing ball and working. But you know what I hated most. The white kids saying, '*Excuse me.*' Excuse me? Shit! They heard you. They understood. Sometimes I'd want to snatch them right over the counter. And they knew what you were saying. They'd go to the movies and laugh at the same shit when Eddie Murphy was doing it—hee-haw! But when you said it, the answer was, 'Excuse me!' That was why I liked New York boys. They'd say, 'Yo, Brian, take this course, it's smooth, you don't even have to show up.' I'd say, 'Goddamn, this guy's all right!' But that was only the New York boys."

He moved back home. Soon after, he was hit while riding his motorcycle. Tribble sued and collected ten thousand dollars. Part of his argument was that the injuries sustained had ruined any chance of a basketball career.

And then an extraordinary thing happened. Cut off by circumstance and attitude from the game he loved most, he found a new entrance into the sport through a deep, true friendship with a man who enjoyed the gifts Tribble lacked, possessed them in the same unaccountable, magical way Tribble possessed good looks: Leonard Bias.

Around eight o'clock Tribble calls his mother one last time.

"Boy," he says, "you talk about somebody not knowing what to do. I thought—I didn't know what to think."

He tells her the doctor has reported Bias has a faint heartbeat and that he thinks everything will be okay. Relaxing, Mrs. Tribble tells him she is going to the social worker and that she won't be home. He hangs up and asks Baxter to drive him home. Baxter agrees; he's eager for any excuse to leave the clenched, antiseptic atmosphere of the hospital corridor.

The drive over is short; Tribble's apartment is in a newly constructed high-rise bordering the steadily receding fringe of woods surrounding the university complex. The young men don't speak again; he seemed sad, not frantic, Baxter later said when asked to recall Tribble's behavior. He lets Tribble off and returns to the hospital.

Tribble enters his apartment. He has lived here six months, but it's a struggle to keep the place. He splits the $680-a-month rent evenly with Mark Fobbs, his roommate, but given his sporadic earnings, Tribble's half is a steep bill. To help make ends meet he eats at home every night. The apartment came unfurnished except for wall-to-wall carpeting. Tribble's additions have been minimal: a bed and television set. The rest of the furniture, a couch, glass table, and floor-to-ceiling drapes, comes from his brother, Junior, who, after a recent separation from his wife, needs a place to store his valuable furniture. The made-to-order drapes are several inches too short for Tribble's windows; the wall sticks out from under them like ankles beneath hand-me-down pants. Still, for a young man without a college degree, the patchwork apartment is impressive, a pad providing freedom from parents or dorm counselors.

The phone rings immediately. The caller is a man named Johnny Walker, a D.C. policeman and an old friend of Bias's. Although Walker and Tribble do not socialize independent of Leonard, the three have spent time together recently, Leonard bringing together his two most intimate friends.

Walker tells Brian he has just received a call from his younger brother saying Lenny is in the hospital. He asks Tribble to tell him what's happening. After a brief conversation Tribble hangs up. Afraid Walker's call is only the first he doesn't want to answer, he decides to crash at Julie Walker's.

Tribble asks Mark Fobbs if he can drive him to Julie's on the way to work. Tribble dresses in shorts and a T-shirt—his usual outfit, the clothes showing his body to advantage—grabs a gym bag, climbs into Fobbs's four-wheel-drive Jeep and heads for sanctuary.

Tribble first saw Bias play when the star-to-be was fourteen. "It wasn't nothing," Tribble says now. "I don't even remember him then. I just know that I met him. He wasn't that good, except for his leaping ability. The young one could rise."

But four years later, when they ran into each other at Maryland, Bias was beginning to display his exceptional talent.

The vision of his friend in action on the court still animates Tribble. "The man was awesome," he says, talking in his parents' living room, where he used to watch ball games with Leonard. He assumes the threatening crouch of Bias's offensive stance, his hand cupped over the imaginary ball; like a good, natural actor Tribble seems to gain heft and stature as he imitates his buddy. "One game he was at midcourt. He dribbled twice, then took off—from this side of the foul line! Flying over everyone! And threw it down! The man was awesome!"

Already friendly with the fraternal leadership of the team—Ben Coleman, Adrian Branch, and Herman Veal—Tribble developed an especially close relationship with Leonard.

"We just clicked. It was like one of us would say something just when the other was thinking about it. We'd be thinking the same things at the same time without telling each other. Like if he wanted to do something, click, I would be thinking the same thing, and vice versa. Hey, shorty, let's get some chicken wings! Click! Hey, I'm going to see *Beverly Hills Cop*. Click! It was weird, man. We would do things that no one else wanted to. I wanted to go to the Prince concert. Everyone else said, Naw, Prince, he's a faggot. I said, 'Damn! the man's awesome! Plays every instrument, writes his own songs, sings, arranges—the man's awesome!' And I never cared about that faggot shit either. Neither did Len. He'd tease Baxter: Come here and give me a kiss, man! He didn't care. He'd say anything. [He'd say,] shorty, your momma makes good pancakes. So we went to Prince."

The friendship grew as Bias's influence on the team increased. Tribble speaks about his friend's emergence as a leader and star with the proprietary air of a coach.

"During the first year he had to get his confidence together. He said he was jumping too high, catching the ball wrong. He said his adrenaline would get him high and his timing would go off and he'd miss the rebound. Then Lefty wouldn't play him and he'd doubt himself. Herman [Veal, an upperclassman forward] helped him on his physical game a lot. Herman would bang you.

You'd go up for a rebound and he'd 'bow you good. He was there. He didn't care. He'd make you cry. He'd make you remember him. But that helped Len. He'd get mad and then he would show signs he could do something great. And also that summer he worked on his jump shot.

"But the other thing was that he got interested in weights. He'd come over here and say, 'Let's lift, man! Get strong!' And that gave him confidence. That was what he needed. Lenny was the kind of guy who knew he did good. He didn't need the crowd. He knew what he could do. After his sophomore year he had confidence because he knew the coach would play him—and once he knew he would stay in a game no matter how he played he had confidence. He'd be mean. He'd get pumped up before a game. If they were going to play North Carolina, he'd say, 'Come on, we're going to get that bitch Daugherty.' "

The player who suffered the most from Bias's success was Adrian Branch, the high-scoring forward who had fueled the team's offense.

"Branch was the shit in high school. He was awesome in high school. But Lenny just took the team over once he decided to. He said, 'Adrian can't do shit, man! This is my team.' And Keith [Gatlin, the team's guard] would always feed Lenny the ball. He'd fake to Adrian, then pass to Lenny. One night Adrian got so mad, he said, 'You all hate me, and I hate you motherfuckers!' He packed his bags. There were things falling out and everything. He went down to North Carolina. Nobody cared. Adrian was crazy. One time Lefty told him something and Adrian called him a motherfucker. He was nasty. A kid would come over for his autograph and he'd scream at them, 'Get out of here, motherfucker!' Or he'd be eating cookies and he'd open his mouth when he passed someone."

Bias's and Tribble's lives were adolescent fantasies come true of games, partying, and shared intimacies.

"Lenny banged everything. Girls just came to him. Lenny would take them all. He'd say, 'I'm going to get her, but I don't care about her.' And that was cool because she didn't care for him, she just wanted to be with Len Bias. So it was a tradeoff. He had a list. The team. He would scratch ones off—cut them, trade them, move them up off the bench to starters. There are old men dying who never got as much booty as Leonard did."

They kept this life hidden from the view of adults.

"His father would lecture him about this and that. Big James, Leonard used to call him: don't mess with Big James. But I think James was a little in awe of Lenny. I mean, what are you going to say to him? The kid's about to make more money in a year than you could ever dream of. Leonard would listen, going, 'Yeah, Pop, yeah.' "

For Bias and Tribble, the draft was only the beginning of what was going to be a wonderful life.

"He called me from Boston. Told me he got me some tennis shoes. He said, 'I'm ready to have fun now.' It moved me that he called because I hadn't expected to hear from him from Boston. He said, 'I'm coming home tonight, man. It's boring here.' I asked him about the draft. 'It was a little scary, man,' he said. 'I got up there and all the little kids were climbing over me and saying, 'Bias, you're the man! You're the man, Bias, you're the man!' He had never been treated like that. He had never seen media like that. I think it shook him a little."

~~~

At about eight, as Tribble is leaving for Julie's, Bob Wagner arrives at the hospital. He is Leonard's high-school coach. David Gregg, another of his ex-players, has told him the news. But Wagner, like everybody else, has discounted what Gregg said to him minutes before over the phone. He is sure either that he misunderstood Gregg or that the boy was exaggerating: Leonard helped recruit Gregg for Maryland and means a lot to him. Gregg must just be hysterical.

Entering the hospital, he sees Terry Long sitting slumped over, face in his hands. Gregg is wheezing asthmatically, as though he has just finished a race, a sign, Wagner remembers, of the boy's being upset. The two are alone.

"Lenny's going to die," Gregg tells Wagner as soon as he sees him. "Lenny's going to die."

Wagner reassures him again. He's a coach handling a kid who has freaked out about something. For all he knows Leonard could have simply sprained his ankle. In any event, he doesn't take the
~~~

situation seriously and just wants to find out what's happening, cool things out. Whatever the problem is, he figures, everything will soon be back to normal. "I'll see about Leonard," he tells Gregg. Then, assuming Leonard will be returning to Washington Hall and that reporters will be coming to interview him, he tells Long and Gregg to go back and clean up the room: he remembers the mess he encountered the last time he visited Leonard in the dorm.

Wagner leaves Gregg and walks down the corridor toward the main hallway. He feels as though he is in a dream. The hall—almost as long as a full city block—is empty, lit by a shadowless fluorescent light. There are no signs and he doesn't know where he is. A University of Maryland policeman approaches, asking whether Bias has taken any drugs. *Why does he want to know that?* Wagner thinks. He begins to worry—maybe Gregg wasn't exaggerating. He turns the corner. A crowd of people surprise him. He advances toward the throng, recognizing faces as he nears the emergency room: Speedy Jones, Keith Gatlin, David Driggs, Leonard's teammates during the last four years. What are they doing here? Each somber stare increases his sense that he has gotten something wrong—that it isn't Gregg who misunderstands what is happening but himself. Everyone is too quiet. People don't greet him, but mumble, look away, answer silently with their eyes. He nears the end of the corridor. For the first time, he realizes he is in the emergency ward. Bewildered, he retraces his steps. As he nears the emergency room for the second time, a looming bulk bumps him. Wagner looks up. Lefty Driesell grabs him, engulfing him with his size and sorrow.

"He's gone," Lefty says.

Wagner is numb. He tries to understand what his old friend has just said. Opposite him, he sees Speedy Jones and Driggs on the phone. Enveloped in Driesell's embrace, Wagner stares at the two boys, finally understanding the nightmare. The silent faces surrounding him mirror an unimaginable new fact: Leonard has just died.

Except for Bias's parents and, possibly, Coach Driesell, Wagner was more responsible than any other adult for Bias's preparation as a player. Bias's "Drill Instructor," he introduced Leonard to the privileges and rigors of professional life. This instruction went beyond the subtleties of zone defense or how to break a two-man trap. Wagner taught Leonard his first lessons in discipline and practical moral judgment, the other tools he would need to survive the professional world. Under Wagner's guidance, Bias transformed himself from a gawky kid who cried and got pushed around a little bit too much (Wagner's words) into a professional trained to earn his living by his athletic prowess—a property, and a valuable one.

Like the other people drawn to Bias, Wagner is a "basketball junkie"; he has an inexhaustible enthusiasm for the game. "I coach, go home, turn on the cable, and this is at two o'clock in the morning, and watch basketball some more," Wagner says today. He speaks in an agitated, compressed fashion, bunching his words and thoughts, his voice wavering with emotion, then attacking the next subject with resolve. "I never get bored. I always see something else that I pick up."

What drew Leonard to Wagner's attention, and what continued to impress Wagner about the player, was the boy's desire to win.

He first spoke to Bias after Leonard had just lost a junior-high-school championship.

"I went over and talked to him. He was crying and hurt—he had tried so hard and he wanted to win so bad. That's the thing that stuck out in my mind."

At the time Wagner had recently been appointed coach at Northwestern High School. The new job fulfilled a teenage dream: always too short to play ball, he had decided in junior high school to teach basketball; after graduating from Maryland's College Park campus he had returned to his old high school as a math-science instructor. Wagner wanted Bias to play for him because, besides the kid's desire to win, he guessed that Bias had an instinct for the game. The boy liked physical contact and he was "coachable," the ineffable, prized quality some players possess of being able to absorb information and respond to criticism by working harder.

Wagner disciplined Bias's aggressive instincts. "I tried to channel his . . . energies, rather than distort them and say, 'Look, you can't play that way.' " He started him weight lifting: "In lifting you become psychologically confident. You feel strong and when you feel strong you feel more confident." He also trained him to use his displays of force selectively. He coached Bias to see game conditions, hostile crowds, unsympathetic referees, unsportsmanlike opponents, as barriers to be overcome. He devoted every moment of practice and play to steeling his protégé against every possible weakness. He turned Leonard into a warrior.

"Leonard had learned that you take it and you take it and you take it—and *then* you give it. You wait for the right time. I tried to teach him that every time somebody hits you, you don't cry about it. You don't let them know that you're hurt. You don't let them see. You wait until you get into the locker room. You don't let your enemy know where your weaknesses are.

"I taught him that the ball is a weapon. You turn and you go into the power moves. If the guy's in the way—if he's going to foul you or whatever—use the ball. Use the ball against him.

"I never tried at the beginning to expect him to be a nice guy on the court. We played teams where they had three or four kids guarding him, literally beating hell out of him, and nothing was ever called. . . . He went through his junior and senior years with that constantly, people just beating the shit out of him all the time. . . . He'd go up for a dunk and they'd knock him down, hit him in the face, stuff like that. He never would have trusted me if I had said, 'Don't do anything back, don't learn how to protect yourself, you're going to have to take it.' So I gave him one shot a game. . . . I told him, Never do it right after the guy turned you upside down or 'bowed you, but when the opportunity comes let him know that you're there, that you're not going anywhere, and you know what he did. . . .

"I sold him and a couple of other kids on the idea that no one can hurt you. We actually ran drills where we would get the football pads and pound and pound on the shooter until they got used to the idea that I *want* you to foul me because I'm going to score anyway. Go ahead and foul me! I'm going to make this shot, I'm going to be on the foul line and I'm going to beat you! I'm not going to run my mouth, and I'm not going to punch you out, I'm going to win the game! That's why I'm here."

The schooling paid off. Bias played the game with raw pleasure. He was proud to lead every drill; he ran the floor, the so-called "suicide" in which players cover larger amounts of the court at breakneck speed, with the manic delight in the punishing exercise that marks a true athlete. In his junior year, he talked to Wagner about a professional career. His coach didn't discourage the notion. He told Bias he could go as far as he wanted to.

By his senior year Bias was a prized property, desired by over 150 colleges. It was Wagner's privilege to guide the nationally touted player through the maze of recruitment.

Wagner had never enjoyed this responsibility before. He approached the recruiting process as though it were a kind of war.

"I told the kids it's . . . almost prostitution, in a sense, because they're going to use your body for athletics, and if you don't get some of your education—if you don't get something in return—then you've been prostituted, you have not been paid. That's crude and brutal to say, but you have to understand that. It's one thing to have coaches hugging you and kissing you and walking you around saying you're the greatest guy. But once you sign, you're just another guy on the team and they're doing that with somebody else."

The first step in the process was to list Leonard's priorities, "education, church, the basketball program, media exposure," and decide what kind of team would best suit and develop his talents. Coaches vary in their specialties; Driesell, for instance, has a reputation as a big man's coach.

Next, Wagner and Leonard picked five out of the 150 suitor schools for serious consideration. Three, Georgia, North Carolina State, and Maryland, belonged to the ACC. The other two were San Francisco, a Catholic school that often recruits blacks, and Oregon State. Wagner selected these two for basically nonathletic reasons. He wanted Leonard to see the country—the NCAA allows schools to pay for a visit from the athlete—and experience living in an almost exclusively white environment.

Finally, Wagner set up guidelines for the recruiting coaches. All contact with Leonard had to be through Wagner. In addition—to preclude the possibility of coaches' circumventing this rule by showing up early—Wagner also insisted that he drive the coaches to the Biases' whenever the recruiters visited the family.

The strictures placed Wagner in conflict with the incorrigibly charming, inexhaustible Driesell.

"Lefty drove me crazy. He said, 'Can't you help us? Can't you do this?' I said, 'Look, if he wants to go here [Maryland], he's going to make the decision.' Even if I tried to influence him to come to Maryland, Leonard would have thought, 'Well, you're trying to tell me what to do so I'll go somewhere else.' "

The final choice came down to Maryland or North Carolina State, an exciting team led by a young, dynamic coach named Jim Valvano, which had surprised the basketball world the previous year by going all the way to the NCAA finals.

Wagner believes North Carolina State was Leonard's favorite. "There probably was a lot of fun and partying going on [there] and he had a good time [visiting the school]. But I think Jimmy made one mistake. [When Valvano visited with the family he said] 'I'm not going to be responsible for your son's education. I have people, academic advisers, tutors, who are going to be doing that.' That didn't go over well with Mrs. Bias. As a parent you are going to say, '*You* are the parent away from home and I want *you* to take care of my baby.' So I think the final decision . . . came down to Mrs. Bias saying, 'Leonard, you're still a little young and immature. You're going to stay close to home. I want you to go to Maryland.' "

The choice was probably more advantageous to both Driesell and Bias than either realized at the time. The two worked well together. Leonard's desire to achieve, his "coachability," fit perfectly with Driesell's program of enforced competition between players. Unlike Baxter, who turned his anger at Driesell inward, Leonard responded on cue to Driesell's manipulations, pouring his furious energy into his game, igniting his performances on court. By the end of his freshman year, he was already a powerful force on the team, demonstrating his leadership when he took and made a last-second shot in an NCAA tournament game.

"He adjusted to Lefty. I said, 'What happened, why are you playing so much better now than before?' He said, 'I've learned more not to feel that he's yelling but to listen to what he's saying.' Some of the guys never got to that point. Terry Long never got there. If Lefty would yell at him . . . Terry . . . took it personally. Lenny learned not to take it personally. He heard what the coach was saying rather than the way he was saying it. And I think he understood that as irrational and emotional as Lefty can be, Lefty wanted to go to the same place that Leonard wanted to—to win the next game. . . . He would say sometimes Lefty would have him so pumped up that he would come out there . . . convinced the team was going to win no matter who" they were playing. "And there were other postgames where Lefty would tell him how lousy he played and [Leonard] would believe that too."

Wagner attended the games regularly, sometimes coaching Leonard behind Driesell's back, signaling moves. Leonard visited Wagner at the player's old high school.

"Most of the time we wouldn't talk about basketball. Maybe he'd just want to walk down the halls and not say anything. He wanted to get away from it all, from peer pressures, academics, the people constantly around you, the press around you, the coach who's constantly on you. It's a little simpler going back to high school. And the kids didn't mob him. They had seen him enough around that, 'Hey, there's Leonard Bias, he went to school here.' It was just like a boy coming back home. I think it was a little bit of an escape for him."

Shortly before the NBA draft, Wagner and Bias met accidentally. Bias was between visits to several franchises that wanted to meet the prospective rookie.

"I was going to eat dinner late one night at a restaurant around here. As I walk up I hear somebody banging on the window. He was in there with somebody, a female. By the time I [was] ready to get seated, he had come up. We just stood there in the front entrance and talked for a while. . . . He told me about visiting the club camps—I don't know where he was going, San Diego, or someplace. I told him a couple of pro assistants had called the high school and wanted facts from all the way back then, how he played, what his attitude was, his work habits. . . ."At that point I didn't think he needed another person asking him the same old questions so I let him talk about whatever he wanted to. I knew he couldn't be going to too much school because he was going through tests [with the NBA teams] and some of them were physical and some of them were just evaluations. Then I said, 'Well, I see you got someone over there and I do too. I guess we'd better sit down.' He was going to be a star. But if you looked at him when he smiled, he was still that simple little kid with that big smile. Even with him knocking on that window, just like a little kid, 'There's my coach! There's my high-school coach! I gotta go talk to him!' "

Mrs. Bias is the first to emerge from the private room near the emergency room; she wears the housecoat she has thrown over her nightgown when she was called that morning. "It's going to be all right," she tells everyone, immediately self-possessed and dry-eyed. "It's going to be all right."

She goes back into the inner sanctum of the emergency room. Wanting to say a last goodbye, Wagner follows her. At the door connecting the waiting room to the emergency operating area stands Johnny Walker. He has glimpsed the tubes coming out of his friend's body and has decided he doesn't want to see him that way. Wagner passes him and enters the medical chamber. In the still room, Leonard lies on the guerney, his father hugging him, pleading, "Wake up, Leonard, wake up, you're my perfect son, wake up!"

Shaken, Wagner holds Mr. Bias, hoping to distract himself from his own grief by soothing the man. Mr. Bias releases Leonard and Wagner guides the man into the waiting room. Even then Wagner remarks to himself on the difference between Leonard's parents. Mrs. Bias remains completely calm. Wagner has not yet seen her shed a tear. But he feels Mr. Bias is going to be angry; the man hurts so much it will be impossible for him not to hold *someone* responsible for the destruction of his son.

Wagner offers to drive the Biases home with Johnny Walker. They usher the Biases out the side door of the hospital and begin the journey back to Landover.

Johnny Walker had been Leonard's friend and mentor for the last eight years. Emotionally and spiritually, he served as Leonard's older brother—a friend, guide, admonitory pain in the ass. He had met Leonard through basketball and like everyone else in Bias's life was proud of Leonard's success. But unlike the others, Johnny Walker saw Leonard's triumph in political and social terms.

For him, Leonard was a warrior. His career signaled a victory over malign influences, external (coaches and agents) and internal (habits and attitudes), that would lead him to failure as a player and a man.

He had met Bias when the player was fourteen. At the time Walker was coaching at the Columbia Rec, a neighborhood boys' after-school club. A mutual friend named Brian Waller, a player whose potential professional career ended after several disappointing seasons in college, brought Bias to the games.

"He did nothing much at first," says Walker today, "except shoot his mouth off." More than any of Bias's other companions, Walker still seems shocked by Bias's death. Lithe and handsome, he speaks in a hushed, passionless voice, occasionally sinking into an abstracted, almost unfathomable quiet, a pool of memory and sorrow from which a visitor sometimes thinks—so still and contemplative are his silences—Walker will never surface. When he gathers himself to answer, he looks away from the interviewer, toward the television, occasionally passing his large hand over his head, cupping his skull in a gesture of utter exhaustion—the *bone* weariness of a child.

It was Wagner who put Walker and Bias together. At the time Bias was planning to attend a high school whose basketball team had qualified for the state finals the last several years. Wagner asked Walker to help convince the boy to enroll at the considerably less prestigious Northwestern.

"I spoke to Leonard. I told him that if he went to the other school he would just be another player in their winning system. But if he went to Northwestern he could make it Len Bias's school. That was all he needed to hear."

Leonard asked Walker to coach him. Saturdays, Walker, Leonard, and Brian Waller played pickup games, the trio ruling the court. Five years older than his protégé, Walker molded Leonard's attitudes toward the game. He went away to attend a junior college in Iowa—"I didn't know how black I was until I went to Iowa"—but returned in time for the drama of Leonard's recruitment in his senior year.

"Leonard wanted to go to North Carolina State. He visited there and liked it. He told me that he had said to Valvano at the airport when he was leaving that Valvano would be seeing him next year.

Leonard's mother said that whatever Leonard wanted was all right with her. But not his father. He wanted Leonard to remain close. And Leonard didn't mess with Big James—that's what he called [his father]. What he says goes."

The first year at Maryland Leonard was miserable.

"Lefty breaks you down. He's stupid, but he wants you to know that everything goes through him. He wants control. He'll yank you from the game and he'll be the one to let you play."

By the Christmas break, Leonard was so unhappy he asked Walker to call Valvano and see if he could transfer. (The NCAA rules forbade Valvano from speaking directly to Leonard.) Walker says Valvano promised to arrange everything, but that Lefty found out; responding to Bias's upset, Driesell gave Bias more playing time, the start of Bias's dominance at the school.

At the same time, Driesell began to spend time with Bias. In Walker's view, the relationship was seductive and corrupting, Driesell luring Bias into the big-time world that awaited him after school, impressing him with a cynical-sounding business philosophy and fancy cars.

" 'Big Chuck,' Len called him. 'Big Chuck's the man,' he'd tell me. 'The fat man's the man,' he'd say. Lefty would drive him around in his car—he has a Mercedes, wears Rolex watches and alligator shoes. He would drive Leonard around and say, 'You're going to be a millionaire, son, you're going to have all this. . . ."

But Walker refused to be impressed by Bias's triumphs. For him basketball is a kind of war game preparing players for the combat of the real world; mental attitudes matter more than points scored. In his view Leonard displayed none of the desire and toughness required to survive.

"I told him, 'You just don't want it enough, man,' " he says, "it" signifying not just the win in a game, but the discipline and self-knowledge that would transform Leonard from being a victim of circumstance to a master of his life. "You just don't want it enough."

Walker insisted on Bias's striving for this perfection. One of their exemplars was Bernard King, a six-foot-six forward whose jumping quickness, sure release, and inventive shooting resembled Bias's. King's career had been checkered. At the University of Tennessee he had been caught driving drunk, an episode followed by drug and sex scandals when he entered the pros. An outcast in the league, King had promised to reform. Now he was fulfilling his pledge, enjoying a dream season playing for the New York Knicks. His vicissitudes, often viewed more sympathetically by blacks than whites, had given him a fabled toughness on the court, a scowl he called his "game face." The entire story had a *Rocky*-like appeal to Bias.

"We were watching TV looking at Michael Jordan. We used to call Jordan 'the king'—not just meaning the best, but Bernard. Jordan had just announced he was going into the pros. I said, 'The king is going, man. The ACC needs a new king.' So Len said, 'I'm the new king.' I told him, 'Not yet. You don't want it enough yet, man. You just don't want it enough.' A little later, the All-America lists came out. His name wasn't on it. I called him up. I said, 'I see the lists. You're not even on second team.' He told me to wait for the tournament."

The tournament was the ACC championship, a prestigious local prize that Driesell had never won. Bias dominated the contests. He averaged fifteen points, shooting well over 50 percent from the field, and grabbed six rebounds a game, a daunting consistency of performance considering that Bias played all but five minutes of the 120 it took Maryland to claim the trophy. In the title game, he scored twenty-six points, missing only five shots.

"So after the tournament he called me. He said, 'You see me? You see me last night? I showed them, I showed them all.' I said, 'Yeah, you're bad, man.' 'Bad? I was *crushing* them.' I said, 'That's what you want to hear, man? All right. You're the king, man, you're the king.' We were laughing."

Fresh from this victory the Terps entered the NCAA tournament. The team was enjoying some hopes of a possible national championship. Instead they were ousted in their second game, losing by a basket to Illinois.

"[Leonard] was crying. I said to him, 'You just don't want it enough, man, you just don't want it enough. You don't work at it. You spend your summer cooling out—chilling as you say. You should be working.' That summer he started going to the stadium and running the steps and lifting weights. Every day we'd go to the gym and we'd shoot. I'd make him shoot from the same spot on the baseline. I'd say, 'Just do that over and over until no one can stop you.' We'd play against each other. Real games. Hard. 'Bowing and everything. And one day I just couldn't stop him from scoring. That fall he got to camp and he called me up and said, 'I'm ready, shorty, I'm lifting, I ran the lines—I was at the front, I'm ready.' "

At the house, Mrs. Bias asks Wagner to retrieve Leonard's belongings—she is scared souvenir hunters will ransack his room. Wagner and Walker drive to Wagner's house to pick up his van. As soon as they enter the campus, they spot David Gregg with another player. Wagner asks Gregg where he is going. He answers that the players are meeting at Lefty's. Wagner starts to drive off. But he feels uneasy about Gregg's guarded, scared response. "Johnny," he says to Walker, "I have to talk to David. I've got to know what went on in there."

They double back and meet the players on the other side of University Boulevard near the golf course. Assuming Gregg won't confide in him, Wagner asks Walker to see if the boy will talk.

Walker refuses, then changes his mind, thinking he might get some information. He has a short conversation with Gregg. When he returns to the van, he is shaking his head and doesn't want to say anything.

The nightmarish fear that he doesn't understand what is going on, the feeling that haunted him at the hospital, returns to Wagner. Worried, confused, he loses his way to the dorm; by the time he and Walker reach the dorm, reporters, campus police, and a swarm of onlookers have gathered at Washington Hall.

Wagner enters the suite with Walker. He tells him he doesn't know Leonard's possessions and that Walker will have to identify things. Walker goes into Bias's room while Wagner waits outside. It is the first time he has been alone that morning and he uses the time to try to sort out the questions that now bother him: What time did the seizure occur? How long did it take to get Leonard to the hospital? What could have caused his death? Reporters are already talking about a congenital weakness in Bias's heart. But if Bias had heart disease, Wagner thinks, he would have shown symptoms during high school when he was playing ball. As for drugs, Wagner is certain Leonard never touched them.

Leonard would only have taken drugs by accident—if someone tricked him, for instance, and slipped something into his beer. The idea isn't entirely implausible. Maybe one player envied Leonard so much he spiked his beer as a joke, not intending any real harm of course. Leonard had told him different players missed meetings and dogged it on the court because they were doing cocaine. Wagner himself has had suspicions about Gregg. Once during the summer league he caught Gregg with beer on his breath; he talked to his parents and they disciplined him. Later that year Gregg appeared wearing a beeper, a sudden fashion among the older kids in the school. *What did David need a beeper for?* Wagner had thought. Who was paying for it? Beepers cost a hundred dollars a month to rent. He asked Gregg and some other kids and they all said the same: they just used them for when girls called and things like that. Beep me, baby, beep me. The answer explained nothing at all.

From Leonard's room, Walker appears with the first load. Minicams following, the men go back and forth past the police line, filling up Wagner's van with the clothes, stereo equipment, records, and basketball paraphernalia that make up Bias's personal effects.

In his junior year Bias moved into the national spotlight. Walker remained the older brother, hectoring, protecting. A lot of their time together was spent playing ball or looking at television. One favorite show was *Taxi*, Leonard particularly liking the impenitently malicious Louie de Palma. When they watched basketball games they argued about players and styles. That year's NBA rivalry was between the Los Angeles Lakers and the Boston Celtics. Walker rooted for the showy, quick, improvisational (and all-black) Lakers while Leonard argued that Walker had to at least respect the slower, more predictable, but physically and mentally punishing Celtics, and especially their leader, Larry Bird.

"I hate Boston. Their fans are so racist. But Lenny loved Boston. So he'd say, 'Come on, shorty, the man can play. You have to give him that.' I'd go along—all right, he can play. Leonard wasn't stingy with other players."

During Bias's last term at school, Walker and Leonard talked constantly about his approaching life in the pros. Why did some players make it and others fail? Where would he play? You had to be careful about going West because unless you were playing for Los Angeles it was easy for the public to forget about you. You had to stay away from drugs—drugs were death. What kind of money could he realistically expect to make his first year? What kind of contract should he demand?

The most important question, the only one the young men could influence in any way, was who would represent him?

The decision was between two agencies, Pro-Serve and Advantage. The two competitors had a complicated history.

Pro-Serve had revolutionized the business of personal representation in sports. Until Pro-Serve most sports agents simply negotiated contracts and handled their clients' legal and financial matters. Pro-Serve was to these small-office, low-budget lawyers what McDonald's was to the corner hamburger shop. Starting by representing tennis players—its owner, Donald Dell, was a serious amateur performer—the agency turned its performers into franchises, organizing tournaments that starred its clients and marketing the performers like movie stars, packaging them for specific audiences and targeting them for selling particular goods. Dell's selling strategy was wildly successful; by the time Bias graduated, Pro-Serve's Washington headquarters had set up field offices in New York, Dallas, Italy, France, Australia, Japan, and Sweden. The firm employed over sixty people, represented 150 clients, and grossed more than $25 million a year.

The most successful example of Pro-Serve marketing strategy was Michael Jordan, the six-six North Carolina guard who ruled the ACC before Bias. Jordan's debut in the pros was a spectacular nonstop high-flying display of dunks and jump shots. Pro-Serve used his pyrotechnics, and his personal charm, to turn him into an icon of the eighties. The agency prints brochures for each client, featuring the performer in a posed, high-gloss photo: a bicyclist gets his lips pinked and is pictured as a Hollywood romantic lead; Pam Shriver, the tennis pro, is shown as the girl-next-door, Ms. Young Republican. In his photo, Jordan is dressed in impeccable black tie. The dusty charcoal of his skin glows against a slate gray background. With casual elegance, he holds a basketball in his upraised palm, his other hand stuck nonchalantly in his pocket, a gold wristwatch gleaming against the tuxedo's black satin. The basketball could just as easily be car keys, a bottle of champagne, or a lady's undergarment: the object is an enticement. Looking at the picture, you expect something to happen. (In a curious way this anticipation reflects Jordan's energetic spontaneity as a ball player.) What you see is style—gorgeous, exotic, self-assured. The image is a startling departure for a basketball player. Jordan isn't pictured as a jock, but a *player*—the street word for mover—whether pimp, drug dealer, or arbitrage expert. He's a star; you either want to be him or sleep with him.

Pro-Serve had negotiated a sneaker endorsement contract for Jordan with Nike. Such agreements usually result in nothing more than pocket money for the player. But Pro-Serve decided to do something different in Jordan's case. The firm convinced Nike to call the shoe the Air Jordan, a pun on the performer's airborne exploits and the footwear's technology, which featured little air pockets in the sole. Before anyone was aware that something unusual was happening, Air Jordans became a fashion fad. Within six months the company sold approximately $130 million worth of shoes. By normal standards the showing was phenomenal. The two million pairs were more than the entire sales of either Keds or Pony and accounted for fourteen percent of Nike's yearly gross. No athlete, and certainly no basketball star, especially a black one, had ever sparked such enthusiastic consumerism. One spokesman for Pro-Serve claims the sales were so great that if Jordan had owned Air Jordans—which he didn't—the product would have converted him almost overnight into the third-richest black businessman in America.

Advantage was Pro-Serve's most important rival. Its president, Lee Fentress, had worked closely with Donald Dell at Pro-Serve before abruptly leaving to set up his own firm with some of Pro-Serve's most important clients. To distinguish itself from Pro-Serve, Advantage cultivated a more intimate, less corporate image than the other firm, locating its offices in a renovated brick complex in Georgetown. Although Advantage had established itself in the business quickly, it still hadn't signed any major local basketball stars. More important, Pro-Serve had shut out Advantage from signing any of the latest top draft picks and exciting rookies, including Patrick Ewing and James Worthy, the new stars of the crucial New York and Los Angeles markets. Consequently the firm had no share of the now wildly profitable basketball sneaker market that had been created by the success of Air Jordans.

Traditionally, Driesell and his players had been associated with Pro-Serve. One famous story recounts how Driesell relied on the talents of Donald Dell to keep his prize recruit, Moses Malone. Malone was eighteen years old at the time, an unsophisticated seven-foot-tall black kid being wooed by the pros at the same time he was preparing to enter Maryland. Of course Driesell was desperate to keep Malone; the giant was a rebounding, shooting, shot-blocking promise of a national championship. So, the story goes, when Moses told him he was about to sign a professional contract, Driesell called upon Dell to help convince Moses a college education was more important than earning a million dollars before he could vote. Dell walked up to the giant, who was sitting, characteristically, with his head slumped down: Moses was notoriously shy and uncommunicative those days. Finding it impossible to get the boy's attention while standing, Dell knelt down, underneath Malone, speaking up into the manchild's face. "Do you know what slavery means?" Dell asked the reticent player. Moses mumbled yes. "Well," Dell thundered, "this contract makes slavery look good!" Dell ended up representing Malone, who years later bolted the firm to be represented by Fentress.

But since 1985 the coach had flirted with the old firm's competitor. In that year, Lee Fentress had helped Driesell renegotiate his coaching contract into a ten-year deal. Shortly after, Driesell was about to sign a new agreement for sneaker endorsements with Nike for $75,000 a year, a 20 percent increase over his previous price. Suddenly Reebok—a company which had dealt successfully with Advantage before—offered him $400,000 for four years. Fentress was quoted in the *Washington Post* as saying, "My advice to Coach Driesell was, 'Accept the offer immediately.' "

For both Pro-Serve and Advantage, Leonard was an important prospective client—a flashy, dramatic, stylish player whose name would attract kids to buy merchandise endorsed by him. As he approached graduation, both companies courted him. But Advantage seemed to enjoy privileged treatment. Driesell personally squired Leonard around the newer firm's offices several times.

With Pro-Serve, he insisted that representatives come to Cole Field House.

Yet despite Advantage's preferential treatment, Walker claims, Leonard was leaning toward Pro-Serve. Bias thought Pro-Serve "was more professional and he liked what they had done for Michael Jordan. But Fentress sold him on Advantage by saying that he personally would take care of him and that he would get more personal attention at Advantage than at Pro-Serve."

Walker and Leonard also discussed the terms of the deal. Advantage charged 3 percent for negotiating the deal, approximately 2 percent for managing his money, and 20 percent for all monies collected from endorsements they got for him; Leonard understood that the high percentage provided Advantage with an incentive for finding top-dollar promotions. One big factor in helping Leonard decide was money. Leonard never seemed to have enough spending money.

"He always needed money," says Walker. "That's why you'd see him working odd jobs. He'd tell me he'd meet guys from other schools and they'd have money—houses, cars, everything. But you never got that at Maryland."

On the day Leonard signed with Advantage, the firm helped him secure a $15,000 loan. The same day, he was issued a bank credit card.

"They used the advance as an enticement to get him to sign because until then he had wanted to sign with Pro-Serve," says Walker. "Leonard was desperate for money. They also gave him a credit card and stuff. But the card only had a five-hundred-dollar limit. He was always complaining to them about the allowance they put him on."

To fill his wallet, Leonard and Walker took a couple of weeks off from Maryland in the middle of Bias's senior spring term and barnstormed through North Carolina, Leonard starring in something called the Across Carolina ACC tournament, exhibition games played for profit, featuring local Tidewater stars.

"That's how I knew he really had no money. We *drove* down to North Carolina. You know how long that takes? No one knew about it. He just told everyone he was going away for a couple of days. I think he didn't tell his agent because then he would have had to give him some of the cut. We took jerseys and posters with us. I would auction them off in the lobby before the games. We'd charge people five dollars to buy a signed life-size poster. After the game we would split the money. The last night we made five hundred and fifty dollars. After the game I gave him the cash. He said, 'That's all right, shorty, you keep it, I got enough.' The brothers who had organized the tournament had owed him several thousand dollars and had paid him all at once.

"So when we got back we went straight to the Lizard Shop. It's in Georgetown. We [bought] all our clothes there. We'd go down there with six hundred dollars cash, for example, and . . . bargain with them—I want these alligator shoes, I want that silk shirt. You could do that because you had cash. Lenny did the same thing with his [gold] chain. He went to a store and got the guy to come down five hundred dollars and gave him twelve hundred and owed him the rest."

Soon after, Bias left for the draft—the kid who, when he first met Walker, "never shot off much except his mouth" now about to claim the glory that Walker had insisted on for him.

"He called me after the draft. It was seven-thirty in the morning. He said, 'You see me, shorty?' I told him I had taped the whole thing. He said he was going to the Reebok thing later. We joked. I told him to get me a pair of Reeboks. He said, 'I thought you didn't like Reeboks.' I told him I could go for a pair of black ones. We talked about some other things. Fooled around. He told me to have some women ready when he came home. I told him I would. Then he said he would be coming home tomorrow. 'I made it now,' he said. 'I'm a millionaire.' 'Yeah,' I said, 'if you're a millionaire then how come you're calling me collect?' "

By the time Wagner and Walker come back to the Bias family's house, reporters are camped outside; inside family and friends are paying their condolences. After unpacking the van, Wagner performs one last obligation. Jay Bias, Leonard's 16-year-old brother, is supposed to play in that night's summer-league game. Wagner asks the boy if he's sure he wants to come to the game. The boy says Leonard has always told him "to stay on the court."

Then, wanting to duck the press, Wagner drives home. With

no more chores to distract him, he thinks of Leonard. He remembers one day in particular. It was when Leonard was still at Northwestern—a long time now, he realizes. He was watching Leonard practice in the gym. It must have been late October, before the regular season started, a six-week period when all the kids' minds are still on summer and no one wants to be indoors canning twenty foul shots in a row. The noises of workout—the squeak of sneakers, sharp bounce of a pass, thump of a rebound—echoed spiritlessly in the drafty gym. The players were taking their shots listlessly, ankles dragging as they ran the lines or made their moves to the hoops. All except one. Leonard. Unlike everyone else, Leonard was having fun—running up and down, dumping the ball, laughing at the others and himself, sweating hard, having a ball, as Baxter would have said. Looking at his star, Wagner realized something special about watching Leonard play: he *enjoyed* seeing Leonard on the court. His pleasure didn't come simply from the way Leonard performed, his style, playing ball the way it should be, the way Wagner had taught him. It was that Leonard *loved* the game. His effort was fully pitched. His concentration, his effort, his strength told the viewer that the work was pleasure, an exultation in power and perfection. "Do me a favor," Wagner remembers telling his prize that afternoon, "if you ever start playing just for the money, get off the court—go draw or do anything that you enjoy, that makes you smile, but give up the game because the pleasure you get from the game is too precious to be spoiled."

His loss is double. Leonard is gone. But with him has vanished something else: the image Wagner had of Leonard's life. Now the ex-coach must admit a truth as painful as the incontrovertible fact of Leonard's death: for all his intimacy with Leonard, in some way he didn't know him at all. The boy he loved, the player he helped to mold, the athlete who inspired him—whose profile as he rose in the air to shoot Wagner can summon even now with his eyes closed—is a mystery to him.

"I asked myself what did I not do for this kid? What did I not say? How could I not see this coming? That's what bothered me the most. Because we were so close. And I never saw him drink a beer or smoke a cigarette or do anything, and he would talk about people he knew who were doing drugs and how bad it was. But he always stayed away from it, and he would talk to the other kids that way. So how could I not see this person who I was really close to? We had grown together. I had grown as coach. He had grown as a player. We both had gotten there. How could I not see this coming? How could it have taken place and I didn't see the signals?"

~~~

At ten-thirty that morning Mrs. Tribble arrives home from the social worker's. She is excited and happy—Priscilla's test results have turned out fine.

The phone rings as soon as she enters the house; it's Dorothy, her next-door neighbor and close friend.

"Did you hear the news about Lenny?" Dorothy asks.

"Brian called me this morning," Mrs. Tribble says. "Everything's okay."

"No it isn't." Dorothy tells her to sit down. "He's dead."

"What?"

"He died."

"What? Somebody's crazy. Something's wrong. Brian said his heart was beating—"

They go through the news reports. Mrs. Tribble hangs up and sits in the chair, not moving. She can't accept the idea that Leonard is dead. She reacts like Baxter—the news is weird, crazy. How can Leonard be dead? She remembers Leonard and Brian sitting on the porch, the voices of the two boys drifting into the house as they talked away late afternoons.

"He never talked basketball. Never talked up himself. Once he came by after he had been suspended from the team for three games. He asked me if I was disappointed in him. He was mad because they had lost a game and he knew they would have won if he had played. I told him he must be disappointed in himself. Another time he came by and said he was worried about the draft—that he might have to go and play in San Francisco or somewhere. But I think he liked to come here because in this house he wasn't Len Bias, but was just one of Brian's friends."

How can he be dead? Brian said his heart—my God, she thinks, Brian! This is his best friend. He doesn't know anything about
~~~

death. How is he going to respond? Junior comes in and she tells him to find Brian.

"What's the matter?" he says.

Mrs. Tribble repeats the news. Junior suggests they call Brian's apartment. Brian still isn't home. The voice on the other end of the line tells them that he went to Julie's and that somebody has broken into Julie's apartment.

Junior goes to get Brian. When he comes back with him, Brian is pale and stricken.

"He walked in the door and I swear to God I hope I never live to see him look like that again. Never. Never. Never."

"Brian," she says.

Her son hugs her, collapsing into the enfolding comfort of her soft skin. "Oh God, Momma," he says, "he's dead."

She comforts him, sheltering him in her short, strong, stout arms. For Mrs. Tribble and her son, Leonard's death marks only the start of the tragedy—their ordeal has just begun.

INVESTIGATION

The first newsman arrives that afternoon. Mrs. Tribble shoos the reporter away, but others soon follow. An irreversible process has begun. In the next several days her ordinary son will be transformed from just Brian to Brian Lee Tribble, the mystery friend of Len Bias, an ex–College Park student who drives a Mercedes Benz, rents a high-rise luxury apartment, dresses expensively, hangs out at fast-lane nightclubs, has no visible income, and is the prime suspect wanted by the police for the "suspicious death" of Len Bias.

"Somebody came by to see what had happened that morning," Mrs. Tribble remembers. "I told him I was sorry I didn't have any comment, didn't know what they were talking about, and I shut the door. Then I told Brian, 'Look, this is going to go on, so go on over to Gloria's.' He went over and stayed the night and I think the next morning he went to Baltimore and stayed in Baltimore that weekend. That's when the police said he was hiding out. From that day on it was downhill about everything. Things came out, one after the other. Every time you looked it was something else. And things were so unreal. I would just sit and tell reporters, 'It's not true.' Finally I felt like I was demented and something was wrong with *me* because all I could say was that it was a bunch of lies. Which it was! But nobody believed me because I was just a mother. If it had been the truth I would have said it was the truth. But it wasn't! Everything was lies—damn lies! It was so incredible, man, I can't even begin to tell you."

From the first, Bias's death was news—not a sports story, but a national event, a tragedy, scandal, and mystery commanding lead columns and the opening segment on the seven o'clock news.

"At first everybody was in town," remembers Sally Jenkins, a sports reporter for the *Washington Post* whose freshman assignment was to cover the team in Leonard's senior year. "The *New York Times* was there, the *Daily News*, the *Boston Globe* turned up for the grand jury." A PR person for the university recalls the siege. "Everyone thought it was their story," she says. "We'd get weird requests. A radio station in Tampa would call saying they wanted the chancellor for a four-hour call-in show starting at midnight."

Bias's death made great copy. A 1940's Warner Brothers screenwriter couldn't have invented a more vivid scenario of the vanity of human wishes than this chronicle of success and destruction. Even more important, Bias's last night presented a genuine riddle. Who was he with? What did he do before the party began in the dorm room? How did he die? Answers only prompted more questions. When the coroner declared cocaine the cause of death—"cocaine intoxication" was the elegant phrase—the mystery increased. The story became an Arabian Nights of speculative leads and philosophical commentaries. How did he get the drugs? Did someone dope him? Was it his first time? If he got high regularly, then who was his dealer? And why was he taking drugs? How often? Did anyone know? Driesell? Bias's teammates? How could *Len Bias* die of a cocaine overdose? The drug wasn't lethal—especially for a healthy-as-an-ox twenty-two-year-old who has just passed several physical exams, all including drug tests. Besides, Leonard was an all-American, born-again Christian. "The fact is that Len was perceived as a man-of-the-year type," says Sally Jenkins. "The incredible schism between the image of Len Bias and the circumstances of his death was a profoundly disturbing event. People were just unnerved by it."

Trying to provide answers, the media spotlight shifted from one area of investigation to another. Like any good drama, the story very quickly expanded outward, leaving the immediate circumstances of his death to touch on the basketball team, the University of Maryland, and state politics. "For the first couple of days the story was 'Len Bias died,' " says Mark Hyman, a *Baltimore Sun* reporter who had just joined the paper that spring. "Did he die of drug use? *That* was the story. [Then] it became . . . larger than Len Bias. . . . From a very personal story it became an institutional story." As the complications of the plot unfolded, different characters emerged as the main protagonists. Each was presented as a media stereotype. Tribble was the mystery man, a cool, good-looking black hustler capable of almost anything. Arthur Marshall, state attorney of Prince George's County, was the prosecutor, wily, naive, incorrigible. Driesell was the coach, simple, folksy, emotional, a father figure besieged by—depending on your view—an errant past or a too insistent, opportunistic press. He was the first of a series of Reagan culture heroes cut down by vanity (Boesky, the evangelicals, Meese, *et al.* were to follow).

The *Washington Post* treated all this as a major event, running over four hundred Len Bias–related articles in the next nine months; the attention given to the event by the country's second paper of record stamped the episode with an imprimatur of national importance it would never have received if Bias had come from, say, Kansas City. (Ironically, though, the *Post* pushed the story mainly for a more parochial reason. The paper was locked in a circulation war with the *Baltimore Sun* for control of the ever-expanding Beltway suburbs. The playing out of the repercussions of Bias's death, this long-running soap opera, sold papers. It still does. "My God," said a College Park official recently, "we're still surprised when a story in the *Post* doesn't begin 'Even two years after the death of Len Bias, the campus at College Park remains etc . . .' ") The final element that made the story news was timing: Bias's death coincided with a national furor over cocaine.

At the turn of the century, cocaine had been among the most popular of nostrum drugs in America. Then it was banned; for the next fifty years its use was marginal. But in the seventies, the drug saw a remarkable revival and was transformed from a guilty pleasure enjoyed by a privileged few into a staple of American consumerism. By the time of Bias's death, over 20 million Americans had tried it at least once, compared to about 5½ million twelve years earlier. Twenty percent of the 1984 graduating high-school class had tried coke, and 13 percent of these had used the drug within the previous year, 7 percent within the previous month.

The drug had become a standard feature of American cultural life. Politically, coke had become an integral part of the debate over the Reagan Administration's Central America policies, left and right accusing the other of trafficking with the "narcos," the thriving bands of entrepreneurial drug manufacturers and exporters transforming the South American interior into a vast cocaine factory. Socially, it had toured Reagan America, descending from the heights of Hollywood and pro sports royalty through the *Bright Lights, Big City* nightlife of young professionals, finally settling in the urban squalor of the homeless, jobless poor of mideighties America. Morally, it had provided a focus for a debate over values: acceptance of drug use was stigmatized by conservatives as a sixties atavism, a kind of domestic Vietnam syndrome, embodying the shallow principles that had led the country astray. Athletes were drafted as the nation's moral standard bearers. Why and how they were assigned this role was never questioned. As Bobby Dandridge, an ex–pro basketball player, said at a hearing at the House of Representatives Select Committee on Narcotics Abuse, "For some reason society has given [professional athletes] the dubious task of being the only role models in this nation." In Pittsburgh the summer before Bias died the trial of a drug peddler accused of selling drugs to major-league baseball players attracted national attention; the proceedings quickly assumed a naming-names, McCarthyite cast, often with journeyman players identifying other users—"You're not looking for Communists," Dalton Trumbo accused his accusers back in the 1950's, "you're just looking for jobs!"—while prominent athletes confessed to their own addiction but refused to point fingers. The spectacle resulted in calls for mandatory arbitrary drug testing, a crusade that climaxed when a California preteen turned in her pot-smoking parents after hearing an after-school lecture on the perils of addiction.

Still, even with all the breast beating, the public remained by and large unconcerned about drugs. Then, in the spring of 1986 crack—a new, more virulent form of cocaine—was introduced to American cities. Almost instantly drugs became an issue of national concern.

Sold in vials and plastic baggies for five to fifteen dollars apiece, crack is a mass-produced, easily marketed, extremely concentrated form of cocaine. Its genius is that, unlike powder cocaine, it can be smoked, which is the quickest, most potent way of bringing the stimulant to the nerve centers of the brain where it works its magic.

When crack appeared, the police were caught by surprise. "No one anticipated the spreading of crack," says Ed Jurith, the staff director of the Select Committee on Narcotics Abuse and Control. "It was kind of funny. It took a while for somebody to figure out what the hell the stuff was. We were getting reports, but even analysts at the Drug Enforcement Administration [DEA] couldn't figure it out. They knew it was cocaine, but they didn't know how it was being processed."

Crack's popularity was enormous and instantaneous. Within several months crack had become the new drug of choice, adopted by blacks and kids, markets previously denied to cocaine because of the drug's high price. Testifying before the Select Committee, a Detroit police department narcotics inspector said, "The problem with crack is we don't have a measuring stick. . . . [Is it] something like heroin was in 1970? Well, that don't fit. Or is it something like marijuana was back in 1950. That don't fit, so there is no measuring stick. . . . We don't know [what we are dealing with]. Ten months ago, it wasn't even in the streets of Detroit, and now it constitutes eighty-five percent of our enforcement effort."

In the drug world, crack was simply an invention designed to solve a vexing business problem: the oversupply of cocaine in the American market. This glut was causing a sharp decline in profit. (A hothouse of entrepreneurial industry and unfettered exchange between buyer and seller, the cocaine market is a laissez-faire economist's dream.)

Crack, the answer to this excess, was, in business terms, a loss-leader. Powdery cocaine burns too quickly to be smoked, because of the hydrochloride salt that is part of its chemical composition. Crack solves this problem by extracting the hydrochloride salt from the "product," as everyone in the business calls the drug. In the process a percentage of the bulk of the original material is lost. But this short-term loss is compensated for by other commercial virtues of the drug.

The first is crack's marketability. Because of its traditionally high price—a gram traditionally costs approximately $100—cocaine has previously been limited to a rich, narrow audience. Crack significantly widens the audience for cocaine. It can be purchased by casual buyers and, most important, experimenting kids.

Second, the drug is more potent than powder cocaine. It acts more quickly and dramatically. Heightening one of cocaine's particular powers, it evidently helps to form addictions in record time. The chief epidemiologist for the New Jersey State Department of Health told the Select Committee of a sixteen-year-old girl who claimed crack took complete control over her life only five days after her first whiff. He described a robbery to dramatize the monomania produced by the drug. "The first thing the robbers, undoubtedly crack users themselves, did was to shoot the proprietor to death as they shouted for everyone else to 'freeze.' While one held a weapon to the almost two dozen users in the house, the others gathered up vials of crack and money. At least four people continued to smoke crack while the robbery was in progress. For these people to continue to smoke, to get as much of the drug in their system as they could, while in the midst of such a life-threatening situation is nothing short of astounding. And as a final fillip, the robbers took a shopping bag and collected the pipes containing crack residue from everyone in the house as part of the booty. This is akin to a robber collecting pennies from the customers while robbing a bank." The most horrific instances of the drug's power involve family violence: a user hanging his two-year-old from the window, another raping his eight-months-pregnant wife, an addicted mother giving birth to a physically impaired baby and naming the infant, "Kookene."

Finally, the drug exudes a kind of perverse allure. For the poor it is instant money, like finding oil in your backyard. Producers don't need much capital or equipment to go into business. Franchises—we are in the age of franchises—are started on street corners. "I was asked to be a partner," says a seventeen-year-old Washingtonian interviewed in 1988. "I would give them two hundred and fifty dollars and they would put their two hundred and fifty and then we'd go buy the stuff from the Big Man"—the generic name for big-time dealers—"cut it, cook it, and sell it. And we'd make a thousand."

In the spring of 1986, for the middle class the drug was also a new thrill. Even the news reports—like Victorian accounts of prostitution—titillated while condemning. Through them, viewers and readers entered an exotic, deadly world mixing nineteenth-century degradation and modern business know-how, where runners with beepers delivered brand names such as "White Cloud," "Cloud Nine," "Based-ball" and "Serpico" to "crack houses," reincarnated opium dens where users "hit the pipe" (to use the phrase from the 1870's) for days at a time, sunk in a claustrophobic madness of drugs, money, and sex.

Crack was everywhere that spring. The month before Bias died, crack accounted for two-thirds of all coke analyses made by police and 40 percent of all felony narcotics indictments in New York City. Drugs became a major issue. "People were generally fat and happy," one congressman told the *Washington Post*. "They had nothing really bothering them except some esoteric matters about the deficit. The one issue they talked about with emotion was drugs."

Bias's tragedy occurred at the height of the public outcry. His death dramatized the destructive potential of the drug and spurred legislative action. Within months of the tragedy the first comprehensive drug bill in years was passed, providing over four billion dollars for drug enforcement, education, and treatment. "Tip O'Neill and Jim Wright had reached out to the committee in the spring of eighty-six," says Ed Jurith, "and we had started a dialogue about a drug bill. Jim Wright particularly was interested in what this committee could offer. So the train was moving down the track. . . . Bias just pushed [the issue] to the top of the public agenda." Bob Weiner, the press information officer for the Select Committee, is less equivocal, asserting that "it took the Len Bias incident to pass the bill. That was a motivating factor. That guy was a hero. He was a hero-to-be. It got enormous coverage. No one could ignore it." The *Washington Post* summarized the drama of the Bias death aptly: "Several lawmakers said the House was responding to a public perception that drugs—particularly cocaine and crack—pose a threat to every segment of society." Bias symbolized every parent's nightmare, "an all-American kid, from a nice family, a good person from all indications, who got involved with a drug and quickly he was dead."

In many ways, of course, this was not accurate. As a drug victim Leonard was anomalous. "Every kid," and certainly most drug victims, don't get Reebok contracts. Neither do they die of "cocaine intoxication," as the coroner referred to the cause of Leonard's death; they "OD," overdose. What the media really meant was not that his tragedy suggested what might happen to other good, middle-class kids; rather, what Leonard's death accomplished was to cast attention on those who were dying. In this sense his death was a heroic sacrifice, transforming an ordinary event, the death by overdose of a young black man in a big American city, into a national tragedy.

Yet for all the attention given to Leonard's death, the dimensions of the plague symbolized by his disaster increased rather than diminished in the next years. By 1989, the crack-cocaine epidemic had become, after the budget deficit, the most abiding legacy of the Reagan Era. Its main and most drastic effects were in the black community. There the drug was as powerful an agent of destruction as, say, the European diseases the conquistadors brought with them to the Native Americans. Crack created a generation of addicts, eroded the stability of black communities, added immeasurably to the fears and furies that generate white racism, and threatened to destroy the moral and political legacy of the black American struggle for freedom.

Some reporting—the *Washington Post* coverage was one notable example—tried to gain a perspective on this plague; but most media discussion was limited to basically sensational reportage, often way behind the event. There was practically no attempt to trace how the devastating new phenomenon had occurred. Instead, the media reported on the plague by mystifying it, making the drug seem to come out of nowhere like H. G. Wells's Martians—and disappear like them too, whenever the media sensed the shock value of the subject had worn thin.

This same attitude colored the reporting on Leonard's death. In examining the case, the press and police concentrated on the personal details of Leonard's drama. Investigators asked only one question: *Who* killed Len Bias? They neglected the more relevant issue of *how* he died. They never asked how cocaine had come to be the drug of choice for a young man like Leonard in the first place.

But in the long term the narrow details—who gave him the drugs, how long he had taken them—mattered considerably less than the broad outlines of his fate: How come he was taking this drug now? Whatever Leonard's personal motivations for getting high that night, the likelihood is that fifteen years earlier he would have been smoking pot rather than snorting coke and the odds of his dying would have been infinitesimal. What counts most in understanding Leonard's death is not private details, but public facts; not an unknown villain—Tribble, or a mystery man who doped Bias's beer, or Bias himself—but the conflicts in Bias's life that climaxed in the tragic resolution of his death. In this sense his case is like the drug crisis itself. The cocaine epidemic is not explained by a mystery—the machinations of the CIA or a secret drug cabal. Rather, this plague came about through the completely observable workings of American medicine, business, politics, social policy, and social prejudice. Untangling the role of these elements that combine to produce the cocaine plague reveals a criminal negligence much worse than any possibly contributing to the death of Leonard Bias: the failure of the major institutions of American society—science, law, and government—to stop an unfolding event of disastrous consequences.

At the hospital, a double reality rules. Everybody knows that Leonard took cocaine the previous night. The players have forced the truth out of Gregg and Long. Long, the center, has told one of the nurses working on Bias. The obvious conclusion is that the drug must be at least partly responsible for his death. But no one admits any of this publicly. Vague rumors are floated that Leonard has died of Marpham's syndrome, the exotic killer disease of tall, thin young people. (A previous Maryland basketball player is one of its victims.) A hospital authority enters Leonard's death certificate as a John Doe, presumably to lessen the publicity.

"The police knew within minutes, as I recall," claims Arthur Marshall in 1988. Marshall is the state attorney who led the official investigation into the case. "They knew right off the bat that things were not right, that evidence was missing, that the room had been cleaned up. . . . They had been at Leland Memorial Hospital when people were running around saying tell the truth. The doctors knew it, the staff knew it, Driesell knew it, but no one would talk to the police."

At the center of the dishonesty is Driesell.

In the immediate aftermath, Driesell deliberately obscures his knowledge about what happened. Known for rising to the occasion—"Lefty's one of those guys who's best coaching when things are going worst," says Sally Jenkins—the coach meets this grave personal and professional crisis with a performance of Nixonian proportions: brazen, sentimental, self-deluded, calculated, profoundly cynical, preposterously disingenuous. And damaging. His statements inadvertently heighten the drama of the revelations about Bias that follow the star's death, ruining, perhaps permanently, Leonard's reputation. They also set the investigation of his death off on a disastrous, misguided course.

"If the Prince George's County police," says Arthur Marshall in 1988, "had developed the fact—which they would have—that Lefty Driesell knew about [Leonard taking cocaine that night] and [Driesell had] come forth shortly after . . . I don't think anybody would have gotten charged with anything. I really don't think so."

Since the morning of June 19, 1986, Driesell has publically recounted the events of the day three times: directly after Leonard's death, in interviews with the press during the following autumn after he testified before the grand jury, and one year after the tragedy, in court testimony. Otherwise he has refused to speak about the event. But his public announcements have not been candid. He consistently withheld vital information. Less than twenty-four hours after Bias's death, he said he didn't know whether Leonard had been using drugs. The next day he said that the police had reported that there had been traces of cocaine in Leonard's urine, but that if Leonard had been using coke, he would have been "completely shocked." Four months later he acknowledges participating in an attempt to clean up Leonard's room the morning of his death. Finally, at the trial of Brian Tribble, he testifies that he was aware almost immediately—within less than four hours of Leonard's death—that Leonard had taken coke that night, directly before his seizure. These are the things that are consistent in Driesell's various accounts.

He hears about Leonard upon returning from a daily constitutional he takes with his wife. He gets a call from a nurse saying she has a player and wants the name of the trainer. So he calls again and speaks to another nurse who tells him that it's Leonard and that the family wants him to be there. He goes to the hospital and meets near the emergency room with Mr. and Mrs. Bias and some family friends. When Leonard is pronounced dead, athletic director Dick Dull suggests the players meet at his office because the players are emotionally upset.

When Driesell arrives at the campus gymnasium, Cole Field House, he speaks with Lee Fentress, the managing director of Advantage. As Driesell recounts to *Sports Illustrated* that fall, he tells Fentress that Bias has died, "and that 'I had heard at the hospital that he might have been fooling with some cocaine.' "

Fentress's reaction, according to Driesell, is to become "hysterical." Fentress advises Driesell to "tell an assistant coach or someone to go over there and clean up the room.' " (Fentress confirmed this account to *Sports Illustrated* but said it was an offhand remark made at an emotional moment without consideration of the implications.)

Driesell listens to the advice. "Put yourself in my position," he explained in the *Sports Illustrated* interview. "He is Leonard Bias's attorney, and he had just negotiated my contract with the university before that, so he's my attorney too." (In his accounts, Driesell—a man who's a coach, after all, one of the ultimate big-boss positions in the society—never initiates anything. Instead Fentress calls *him*, tells *him* to go clean up the room.)

According to Arthur Marshall's recollection of Driesell's testimony to the grand jury, Driesell doesn't take Fentress's advice immediately. This hesitation is sensible. The press is already at Cole. Besides, at this point, Driesell doesn't know the extent of the cocaine use. He hasn't had a chance yet to interrogate Long and Gregg. All he knows are rumors.

So he tells the players to go to his house. (Speedy Jones refuses.) There the coach and players pray for Leonard. Afterward, Driesell holds a private meeting with Gregg and Long. He quizzes the two players—this is around ten-thirty that morning—in the basement.

"They had a meeting that same day right after the death at Driesell's house," Arthur Marshall says. "Nobody told [the police] about that. . . . Driesell was downstairs with I guess Gregg and

Long. Nothing wrong with his original reaction. Nothing wrong with bringing Long downstairs and finding out what happened. What was wrong from that moment on was not telling the police. . . ."

At first Long is afraid to speak. He has never been able to distinguish between Driesell's bark and his bite. "If Lefty would yell at him," Wagner says, "that was it, Terry could not handle it. He took it personally." The substitute center must be afraid that if he tells the truth the coach will punish him. Only the intervention of Gregg convinces him to talk. In tears, Gregg implores Long: Terry, he begs the bigger player, you got to tell Coach what happened, you got to! Don't be scared, man, don't be mad, just tell the truth!

So the story comes out. In the days to follow the tale will be repeated numerous times, one player telling another, different variations embroidering the basic events.

The first part is always consistent. Bias entered around three that morning, waking up the guys, telling them they were going to celebrate. Leonard was with Tribble. (Driesell claims Gregg and Long told him Tribble brought the coke, but neither Gregg nor Long testifies to this.) Crowding into Long's room, they start hitting the pipe. After a while Lenny leans back. Brian warns him not to, tells him that putting your head back can induce seizures. Lenny laughs. One can imagine him stretched out on the bed, relaxed and excited from the drug, exhausted from the thrill and grind of the last twenty-four hours. Seizures! he scoffs at Brian. The idea that *his* body, this perfect engine just drafted by the Celtics, might go out of control is too ridiculous to contemplate.

And now the variations begin, each adding some detail to the drama. In one Leonard has already been hitting the pipe hard. The other kids warn him to go easy. No, he shrugs them off, I can take it, I'm a bad motherfucker, I can take it. In another he simply reclines and closes his eyes, as though drifting into sleep. In a third he slumps back, faking an exaggerated palsy, pretending to be Brian going into a fit. Or so the boys think. This is Lenny clowning around, the joker who fell down in front of the store claiming Baxter hit him, who calls Lefty "Big Chuck," who doesn't care if Prince is a faggot, the player who makes his own rules. So they are laughing at him. Then his foot flails out, knocking over the stereo at the end of the bed. They realize that what's happening is real. Long, remembering emergency first aid, kneels and uses a scissor to keep Leonard from swallowing his tongue. He begins to administer mouth-to-mouth. Brian calls his mother. The terror has begun.

Acting with customary bold assertiveness, he follows Fentress's advice. He calls on Oliver Purnell, a first-year assistant coach, and the only black on the Terrapin basketball coaching staff.

"Purnell was standing upstairs," says Marshall, "trying to go downstairs—something like that—and they told him he couldn't go downstairs."

Now Driesell tells Purnell that Fentress has said to go clean up the room. "I didn't even think about it," Driesell explains later in an interview, "because here's a lawyer [i.e., Fentress] telling me what to do. The guy's supposed to be a lawyer."

Purnell "didn't say no," remembers Marshall. "As I recall he started to go and he said, 'That's wrong.' " But Purnell goes.

In any event, when Purnell arrives at the room there is nothing he *can* do. The university police have already cordoned off the area; besides, the room is spotless, without any evidence of drugs, not even a beer bottle except for a half-empty one in the refrigerator, later identified as Baxter's.

Meanwhile the meeting ends. When the players emerge and speak to the press, none, not even the most independent of them, tells the truth. A shocked Jeff Baxter quite sincerely informs a local television interviewer that he knows nothing about Leonard doing drugs. Speedy Jones tells the *Baltimore Sun* that Leonard had woken Terry Long up at about six that morning, spoken to him for several minutes, then laid back and "closed his eyes and started shaking." All cloak Leonard in innocence to protect his image, the University of Maryland, the basketball team, themselves, even perhaps their pride because some surely must have felt angry, betrayed, or humiliated to discover they were excluded from the intimacies of the person they considered their best friend.

Only Gregg and Long are nowhere to be seen. Bob Wagner explains. "That evening, I think, Oliver or Ron [Bradley, another Maryland assistant coach] asked would I keep Terry and David at my house because they knew just me and no one else lives there. I didn't even question their actions. I just thought it was to keep them away from the press. And I had a summer-league game that night, so I said okay. They got some sodas and went upstairs . . . they were out just like that, in a few seconds."

Later, on the way to the summer-league game in which Jay, Bias's younger brother, is going to play, Wagner runs into David Gregg's stepfather.

"[He] wanted to know if I knew where David was. I said, 'He's at my house, if you would have called the basketball office they would have told you where he was.' . . . But that bothered me that he didn't know where his own son was."

Then, on the way back, "I hear on the radio that the police don't know where they are and all this kind of stuff. Well, when I got in, I said, 'What the hell is going on with you guys?' They said they just talked to Detective whoever and let them know where they were and they were going to see an attorney the next morning. . . . They said they were going to cooperate with the police and they were going to tell everything they knew. They weren't going to try and play any games, they weren't going to lie or any of that kind of stuff, and that was the end of the conversation."

The next morning the two are gone. "I don't know if they left before I got off or when I was working, but they had that appointment and [David Gregg's stepfather] came over that morning, early, six-thirty, seven, whatever, and they went to wherever the attorney's was."

None of this information is given to the public.

Not that Driesell isn't talking publicly. On the contrary. The afternoon of Leonard's death he goes to Cole Field House. In the large rectangular foyer, before a battery of microphones, he holds a quick press conference. There, the large, formidable coach who has the bulk and bearing of a World War II general or an old-fashioned sheriff speaks with a disarming grief, impressing several reporters present with his emotional vulnerability.

"I really don't know whether I'm up to this, but I guess Leonard would want me to say something," he begins. Then he pauses, dabbing at a tear. The next morning the picture makes papers everywhere, Driesell's small eyes shuttered in pain, a portrait of humble, manly grief.

When he gathers himself, he eulogizes Bias. Leonard was like a son to him, he says, the greatest player in ACC history, an athlete who constantly improved himself. "But . . . more important than that, the last five or six years we've had a religious retreat up in the mountains. Leonard was a born-again Christian and he gave his life to the Lord. That shows you what kind of man, what kind of person he was."

The questions start. Cocaine is the reporters' concern. They have heard the same drug rumors as everyone else; they are desperate for confirmation. What does Driesell know about Leonard using cocaine? Does he think drugs or alcohol played a part in Leonard's death?

"I don't know. . . . I'm not really concerned with that right now," Driesell answers. He expands his denial, asserting that there "has never been an indication of anybody involved in the men's basketball team that have been involved with drugs." After detailing the university's testing policies, he returns to his sorrow. "As my wife said, he's in a better position right now than we are. He's at home with the Lord. I really sincerely believe that, and his mother is a very, very strong Christian woman, as is his dad. I'm sad, but I'm not even worried because I know where Leonard is, I know he's in heaven. We'll miss him, I love you, Leonard, and I miss you. I'll see you in heaven one day."

With that, Dick Dull, the University of Maryland athletic director, takes over. An ex–javelin thrower with a handsome, Kennedyesque youthfulness, Dull speaks with a calm, assured openness, drawing upon a seemingly infinite well of genuine feeling. But he continues Driesell's stonewalling. "Right now we're grieving the loss of one of our own," he answers when asked the obvious question about drugs, adopting a high moral tone as though the query is inappropriate, unworthy of their attention. "We're less concerned as to how it happened."

Dull compounds Driesell's obfuscations. He says Bias was nine or ten credits short of graduation and was going to summer school. Actually, Bias has attended almost no classes that spring term and needs twenty-one credits to graduate. Being short credits is a commonplace among college senior ball players. In his final term, Bias has been preparing for the draft, enjoying his notoriety—witness his trip to North Carolina with Johnny Walker—traveling to interviews with NBA teams, and deciding professional problems such as his representation that would affect his future for years to come. It would take a mind more powerfully disciplined and stringent in moral rectitude than Increase Mather's to concentrate on finals while handling these tasks, to say nothing of ignoring the sheer distraction of the million-dollar contract awaiting on June 20th. But Dull's discrepancy, when it is discovered, suddenly makes the athletic department seem completely untrustworthy—especially to the Biases, who were ignorant of Leonard's academic standing and want to know why they weren't informed.

By now any attempt to hide the cause of Bias's death is doomed to failure, since the police and several hundred reporters are searching for the proof that will confirm what everyone believes. Still, Driesell is undaunted. The difficulty of the situation has brought out the battler in him. "People always say about Lefty, he'll do more with less than anybody," comments Sally Jenkins. "There are plenty of stories about how he used to do things like change light bulbs in the opponent's dressing room, screw in thin white bulbs so that when they came out on the floor the glare would get to them, have a center change jerseys with a guard to try to confuse people, things like that . . . his entire philosophy and demeanor [are expressed in] a sign on his desk that says, 'If the going gets easy, you ain't climbing.' That's Lefty. A tough old streetfighter, that's what he is."

The next morning, on "Good Morning America," Driesell continues the campaign to obscure the truth. The tough old streetfighter is filmed in front of the appropriately vast and empty Cole Field House, the symbolic void once filled by Bias. He wears a distracted, somber expression, that of a man who is grieving but will fulfill his duty and speak to the public anyway. In the studio, the interviewer, a young man with model-like good looks named Stone Phillips, leans forward intently from the mock living-room set of the sound stage. In light of what is now known about Driesell, the moment is almost unconscionably false. Not only are all the trappings—the phony set, the fake first-name intimacy between host and guest—untrue, but what Driesell is about to say is a series of untruths. The solemnity of the occasion, the human loss and grief that are the subject of the interview makes the otherwise usual acceptable fraudulence of television staging monstrous.

"Coach Driesell," Stone Phillips asks, "have you reconciled

yourself yet to the loss?" One of the curious emotional miscues in the numerous television interviews of Driesell, Dull, and Auerbach is that the reporters direct their condolences at these men rather than at the victim's family. They thank them for appearing on the set, commiserate with them about their loss, transforming them by this emotional alchemy into the victims. Only K. C. Jones, the Celtics coach, a model of tact and honesty, declines to enter the center of the tragic stage. Pressed time and again by one interviewer, Jones patiently and modestly keeps focusing attention on the Bias family.

Hands clasped before him, looking down and squinting as though he really doesn't want to be in the public light, Driesell is ready with his answer. "I guess I know I'll never see Leonard running or jumping or dunking or happy again and it's hard."

Cautiously Phillips asks about stories that cocaine was involved.

"I would be very surprised," Driesell answers. He uses a mild, almost affectless tone of calm assurance. Either he really believes he can bamboozle the public or he is so panicked that, like a child caught in an impossible situation, he figures the only way to escape his first lie is to keep telling fibs. "Leonard had just had exams in Boston, New York, and with the Golden State Warriors, and I'm positive there were no drugs there. And it's completely out of character. That's one thing I told Red—they didn't have to worry about drugs or alcohol with him. That he was a born-again Christian and a great person. It would be completely out of character."

There's a report in the morning's *Boston Globe*, Phillips says, that Driesell had called Auerbach last night and told him the police had reported traces of cocaine in Bias's urine. Perhaps, Phillips suggests delicately, Leonard was taking it for the first time.

Driesell's answer is unequivocal. "No," he says matter-of-factly, his voice tinged with a little exasperation at having to set the matter straight. "I told him that they said in the urine there was a trace. But if that's the case it's completely out of character for Leonard Bias. I would be completely shocked."

Then there's no reason to believe he might have been experimenting? the interviewer presses.

"I really couldn't tell you that until the autopsy is done," Driesell replies, wanting the inquiry to stop.

He gets his way. "Coach, what made him such a great player?"

Driesell gives the familiar litany, ending with the by now familiar reference to Leonard as a "born-again." There is in his voice a sense of exhaustion. Perhaps even he is beginning to tire of the ordeal.

There's going to be a scholarship in Bias's name, Phillips mentions, finishing the interview on the appropriately elegiac note.

Well, Driesell explains, wrapping up, Leonard was going to do a lot for his brothers and sisters. Now the university is setting up a fund to take care of their college education.

The final note of the sound bite, this is also not true.

The University of Maryland was not, then or later, associated with any scholarship fund bearing Bias's name. Advantage does collect money. Eventually the fund totals twelve thousand odd dollars, ten of which are contributed by the Boston Celtics.

Except for a eulogy he delivers at Leonard's funeral, and a press conference on June 25, Driesell's appearance on "Good Morning America" is his last public statement for the next several months about Leonard's death. From almost the moment of Leonard's death, the coach's method has been undeviating: to present Leonard as a Christian young man and himself as a coach who had no idea at all of any drug use by Leonard or any other player on the team.

It would be wrong to suggest that this effort at misdirection was guided simply by a desire to cover himself.

To begin with, even the issue of self-protection is cloudy because by protecting himself Driesell, like his players, was of course also shielding Leonard, guarding the player's good name. And it is undoubtedly true that Driesell had genuine feeling for the player who had starred so successfully in his program. "My perception . . . is that Lefty was quite sincere in his remorse over what had happened to Len," says Bennie Thayer, the owner of a sporting-goods store in Landover who has been involved with local politics for a long time. "I think Lefty had put quite a stake into Leonard's career and I think he was devastated by what happened to him. He was remorseful. I can tell you he was remorseful then. At a later time he seemed somewhat removed."

But Driesell's contempt for the truth about Leonard's death also stems from his character and his long relationship with the University.

Driesell is a supremely self-confident man. His country-shrewd manner wins people over. It is almost impossible to find someone who doesn't like him. People disagree with him, criticize him, think he's a bad coach, but there are few who don't give him the benefit of some spontaneous goodwill. One comment you hear constantly about Driesell is, "That's Lefty!" The words are said with ironic acceptance. People will tell you he "wears you down"—wears down his assistants by working them too hard, wears down his recruits by answering all their fears about his program, wears down the reporters by his fearless confrontations with them. He wears down people's hesitations about him too, winning his audience over slowly. For all his extravagant posturing, he elicits acceptance.

"When Lefty reacts," his colleague and ex-student Wagner says, "he reacts from down in his gut. . . . That's his strength and his weakness. . . . When you see him coach, you don't see him sitting there calmly watching the game—he's up, he's got nervous habits, he's involved one hundred and fifty percent . . . and I think that's why people perceived him as—you either loved him or hated him, because when Lefty stands out there and coaches, he . . . stands there totally naked in a sense . . . he doesn't care who's in the stands. . . . What you see with [him] is what you get. He is right there. He's not playing with you."

"I don't think he is capable of very serious deception," says Mark Hyman about Driesell. Hyman is a *Baltimore Sun* reporter who covered the University of Maryland athletic department the summer of Bias's death. "People look at him and they think: nobody can be this way. But he is. I think he feels, in his heart, that he provided for those kids everything that he could provide for them. He offered the kind of leadership that was appropriate. And I think he feels that he did nothing wrong. Throughout the whole episode. I'm sure of it in fact . . . I've talked to him about it. He doesn't feel any guilt about the death of Leonard Bias. . . . Whatever Lefty did . . . on behalf of Bias, I'm sure he sincerely feels was in Bias's best interest, and if he happened to benefit as a result

. . . I don't think he feels badly about that. That's the thing you have to understand about Lefty. Jewish guilt is not a big part of his makeup."

There is another aspect to Driesell's response to Bias's death. Permissive and protective toward his players, Driesell had acted as an independent agent within the university for many years. "When Lefty started out at the University of Maryland he was . . . younger and he was recruiting kids he had a lot in common with . . . kids who came from middle-class backgrounds, who were fairly bright," says Molly Dunham today. Dunham is a reporter for the *Baltimore Evening Sun* who had covered the team for three years when Leonard died. Driesell "would outrecruit everybody just by outworking everybody. He'd be on the road twenty-four hours a day. . . . The NCAA rules changed and restricted the business and suddenly the rest of the coaches started catching up to Lefty because Lefty couldn't outwork them anymore. And rather than Lefty coming down a bit, they came up and suddenly the pool of talent was limited and [Lefty] started saying I gotta pick this guy—even if I don't think he's the right type of person, I've got to take him for my team. And I'd say since seventy-six Lefty's recruiting started going downhill and the character of the players started going downhill and I think he would come close to admitting it, but doesn't come out and say it exactly. And I don't think ten years ago Lefty would ever have recruited Terry Long, ever. He wouldn't have even given him a second thought."

But no one in the university administration confronted Driesell about the change in his recruits. He "had a great constituency among the alumni," explains Mark Hyman, "and he was more closely identified with the institution than any of his superiors. . . . So [Driesell] was able to make the rules to a larger extent than he should have. . . . As long the team was winning and there were no disastrous consequences, I think people were content to let Lefty do as he wanted to do. . . . Over the years—as the kids' academic profiles became worse and worse and worse, and their ability to stay in school got worse—[this policy] created a program where kids were, you know, flunking out almost as fast as he could bring them in. . . . And for a variety of reasons, Dick Dull and [university chancellor] John Slaughter didn't act forcefully in letting Lefty know that there weren't going to be exceptions made for these kids, that if they didn't meet minimum requirements they weren't going to get in. . . . They sent all the wrong messages to Lefty. When he appealed certain admissions decisions, they were readdressed and in some cases kids were let in who initially were rejected. . . . The academic counselors would tell the coaches the kids were failing, or skipping exams, or skipping tutorials. And the coaches [had] an opportunity to say to the kid: If you don't pay attention to schoolwork I'm going to sit you down for a game or suspend you or something." But the kids got a clear and opposite message: As long as you can stay eligible and you're productive on the floor, I'm going to protect you." Hyman cites the rape charge made against Herman Veal as an instance of Driesell's power on campus. Driesell's attempt to get the young woman to drop the allegation "was clearly inappropriate behavior. Yet if he got reprimanded at all by the chancellor, it was a very mild reprimand. . . . [People] just sort of thought it was Lefty and that was okay. . . . I mean they gave him a ten-year contract. . . . And I think he got the message that, well, if no one is saying anything about it, then this must be acceptable to them."

It was also not unusual for Driesell to get away with stretching the truth. Shortly after Bias died, for instance, the *Washington Post* published a four-part series on Maryland athletics, prepared before Bias's death. One of them described Driesell's tactics as a recruiter and gave numerous examples of Driesell's gift for mistruths. In a letter to one recruit he wrote that he had no doubt the team would win four national championships if the kid attended Maryland. When the reporter asked him whether or not he really meant this, Driesell at first suggested the letter was forged, then, when shown a copy, claimed an assistant wrote the message, and finally allowed he might be the author "because it sounds like me." To other recruits he boasted that Moses Malone, the great professional center, was a member of his program, though Malone never actually performed for a minute wearing a Maryland jersey. He told one recruit he was the "Number One player in the country that I want in a Maryland basketball outfit"; a few months later he sent a letter to another recruit, saying, "We consider you as our top prospect." When he was asked about the two invitations to sign, he said, "I don't know how I could have said that."

So when Bias died Driesell simply acted in character. The death didn't make him act irrationally or thoughtlessly. Rather, he was true to his nature. The problem was he misread the event. He imagined things would continue as usual and that people would react to him as usual. They had said, That's Lefty! so long that he must have figured, What the hell, they'll say it again! He was unprepared—by experience or imagination—to realize that this time his way was not going to work.

In nature, cocaine performs the most modest of functions. It's a scarecrow. It protects the coca plant, warning—in the words of one government report—"insects and herbivores to stay away through bitter and intoxicating experiences."

But in society cocaine takes on the aspect of the perfect drug. Not in the sense that cocaine is harmless; no drug is without some danger: the seventh and eighth most commonly named drugs in hospital emergencies are acetaminophen and aspirin. But cocaine—although this wasn't clear until recently—embodies the quintessential idea of a drug: a substance mysterious and erratic, capable of producing profound inner change, including pleasure bordering on ecstasy and harm bordering on evil. It is commonly believed that Robert Louis Stevenson wrote *Dr. Jekyll and Mr. Hyde*—a classic allegory of drug abuse—while he was using cocaine.

Its powers are diverse: unlike the dulling opiates, cocaine both stimulates and anesthetizes, activating the central nervous system while numbing the local area of application. Its preparations are multiform: absorbed into the body through any mucous membrane, cocaine can be drunk, smoked, snorted, shot into a vein or under the skin, or otherwise exotically ingested. One witness before the Select Committee spoke of a young woman who applied the drug regularly with an eyedropper to her anus; and as early as the turn of the century users were applying it to their genitals. Its effects are protean: more than most drugs, cocaine produces a dramatically wide range of response, one user's paranoid psychosis the extreme manifestation of another taker's pleasant rush of energy and alertness. "I could not fail to note," mentions Sigmund Freud in his famous paper "On the General Effects of Cocaine," ". . . that the individual disposition plays a major role in the effects of cocaine, perhaps a more important role than with other alkaloids. The subjective phenomena after ingestion of coca differ from person to person, and only few persons experience, like myself, a pure euphoria without alteration."

Cocaine has had a complicated history. Discovered in the 1850's, it was hailed as a wonder drug; twenty-five years later it was condemned as "the third scourge of mankind." Outlawed, it fell into disuse until the last fifteen years when, almost as a centenary celebration, it repeated its previous rollercoaster ride of approval and rejection. In the literature on the drug—from one hundred years ago and in current writings—a siren song of acceptance accompanies horror stories of epileptic seizures, violent personality disorders, and mad obsessions. A desire to idealize the drug, reinforced by the fact that many users don't become addicts, vies with a passion to denounce it.

Yet even now there is relatively little precise scientific knowledge about cocaine. The exact way it affects the brain remains a matter of speculation. Researchers are still experimenting, for instance, with the mechanisms causing the seizure that killed Bias, suspecting, but not certain, it is the drug's potent combination of stimulant and anesthetic that occasions the lethal attack. Even the seemingly simple question of how the body misfunctions in these convulsions—does the heart stop beating or the lung breathing?—is yet to be answered conclusively.

What is known is intriguing. Cocaine, in the words of the specialists, *potentiates* the dopamine system. Dopamine is a neurotransmitter, a chemical that facilitates the passage of electrical impulses from one nerve to another. Dopamine neurons are channels in particular areas of the brain. Although relatively discrete, these areas are associated with a wide variety of behavior, from motion and our processing of sensory information to memory, intellect, and emotion; they are part of the borderline at which the biological, chemical, and electrical processes of our bodies are transformed into the mystery of our individual selves.

In normal operations, the dopamine is released to allow the passage of an impulse, then reabsorbed into the receptor. Cocaine blocks this process of "re-uptake." Instead, the dopamine continues to flood the system, setting off various reactions and activating other chemical systems. "What happens," explains National Institutes of Health (NIH) scientist Sue Weiss, "is that you've got neurons potentiated by cocaine. They're connected to other neurons. The cocaine starts a whole chain of events." Imagine the brain as an orchestra, an ensemble of instruments and players working harmoniously to produce a sound—the mix of temperament and experience that is defined as *us*, our being in the world, our soul or character. Cocaine alters that harmony. It changes who we are, both as individuals and as a community.

Researchers have not yet mapped the exact sequence of events, a critical step toward understanding what the drug does and toward formulating ideas on how to fight its addictive properties. Scientists know, for instance, that animals that have developed a dependency on the drug will stop taking it after a section of the brain called the nucleus accumbens is cut, though the reasons for this are still a mystery. But they do understand how taking cocaine develops into a craving, though this discovery is fairly recent.

One area navigated by the dopamine neurons is associated with reward, a pleasure center. The flood of dopamine produced by the taking of cocaine maximizes the sensation of pleasure, producing the euphoria that is the prime delight of the cocaine taker. Liking this sensation, the user wants more. "Whenever I have been around groups of people with access to large amounts of good cocaine I have noticed how difficult it is to leave that substance alone," Andrew Weil, a Harvard researcher, wrote in the mid-seventies. "One expression of this difficulty is that any amount of cocaine set out for use gets used: it is unheard of for any to be left over. And it seems very easy to get into a pattern of taking cocaine all the time if a lot of it is around."

This coolly reported phenomenon is called reinforcement, or self-reinforcement, the power of the drug to make the user want more. It is the basis for the frightening binges of crack addicts, the lost days spent in the monomaniacal bedlam of the crack house. Experiments have demonstrated the devastating power of cocaine's self-reinforcement. In a series of bizarre tests, caged, harnessed monkeys self-administered an array of drugs that included morphine, codeine, mescaline, salt water, and cocaine. With cocaine—and only with cocaine—the freedom to take as much as possible proved lethal. "Two monkeys began administering cocaine at a dose of 0.25 mg per kg, and three others started at a dose of 1.0 mg per kg," write Harvard researchers Lester Grinspoon and James B. Bakalar in their important study, published in 1976, *Cocaine, a Drug and Its Social Evolution.* "The course they followed was a rapid but erratic increase in consumption ending in convulsions and death within 30 days. The pattern was self-administration around the clock for 2 to 5 days, followed by exhaustion and abstinence for periods of 12 hours to 5 days. The largest intake in any 24 hour period was 180 mg per kg. All the recognized symptoms of cocaine abuse appeared, including apparent tactile hallucinations and weight loss. The toxic symptoms quickly disappeared when cocaine was discontinued (none of the animals discontinued it voluntarily)." (The brutality in drug experiments is almost incomprehensibly sadistic. In one famous marijuana experiment, cited by President Reagan to prove that the drug kills brain cells, monkeys were strapped into gas masks and forced to breath in smoke from thirty marijuana cigarettes in five minutes. "No smoke was lost," writes Abbie Hoffman, "the monkeys inhaled it all. Not surprisingly, within ninety days, death occurred." In another, a monkey was programmed to press a lever over twelve thousand consecutive times before receiving his cocaine fix.)

At the same time the drug has an opposite and equally devastating effect. The body reacts to opiate drugs by tolerating them: the user needs more of the drug to produce the same effect. Cocaine works in the opposite fashion, which is called "reverse tolerance." The body becomes more sensitive to the drug, the same dose stimulating increasingly more extreme responses. This reaction is called kindling. In animal experiments kindling develops progressively. Given smaller doses of chemicals (or electrical stimulation) the functioning of the animals becomes increasingly impaired, their symptoms increasingly extreme.

This reaction is similar to what Oliver Sacks witnessed among many of the Parkinson's disease patients described in his book *Awakenings.* Many symptoms of Parkinson's are caused by a lack of dopamine, and Sacks was involved with a then new treatment that consisted of giving a drug called L-DOPA, "the natural precursor of dopamine." Many of his patients, trapped in a fantastic complex of crippling physical and psychological ailments, responded to the drug in a speeded-up version of the development of a cocaine habit. Their first times using the drug were miraculous; they experienced the euphoria that is the main seductive power of cocaine. Shortly afterward, however, changes produced by the drug became wildly exaggerated. One patient was an avid reader. L-DOPA shortened his attention span so much that he found he could only retain what he had read by closing the book after each sentence. As with cocaine, lessening the dose didn't modify the response. "What we see, in every patient maintained on L-DOPA," writes Sacks, "is that his tolerance for the drug becomes less and less, while his need for the drug becomes greater and greater: in short, that he gets caught in the irresoluble vicious circle of 'addiction.' "

Reverse tolerance has one final, insidious quality. A seemingly positive aspect of self-reinforcement is that the user doesn't react to the absence of the drug with physical symptoms. Because of this users can take the drug intermittently, convincing themselves that they are not dependent on the chemical. But researchers have found that reverse tolerance only occurs when the use is intermittent. The very aspect of the drug that seems to demonstrate its harmlessness ensures its power to destroy.

These theories fall short of explaining all the behavior occasioned by the drug. "No one really understands the mechanism of reverse tolerance," NIH's Sue Weiss says. Furthermore the dependency doesn't follow a sure course. "You can have tolerance and reverse tolerance at the same time," she continues. "A user could be becoming less tolerant to the euphoric effects and more tolerant to other effects."

All of this is far from Bias of course—though, actually, one NIH researcher theorizes that kindling can help explain Bias's death—but not from the issues highlighted by his tragedy or the widespread use of the drug. Drugs are usually thought of as substances with inherently good or bad powers. But the questions raised by cocaine cannot be understood, much less resolved, by an objective judgment of the drug itself. In this respect cocaine, and the addiction it causes, is similar to what Olivers Sacks says about patients with post-encephalitic Parkinson's disease: "Thus, post-encephalitic illness could by no means be considered a simple disease, but needed to be seen as an individual creation of the greatest complexity, determined not simply by a primary disease-process, but by a vast host of personal traits and social circumstances: an illness, in short, like neurosis or psychosis, a coming to terms of the sensitized individual with his total environment."

Shortly after Driesell appears on "Good Morning America" on June 20, the police sift through the waste in the huge dumpsters stationed behind Washington Hall. They salvage a pizza box bearing Keith Gatlin's name, an empty bottle of Private Stock malt liquor, some cut straws and empty vials. Meanwhile, in a university parking lot, newsmen have located Bias's cobalt blue Nissan X-Z. They notice white flakes on the passenger side of the floor. Wanting to search the vehicle in private, a university cop calls a tow truck to haul the car to the university police station. The newsmen, worried that the cop will overlook what should be the focus of his attention, follow behind. When the cop begins his examination, they call out suggestions, telling him to look on the passenger side. Finally he takes the advice. He reaches up and under the plastic hood. White powder trickles down, sprinkling the floor. The cop sticks his hand up farther and extracts, packaged in a crinkled plastic wrapper, the cocaine everyone has been waiting to find.

A little later Major James Ross, the policeman leading the investigation of the "suspicious death," calls state attorney general Arthur Marshall, who is spending the weekend, along with all the other legal actors in the coming drama, at an annual convention of the local bar in Ocean City.

"They said he died as a result of a cocaine overdose," says Arthur Marshall today, ". . . that the faculty and staff of the University of Maryland were not only uncooperative but that they were hiding evidence. . . . It was clear they were just not able to conduct the investigation properly. I told them I was going to be home on Monday. . . . And probably at that time—I think they called back the following day, Sunday, to say that they still were getting a runaround and they confirmed at that time that it was a cocaine overdose. . . . So I said the only thing we can do is if you're interested in using the grand jury then let us know."

Arthur (Bud) Marshall had been a fixture in the political world of Prince George's County for a quarter of a century. In 1986 that cramped, fiercely competitive world was changing radically. The bit of Maryland you enter if you keep driving straight down the wide thoroughfare of Pennsylvania Avenue, Prince George's County—PGC to the natives—is a twenty-by-thirty-mile hump to the east of Washington that, like a European country, manages to include an impressive contrast of landscapes, peoples, and economies. The districts closest to Washington extend both the slums and middle-class tracts of the city. This is surrounded by another belt of expanding suburban malls and housing projects. Finally, the building thins out. (Not stops; PGC prides itself on having one of the highest rates of construction in the country.) The lush, spreading countryside of old PGC emerges, with low, wide trees, broader than their northern cousins; sloping, tilled fields; and handsome red barns. It's tobacco and horse country—the county seat is called Upper Marlboro—noted for its good old boys.

An outsider—he came to PGC from Manhattan's Upper West Side—and he had been the top legal officer of this explosive mix of new money, old landed gentry, and enduring poverty since 1962, when he won election on a reform plank. Under his control the state attorney's office had expanded from a small operation to a floor of the county executive building, Marshall building a staff that commanded the respect of the state's top barristers. But he had been unable to capitalize on this success. His first official position remained his only one. In subsequent campaigns he had lost tries for county executive, the House of Representatives, and the circuit court, even after a change of party affiliation. Opinions about him varied wildly. One Baltimore columnist considered him a buffoon, saying Marshall's behavior during his most famous trial, the prosecution of Arthur Bremer for the attempted assassination of George Wallace, "was, in twenty years of covering such things, the single most embarrassing performance I've ever seen in a court. Marshall couldn't even introduce a question properly. . . ." A local politician called him a Machiavel: "He has always had impeccable timing, somehow making lightning strike around election time." To Alan Goldstein, the lawyer who represented

Gregg and Long and who is an old-time observer of PGC politics, both these judgments are unfair. "He's heavy in court. He's Wagnerian. But he's very shrewd. He'll lay traps for you and then get you."

At the time of the Bias case, Marshall needed a trap. He faced the most significant challenge of his elected career. With blacks making up almost 50 percent of PGC, the black Democratic caucus (in effect the Jesse Jackson bloc) had targeted his position to become the first county-wide office held by a black; they'd chosen a younger man named Alex Williams for the job. In Democratic PGC, the primary counts as the election. "Marshall's persistence in death penalty cases appears out of tune with the views of the community," a black Democratic member of the Maryland House of Delegates explained to the *Baltimore Sun*. "There is a sense that he has been around too long. He is not an innovator."

The caucus hoped to make this switch without a fight.

"The Democratic party in Prince George's County had worked out a deal," Marshall explains. "The judge who was the judge is now retired, Jimmy Taylor. Jimmy was a friend of mine—in fact Jimmy worked for me many years ago. And they had made arrangements that Jimmy would step down the day prior to the filing deadline. I'd withdraw as candidate for state's attorney, I would file for Jimmy's job, I'd run unopposed."

But Marshall is known for not quitting. In Korea he fought and survived Pork Chop Hill. (He is one of the characters in the Gregory Peck film made about the battle.) Like Driesell, who was shortly to become his main adversary, Marshall is stubborn, vain, loyal to his sense of himself.

Contrary to common sense, he refused the offer.

"I told Sally, my wife. She said, 'Boy that's tacky, that's not the way to become a judge.' Of course she's a Republican. So I said no . . . on the morning that I left to go to the state's attorneys' meeting at Ocean City, which was the week Bias died."

When Leonard died, local politicians thought that Marshall's uncanny luck had struck again. The Bias case presented the state attorney with an excellent campaign opportunity to steal the drug issue away from his black opponent while not alienating white supporters.

"The original perception was that the citizens of the community wanted their local college cleaned up," says Alan Goldstein today. "*That* was the perception of where the political interests lay. Here were all these parents of Prince George's County young people who were out at that school where drugs were supposed to be running around rampant and *they* wanted guys like Tribble to be brought to justice. And they wanted that campus to be cleaned up of drugs. And evidently that was wrong. . . . If there was white resentment against [Marshall] it was for dragging the university through the mud. It would have been interesting to see if it were white ball players what the reaction would have been. . . . How would the white community have felt about prosecuting a black dope dealer, or even a white dope dealer, who killed a white kid? And then if it's a question of besmirching the university or nailing the sonofabitch that did it, how they would feel. Take a hypothetical. Suppose Danny Ferry [currently a white star at Duke, and the son of the general manager of the NBA Washington Bullets] comes out of Damatha High School [a D.C. basketball shrine] and instead of going to Duke, he goes to the University of Maryland. His father is connected with the Washington Bullets, he's a hometown kid, he comes out of the local parochial schools, and he hits it as big as Danny Ferry did at Duke. And then he dies the day after he's drafted. Wha-hoo! My argument would be that I think the white people would have a different perception of their priorities. That's what I'm saying. The old-boy white network that was protective of the university, was placing the black ball player second place."

The case hit Marshall in a personal way, too. Several years before, one of his seven children had been arrested on drug charges. Marshall had appointed a special prosecutor, who had won a conviction, and Marshall's son served a year in the Prince George's County jail.

"It affected me," says Marshall. "I have very strong feelings about drugs."

"[Marshall] wanted the campus cleaned up," says Goldstein. "He knew *he* did. . . . He constantly was talking, early in the case, as a parent."

Working with Marshall on the investigation was Jeffrey Harding, the only state official who remained with the case from beginning to end. Harding was a PGC native whose father had been the mayor of the town of New Carrolton; he knocked around in the early seventies before joining the Marines. The Corps provided him with the discipline and purpose he had lacked previously and remains the key influence in his life. He still goes "splat-gunning" on weekends, and empty cartridges line the edge of his desk in the prosecutor's office.

For Harding the case also presented an opportunity.

"I got out of law school in eighty-four and came back here," Harding explains today. "Bud hired me while I was taking the bar, passing the bar. Very early on Marshall apparently thought I was some kind of whiz kid or something and gave me all this responsibility. . . . When you pass the bar you go to district court for twelve to eighteen months. . . . Then you go to juvenile court which is felonies but for kids. . . . Then you go up to circuit court, where I am right now, which is serious felony crimes. I passed the bar, went to juvenile for five months and right up to felony trials, right next to Mr. Marshall. . . . I handled a couple of big cases for him prior to this. . . . I was his legal left-hand man. . . . So, when Bias died and when he decided to go, I was his logical choice."

Alan Goldstein disputes this version of Harding's career. Harding had been "in child support—the Siberia of the office," says Goldstein. "Then he was sort of made like Bud's political assistant. He was not given any real case assignment. He'd never been in district court, which is where everybody usually goes to start out [and] learn the ropes. He had none of the experience. . . . He was there because Bud was just going to let him do shit work." If Marshall had needed somebody who was trial-trained, "he could have reached down and pulled out a million guys that were more experienced than Jeffrey."

In any event, Harding was unprepared for the responsibilities that were to come with the Bias case. He "was like a kid with a toy," says Goldstein.

For the press, the half-ounce of coke in Leonard's car proves what everyone already believes: that Leonard was using drugs.

The reporters knew there was cocaine "from the first day," says Sally Jenkins. "We had it in the very first story. . . . We just didn't know anything about why. Was it a first-time deal? Did he have a heart problem? At that point, people just didn't feel you were dead of cocaine use. Cocaine was still the perfect drug, a recreational drug that was not necessarily highly addictive. A bunch of doctors thought different. But for the most part we and most of the people who read the *Post* didn't realize that cocaine was a killer. So I guess that was our assumption. Could cocaine really kill a six-foot-eight, two-hundred-pound guy? Len was so huge, so substantial. It was unfathomable that something like that could have done him in."

Treating the event as a major story, editors assign reporters from both the sports department and metro news to uncover details about the young star's secret life.

"We were going to introduce some medical stories," says Jenkins. "And we had to do some stories on where exactly he had been that night, what he had done, try to find out what kind of coke was it, whose was it, was it Lenny's first time, was it his fiftieth time. There were a million questions to answer. The story went off in so many different directions we didn't know where to start. . . . I wrote in a straight dash from June nineteenth on." A few days later, when her boss suggested Jenkins take a day off and let another reporter write the story, "I said, 'Over my dead body.' Because you felt like if you took one day off you'd get left behind. . . . New information was coming in every day that might turn out to be important at some other time." For Jenkins, there was "so much to find out."

As more information comes out, Leonard's public image changes dramatically: a superstar on Wednesday; tragic victim on Thursday; dumb innocent on Friday; possible longtime coke user, frequenter of a D.C. "drug bazaar," and dealer's best friend on Saturday. At times it seems there is a race between the police and press to uncover the new Leonard Bias before the old one is put to rest. The period that should be a solemn mourning time for Bias, the days after his death leading up to his funeral, becomes instead a storm of denial, discovery, disbelief.

At first he is praised without reservation. John Slaughter, chancellor of the University of Maryland, says, "Leonard Bias was a wonderful young man who made a positive impact upon everyone he met. . . . I told Lenny last year that the thing that I admired most about him was his selflessness and his support for his teammates. He received his greatest pleasure in seeing them succeed. He brought joy to our university not only by being a superb athlete, but more importantly by being a fine person who enriched us by his presence." The *Washington Post* devotes an editorial to him: "He was a gentleman and a good kid, say those who knew him best. His worst confirmed transgression: missing a team curfew at an away game when he visited old friends." Driesell constantly reminds his listeners that Leonard was a "born-again Christian," as though Leonard's religious persuasion should blanket him from any accusations of moral failure. The presumption of unblemished virtue is shared even by the nondenominational *Washington Post*. "Len Bias was a born-again Christian, and a spiritual leader . . ." they write in their eulogy. Would they have said the same if he had been a Black Muslim? Adrian Branch, the player from whom Leonard had seized leadership of the team, says Leonard was on "his way to being an American hero like Martin Luther King and Babe Ruth."

In the bright light of this praise Leonard's soon-to-be-discovered questionable behavior casts long shadows. The revelations of his real life make him seem hypocritical, a liar and trickster rather than a young man struggling to find his own way in a number of new worlds—professional basketball, his own celebrity, the Beltway social circuit of young blacks—whose only common feature is an often profound corruption. The fact that the all-American Len Bias people imagined him to be never existed, that his golden-boy image was only a vision created by others' (often intentional) blindness doesn't matter. The living don't see that they failed Leonard through their lack of understanding; in their judgment, Leonard failed them.

"I mean what else could you do for what he had set out to do?" asks Bob Wagner. "If I could have a wish . . . [I would want] two things . . . to talk to Leonard and find out what happened. What did we not do? Why did you let something so stupid happen? And to communicate with him, to know that if he could talk to us [he would] say, I'm sorry that this hurt so many people. For him to have the opportunity to talk to certain people and say, Look, I'm sorry."

Wagner's private incomprehension is mirrored in public attitudes. George Michaels is a sports journalist for local Channel 4. On the night of Bias's death he is too shaken to read his commentary; while on the air he asks for a moment off-camera to collect himself. A day later, as the news of the cocaine comes out, he again expresses his confusion. "For someone who's always known Len Bias to be a good guy this has just been completely frustrating," he says on the eleven o'clock news. Auerbach offers a different reading. If it was drugs, he says, "it was undoubtedly a first-time experiment. He was so happy, you know. Somebody must have talked him into it." (Why was Bias so happy? "I look at it this way," explains Auerbach. "Len Bias fulfilled his goals. The biggest thing in his life was to be a Boston Celtic. The second-biggest thing was to be the top choice of the Boston Celtics. He accomplished those goals.") What about cocaine? reporters ask Dick Dull. Dull's face settles into an appropriately somber mask of firm lips and unblinking eyes. As the tragedy becomes melodrama—Leonard's death turning into a cops-and-robbers story of police investigation and malfeasance in high places—people adopt poses: stern lawman, concerned authority figure, outraged lawyer. It is impossible to know whether they cloak themselves in these roles for protection or whether they *are* these limited, undeviating stereotypes. *Wait*, you think, watching the videotapes or reading the clips from two years before, *you don't mean to say that!* It's too pat, too predictable! They never listen. Each performs their traditional role in the swelling progress of the pathetic drama. What about cocaine? "If there is cocaine," Dull replies, "then it will only be the second part to this tragedy."

The contrast between the idealized and real Leonard even influences the investigation. "Responding to widespread media reports that Mr. Bias had used cocaine before his sudden death Thursday morning," goes a story in the Monday *Baltimore Sun*, "Arthur A. Marshall, the prosecutor, said drug use was out of keeping with the background and character of Mr. Bias and his family, leaving investigators uncertain about the final hours of the young man's life."

But it's not only drugs that casts a shadow over Bias's memory. It's the world of drug dealing. On Saturday morning, the police say they are "trying to determine whether Bias and a friend drove early Thursday to an area in the District of Columbia where . . . drugs are often sold."

The area is Montana Terrace, a poor housing project in Northeast D.C. In the media, Montana Terrace is depicted as a set piece from *Hill Street Blues*, referred to as an "open-air drug bazaar" or a "drug supermarket." "There is no curb service for cocaine buyers at Montana Terrace . . ." begins the first *Washington Post* story that describes the project. "It's a nasty little place," the story continues, quoting a police officer. "We go up there pretty strong and pretty deep. We always take lots of officers. That is not a place you want to go alone as a police officer."

The friend is Brian Tribble.

"I was talking to this guy named David," says Sally Jenkins, "who said, yeah, he'd been with Len the night before for just a few minutes because Leonard had come over to stop by the apartment of a friend of his, had a couple of sodas, and then they had left together. I said, 'What's your friend's name? What's his apartment?' He said, 'It's up in Cherry Hill Road, his name is Brian Tribble.' "

By that weekend Tribble is fixed in the public mind as someone at home in the drug world, a suspicious character, the "mystery man."

"Police say they are looking for a man who goes by the name of Tribble," announces television reporter Pat Collins, a newsman with a Geraldo Rivera–like flair for melodrama. He flashes a triangle showing the people with Bias when he died: yearbook portraits of Gregg and Long, and a black shadow silhouette for the missing friend. No reporter has yet managed to secure a snapshot of Tribble. Then Collins's voice rises with drama. Tribble, he reports, is described as a fancy dresser who drives a Mercedes.

"He was the X factor," says Sally Jenkins. Reporters "knew who Bias was, knew who David Gregg was, Terry Long. We knew all the players on the team. He was the one guy who was not a ball player. A mystery man, you know? We started trying to find out as much as we could, and it immediately became evident that maybe he was kind of the key to the whole thing just because of his lifestyle. . . . Just the fact that he owned a Mercedes made everybody immediately sit up and say, 'Whoa.' "

The other emerging facts of his life only confirm the suspicions.

"I'd see him with Lenny a lot," one Terrapin football player tells the *Baltimore Sun*. "He used to come to games. Lenny would get him tickets. . . . All I know is that he always had money. He had a gold chain he wore that was as thick as the neck of a beer bottle." The article continues: "In his freshman year [the football player] said he and Tribble shared a class: Health 104, Drug Use and Abuse."

By the end of that weekend Tribble is as notorious as the "drug bazaar" of Montana Terrace. When his picture does appear, he *looks* like an outlaw, bearded, with brooding brown eyes and a wary, haunted, handsome, dangerous face.

And, besides, now Tribble is hiding from the police. "Police have been in contact with an attorney for Tribble," the *Washington Post* reports that Saturday. But they say "his attorney would not bring Tribble in for an interview with detectives." Pat Collins adds, "Since Bias's death, Tribble has all but disappeared."

The public revelations affect the Bias family. On Friday night, in a rare interview, James Bias expresses apprehension about the investigation to a reporter from the *Baltimore Sun*. "Something happened," he says, "I don't know what. . . . I just don't know what went wrong." The story goes on to say that Mr. Bias "was prepared to face 'whatever comes out' of the police investigation. . . . 'No matter what anybody says, there will always be an empty space in our life. . . . I still have three children left that I love very dearly. And I'll remember the good things about Lenny. That's all I have to hang on to.' "

The presence of Driesell is the main reason for concern. Driesell is one of the most powerful men in the state. The darling of the Terrapin Club, the alumni association, he has friends of national importance. His attorney, Edward Bennet Williams—EBW in Beltway-speak—is arguably the most powerful lawyer in the nation; and Robert Novak, the syndicated political columnist, likes talking basketball with him. (Several months after the investigation Novak publishes one of his patented paranoid pieces. He defends Driesell against a Beltway media conspiracy, accusing the press of indulging in "an orgy of Driesell-baiting." He says that among Driesell's virtues is that "he is a Christian, and increasingly felt part of coaching is moral values. . . .") If Driesell is guilty of any illegality concerning Leonard's death, it is hard to imagine the PGC police will nail him on it. More than the county's other institutions, the police force remains overwhelmingly white and rural, a throwback to PGC good old days.

The next day Mr. Bias receives calls from Driesell, Chancellor John Slaughter, the campus police chief, and Major James Ross to reassure him "that the university is cooperating with the investigation." But Bias keeps his independence. Walter Scott, an uncle of Leonard's, is quoted as saying the family feels "the university may not have Len's best interests at heart. . . . We feel there may have been something in the dorm room, some playing around in the dorm room or some prank of that sort."

Meanwhile the funeral plans are announced. Leonard's remembrance will be an elaborate twenty-four-hour ritual: a wake Sunday night at the Pilgrim African Methodist Episcopal Church; a funeral Monday morning at the College Park Chapel; the burial at a cemetery in Suitland, a small Maryland suburb; a family gathering—the Biases are a large clan—at the local church; and, finally, a memorial service at Cole Field House, where Leonard's family, Coach Driesell, and his teammates will honor his memory. The elaborate plans reflect a truth about Leonard: a public person, he is mourned by many and different kinds of people who all want a chance to show and share their grief at the loss of him.

One of them is Jesse Jackson.

"I'm fairly close to Reverend Jackson," explains Bennie Thayer, the local political leader. "I had brought him through to speak to one of the high schools involving drugs. . . . He voiced to me that he would at least like to speak to the family or get involved. . . . It was kind of difficult to get through to Mrs. Bias, although once I had told her Reverend Jackson would be calling it was no problem and they accepted the call . . . and I assume it was a natural followup that they asked him to speak."

But Jesse Jackson in 1986 has not yet won the stamp of national respectability he will gain by the presidential campaign of 1988. Besides, he is also publicly associated with the drug issue, which the university has yet to confront openly. His presence is not welcomed by College Park officials.

"There was an initial resistance on the part of the university to having Jesse speak," says Thayer. "It was expressed to me that the university was hesitant to have him come and speak because of the press that would be associated with it." Instead of deferring to the university spokespeople Thayer calls up their boss.

"Chancellor Slaughter is a very, very good friend of mine. My first impression was to call him. Which I did. He assured me Jesse would be welcome."

A day after the funeral Jackson requests a meeting with Slaughter, Dull, and Driesell. While driving out to the cemetary with some members of the team, he has become worried about the young men.

"Now in that meeting," Bennie Thayer remembers, "Dick Dull came in very dressed and professional as one would expect, [and the same with] the vice chancellors, Reverend Jackson, myself, the chancellor of course. Lefty Driesell showed up in denim pants, sneakers, no socks, open shirt, and was very laid back. I was struck in the meeting—having just attended the funeral—where is this man now, coming here like this? First of all, obviously, I believe Reverend Jackson deserved a little bit more than sneakers and denim. But I recall Driesell was very laid back. Jesse asked very pointed questions of him. . . . [And Driesell] rambled in his answers. . . . I recall he was very—'Jesseee,' speaking with his Southern drawl . . . not as specific or as to the point as the reverend and others in the room would have liked in terms of . . . the problem. . . . And there *was* a problem, a problem in terms of the athletes, the permissiveness of the athletes, the fact that dope was present and everbody knew that. . . . Lefty didn't sit up, wasn't erect, not aloof, but casual, comfortable, not tense at all. He had *recouped* pretty fast—let's put it that way."

Sunday night the final rites begin at Leonard's local place of worship, the Pilgrim A.M.E. church, a modest, squat structure whose roof rises only fractionally higher than the tops of the one-family houses nearby. It sits on the corner of a quintessential District block: the street's short length spans the black community. The houses progress from pristine, solid red-brick middle-class homes with neatly tended lawns to battered wood-shingled two-story Southern shacks, their wooden porch columns leaning drunkenly, fronting weedy yards. Mercedes and Caddies are parked next to boatlike Galaxies, as worn down as decrepit pack horses. Around the corner the destitution continues: shattered windows, backyard jungles, packs of kids looking for a friendly buyer.

"I would say there were tens of thousands of people," says Levi Woods today. Woods is the pastor of the church; he had just been appointed in 1986. "We were supposed to close the doors at nine, but . . . [the family] came up and asked me to extend the wake to try to accommodate the people who had traveled so far—all the well-wishers, people who had come from as far as California to pay their respects. So we extended the wake. I believe if we hadn't closed the door there would have been people outside the next morning. People would sit in the pews and others would take their place. But in other respects it was a wake like any other, except that he was so young and his future was so great. I guess you could say that because of his great promise you could not take his loss lightly."

Inside, the mourners—the following day the *Post* estimates a more modest three thousand—move slowly down the eighteen rows of pews, past the laminated wood interior that is broken only by fake U-beams, plastic hollow decorations disguised as structural supports. Each person gets a plainly printed program with a message from the family:

Like a ship that's left its mooring
and sails bravely out to sea
So someone Dear has sailed away
In calm serenity
But there's promise of greater joy
Than Earth could have in store
For GOD has planned a richer life
Beyond the unseen shore

There is a photo of Leonard—wide smile, the smile that always got to Mrs. Tribble, eyes heartbreakingly expectant, eager, confident. Then the printed words:

A SERVICE OF WORSHIP SACRED TO THE MEMORY OF LEONARD (FROSTY) BIAS

On Thursday, June 19, 1986, the book of life unfurled its final chapter upon the beautiful epistle of the life of

> Leonard (Frosty) Bias and he advanced from labor to reward.

At the front of the church, under a plastic stained-glass window of a white Jesus holding a baby lamb, lies the embalmed body.

"His body looked helpless," Jeff Baxter remembers. "That was a sad sight, a sad, sad sight."

"We came in," says Bob Wagner, speaking of himself and Lefty Driesell, "passed, viewed [the body]. It really bothered me seeing him again, I wish I hadn't gone to it. With the makeup on he didn't look like himself. I was left with a vision of him that I thought was real and then I saw this second one that wasn't."

Afterward they went downstairs.

"We talked to Mrs. Bias, and Lefty said, 'Where is Mr. Bias?' He was upstairs.

"So we came upstairs and Lefty walked over toward Mr. Bias.

"[Mr. Bias] says, 'Stay away from me! I don't want to have nothing to do with you! I don't want to talk to you! Get away from me!'

"Then he pointed to me and he said, 'You too!'

"I just said, 'Come on, Lefty, let's get out of here.'

"We walked out the side door and back to the car. That personally may have taken as much out of me as losing Leonard. Because I didn't know about the financial situation, I didn't know about not having insurance, I didn't know about any of that kind of stuff. I could see where I knew he was going to be angry, but I didn't think he'd be angry at me. I had worked really hard with the kid. And then maybe—I'm trying to imagine what was he thinking: well, here's the white high-school coach who sold his son to the white college coach that abused his son. . . ."

Inside the services begin. The next day the public memorial for Leonard will take place. The service will be held at College Park Chapel, an elegant colonial structure overlooking the broad sweep of the campus lawns. The speakers will be nationally famous men—Chancellor Slaughter, Coach Driesell, Jesse Jackson. Afterward the funeral cortege to the cemetery will stop traffic on the highway. That night thousands will gather at Cole Field House. Jesse Jackson will compare Leonard to Kennedy, King, and Mozart. "There are so many memories," Driesell will say. "I can't recall them all. I can see Leonard shooting his picture-perfect jump shot or taking a lob pass from Keith. I can't believe he's gone. But he's not gone. He's just starting over where he is. Leonard's records will have come and gone in one hundred years, in five hundred years. Where Leonard is, he's there for eternity. I think this was all planned by the Lord. All this is planned. Something great is going to come of this." For five minutes the gatherers will rise and cheer Len Bias's memory.

But now, Sunday night, in the church Leonard attended, there is no celebrity. Levi Woods stands at the overly ornate podium, a wooden pulpit with the motto IN REMEMBRANCE OF ME carved into the wood. Behind sit some other ministers, a chorus commenting on Woods's contemplations. "Well," one utters, his rich, deep voice somehow dredging up understanding and wonder from that single, arid syllable. The minister gives the simple message of his congregation, one that can apply to anyone: he embraces Leonard whole, a sinner who struggled for grace.

"We come to celebrate the home-going of Lenny Bias.

"Amidst the fanfare of the sports world and his desire to play pro ball in the NBA, Lenny Bias sought the need for something higher—something above the cry from the grandstand.

"He therefore made the biggest decision of his short lifetime. In the presence of his teammates he walked down the aisle and gave me his hand and God his heart.

"It's not how long you live, but how well. You have nothing to do with the date you were born on or the date you leave this world. But the days in between are your life. It was Shakespeare on one occasion who had one of his characters say, 'Life is a tale told by idiots, full of sound and fury signifying nothing.' Wordsworth Longfellow said, 'No, no, life is real, life is earnest, and the grave is not the goal. Dust thou art and dust thou returnest was not spoken of the soul.' And I'm here to say that Lenny knew life was real, life was earnest, and that the grave could not contain his world.

"Life is a gift from God.

"And since He gave He can also take away. The Bias family had Lenny because God gave him to them. Coach and the school of Maryland had him because God gave him to them.

"So think about the fact that death is real. Twenty years I've been pastoring and I've never told people not to cry. I think it's bad advice. I can tell you that those who don't cry are those who have no hope.

"We're going out tomorrow to commit the body, but we commit not him but his body to the earth. You know when you've been around waiting for a check? And the envelope came and it was all messed up. You're not worried about the envelope. You open it, take out the check, tear the envelope up, throw it away and put the check in your pocket and go to the bank. Well, that's the way it is with God. He's coming back to pick us up!

"Lenny is gone. But mother, teammates, coach, friends—he's coming back!

"And I want to say this. You've seen this crowd for the last three hours. They're still out there. I want you to know Lenny touched many lives on the basketball court, but Lenny did something today he couldn't in life. In death, Lenny brought all of us to church! So hold on! God will come down!"

Afterward, members begin to testify.

"It was a sad sight," Baxter recalls. "Everyone crying. I was fine, real cool and calm. Then, after the preacher had his sermon, Mrs. Bias started talking. Everyone got real quiet. She went, 'I knew my baby, I knew this was going to happen sixty-seven days ago'—something like that—'I knew the Lord was going to call my baby and I'm not high off of drugs, I'm high off the Lord' and all that.

"After that I broke out crying. I just got up, my mother got up behind me, and my brother and sisters and everyone in my family and we went outside. We were in a circle crying. At that point my mother was thinking it could have been me. It was just like—I couldn't think of another word: it was crazy. Jay [Bias, Leonard's brother] came out. We were holding hands. He was like falling out—it made no sense at all."

Cocaine's fatal attractiveness is apparent from the start of its history.

One of the first to explore its effects was William Hammond, a surgeon general of the United States. Like many doctors, Hammond was fascinated by cocaine. Along with dentists, M.D.'s, with their casual access to the drug, made up an estimated 30 percent of the cocaine-using population by the turn of the century. Hammond recommended cocaine as a cure for "cerebral hyperemia due to excessive mental exertion," "the mental depression that accompanies hysteria in the female," and female masturbators, who, he suggested, should have their genitals numbed through applications of cocaine-soaked lint rags. In 1885 Hammond experimented on himself, taking increasingly large doses. His last encounter, eighteen grains in less than half an hour, proved almost fatal.

"In all the former experiments," he wrote, "although there was great mental exaltation, amounting at times almost to delirium, it was nevertheless distinctly under my control. . . . But in this instance, within five minutes after taking the last injection, I felt that my mind was passing beyond my control, and that I was becoming an irresponsible agent. . . . I was in such a frame of mind as to be utterly regardless of any calamity or danger that might be impending over me."

Soon afterward he lost consciousness. The next morning he retraced his steps. His first sight was reassuring. He found he had gone to bed following his usual routine, even putting the match to light the gas "in a safe place." But a shock greeted him downstairs. "I found the floor of my library strewn with encyclopedias, dictionaries, and other books of reference, and one or two chairs overturned." The pathetic, courageous image of the rational man confronting the shambles his unmindful activity has wrought upon the secular temple of his intellect is Jekyll and Hyde come to life.

Hammond's experience was not unique. Another important doctor, William Halstead, a famous Johns Hopkins physician, became addicted while experimenting with the drug's anesthetic powers; he weaned himself on morphine, confessing toward the end of his life that three of his assistants had died from cocaine.

Perhaps the most famous instance of a scientist seduced by the drug is Sigmund Freud. In 1884, when he was twenty-eight and eager, in the words of his biographer Ernest Jones, "to make a name for himself by discovering something important in either clinical or pathological medicine," Freud experimented with the drug on himself. Freud was particularly interested in using cocaine as a cure for morphine addiction. (The possibility caused the writer of a Parke-Davis pamphlet to enthuse: "If these claims are substantiated . . . [cocaine] will indeed be the most important therapeutic discovery of the age.") Freud prescribed some for a friend who had become addicted to the narcotic after using it to soothe a painful physical condition. Freud thought his cure immensely successful. But a year later his friend had become a cocaine fiend—the old term is perhaps the most appropriate, given the debate over whether cocaine is addictive—and Freud later wrote that the one night he spent tending his associate's addiction was the most "frightful" of his life. Chastened by the catastrophe that had befallen his friend, Freud stopped championing the drug. But it is interesting to note as a sign of both his intellectual rebelliousness and also the drug's power that he continued to use it and even to send doses to his fiancée, warning her to take the drug in small amounts. Even after dropping his endorsement, he persisted in saying that "all reports of addiction to cocaine and deterioration resulting from it refer to morphine addicts." (There is a sidenote to the story. In investigating this aspect of the drug, Freud neglected another, less controversial, and more commercially useful property of cocaine: its application as a topical anesthetic. He was envious of his contemporary who was credited for this discovery, and indirectly blamed his wife for his mistake in judgment.)

But experiences such as Hammond's and Freud's didn't retard the marketing of cocaine. (At the time cocaine and coca were interchangeable, and both were dispensed over the counter.) The drug was sold as a remedy for almost every possible ailment, especially the newly popular nervous disorders of the burgeoning middle class. Advertised with a peculiarly American blithefulness—"A harmless remedy for the blues is imperial," announced an 1870 editorial in the *Louisville Medical News*—it came packaged in more ways than McDonald's burgers. The first merchandising effort was a brew called Vin Mariani, created by an enterprising Corsican in 1863 and used as a general health tonic by a distinguished company that included Pope Leo XIII, Thomas Alva Edison, and Émile Zola. The elixir was the flagship product of a line of cocaine-based Mariani products, including coca-laced pastilles and pâté.

Imitators followed. Parke Davis and the German pharmaceutical giant Merck, one of the first cocaine manufacturers, sold the drug "in cigarettes, in an alcoholic drink called Coca Cordial, and in sprays, ointments, tablets, and injections." One popular concoction was called Metcalf's Coca Wine, which "claimed to be capable of alleviating or curing, among other things, phthisis, typhus, scurvy, gastralgia, anemia, enteralgia, the opium habit, alcoholism, and indigestion." The Metcalf label instructed readers that South American Indians used coca "from the earliest times for every malady from headache to neuralgia," that "Public Speakers, Singers, and Actors" found the nostrum a "valuable tonic" for their vocal chords," while athletes found it to "impart energy" and "elderly people have found it a reliable aphrodisiac superior to any other drug." Coca-Cola itself began as one of these "wines." Its inventor, a Georgia pharmacist named John Styth Pemberton, enhanced his product by substituting coca extract and caffeine for alcohol in his French Wine Coca. His calculated entrepreneurial daring proved profitable two years later when he sold the rights to his "wine" to another pharmacist who founded the Coca-Cola company. The new formula was so successful that drugstores began to install soda fountains to dispense the syrup, transforming the local pharmacies into popular-culture versions of the health spas that were the pride of the European bourgeoisie.

By the turn of the century cocaine was available to everyone. A 1903 report—tainted by opposition to the drug—issued by the American Pharmacologist Association claimed customers at one Philadelphia drugstore signaled their needs simply with finger-signs. "Holding up one finger means the party wants a 'five-cent powder'; two fingers, ten cents worth; three, fifteen cents, and so on." By this time cocaine was probably the most widely used "psychoactive drug" in America. Treasury statistics from 1906 show that enough coca leaves were imported to make approximately 21,000 pounds of cocaine. "Its use spread downward as well as upward in the class structure. . . . Its users were described as 'bohemians, gamblers, high-and-low class prostitutes, night porters, bellboys, burglars, racketeers, pimps, and casual laborers.

. . . Bartenders put it into whiskey on request and peddlers sold it door to door." Cocaine experienced the same kind of boom that marked its comeback eighty years later. And its unrestricted sale resulted in other modern equivalents. At the turn of the century, "Daily dosages of cocaine addicts sometimes reached over 12 grams, doses . . . that would not be seen again until the discovery of smoking cocaine freebase."

Attacks on the drug increased with its popularity. By 1890, there were reported cases of "cocaine psychosis with tactile hallucinations ('coke bugs')." There were also numerous instances of the drug provoking irrationally violent behavior. "Some think the original dope fiend—a caricature once used to justify prohibition of marijuana and opiates as well as cocaine—was in fact a hyperactive, paranoid cocaine abuser." By the start of the 1890's reports of death by cocaine intoxication and cocaine poisoning numbered in the hundreds. In 1902, socialite Annie C. Meyers published her sensational *Eight Years in Cocaine Hell*, an exposé that included a scene in which she uses a pair of scissors to pry a gold denture from her mouth, pawning the tooth for eighty cents to buy her daily fix of "Birney's Catarrh Remedy." In 1903, the year Pemberton introduced his world-colonizing drink, the *New York Medical Record* claimed, "No medical technique with such a short history has claimed so many victims as cocaine." By the twenties, a Zurich doctor named Maier claimed to have studied one hundred "cocaine psychoses," and announced a syndrome he called "cocaine insanity," many symptoms of which sound like the fierce and incomprehensible behavior of crack addicts: "optical and auditory hallucinations, delusions of persecution and grandeur, jealousy, violent tendencies—often with clear consciousness and insight on the part of the abuser. In this condition minor frustrations may cause energetic suicide attempts. In the late stages of cocaine intoxication, there may be spontaneous abortion, twitches, cold extremities, and even paralysis."

These reports fueled a growing campaign, inspired by both reformist zeal and corporate greed, to regulate the drug business.

Crucial to the propaganda against the drug were stories associating it with blacks.

Blacks did of course use cocaine. "Sometime in the late 1880s or early 1890s . . . black stevedores in New Orleans began taking the drug in order to 'perform more easily the extraordinarily severe work of loading and unloading steamboats,' a task at which they toiled for up to seventy hours at a stretch . . . without sleep or rest, in rain, in cold, and in heat,' " writes one historian. Another claims plantation bosses supplied their slaves with cocaine, and also quotes earlier speculative sources that blacks "turned to cocaine when most of the states passed legislation which effectively barred them from access to alcohol." The same writer quotes a 1902 article from the *British Medical Journal* entitled "The Cocaine Habit Among Negroes": "On many Yazoo plantations this year," the British observer commented, "the negroes refused to work unless they could be assured that there was some place in the neighborhood where they could get cocaine. . . ."

The propaganda of the turn of the century played upon these stories, trying to make cocaine as synonymous with blacks as smoking opium was with Chinese. A 1903 report by the Committee on the Acquirement of the Drug Habit, set up by the American Pharmacological Association in response to a previous warning against "Negro cocainists," mentioned wide usage among Negroes and observed that "Georgia reports almost every colored prostitute is addicted to cocaine." In the same year a Colonel Watson of Georgia wrote the *New York Herald Tribune* that "many of the horrible crimes committed in the Southern states by the colored people can be traced directly to the cocaine habit." In 1910, Hamilton Wright, one of three American delegates to the Shanghai Opium Commission, "sought to secure passage of [an antinarcotic bill] through scare tactics. . . . He especially stressed the danger to white women posed by black cocaine users." The *New York Times* carried several articles demonstrating and doubtlessly encouraging the popular fear. One, published in 1908, said, "There is little doubt that every Jew peddler in the south carries the stuff. . . ." And a 1914 article entitled "Negro Cocaine 'Fiends' Are a New Southern Menace" stated, "There is no escaping the conviction that drug taking has become a race menace in certain regions south of the [Mason-Dixon] Line." The author, a doctor, observed that the drug produced violent behavior. "Stories of cocaine orgies, followed by wholesale murders, seem like lurid journalism of the yellowest variety," he wrote. "But in point of fact there was nothing 'yellow' about . . . these reports." He particularly mentioned the cocainist's inhuman strength, citing the case of an Ashville, North Carolina, sheriff who, "informed that a hitherto inoffensive negro was 'running amuck' in a cocaine frenzy," drew his heavy Army revolver, placed it over the victim's heart, and fired, intending to kill the man, and found instead that the bullet had "little effect in stopping the negro or checking his attack." These are turn-of-the-century crack stories, presenting the then underclass as alien and out of control.

The campaign to outlaw cocaine proved successful. In 1906, Congress passed the Pure Food and Drug Act, forbidding interstate shipments of cocaine and opiate products; eight years later the Harrison Act, the cornerstone for all future narcotics policy, was voted into law. By then forty-six states had already passed legislation against cocaine, establishing the drug as the most dangerous substance of the time.

By the twenties cocaine's popularity was doomed by rising prices. The drug became unaffordable to the working class and the poor. Heroin took its place. "Heroin was doubly attractive," writes one historian. "It was cheap, and it was taken in the accustomed fashion, sniffing. Any unpleasant symptoms, particularly depression, that the regular cocaine user might experience on discontinuing use of the drug were alleviated by the tranquilizing and mood-elevating properties of heroin." The image of the junkie—a 1920's coinage to describe New York addicts who maintained their habit by selling metal scraps gleaned from industrial garbage piles—was fixed: young, male, lower-class, a street rat, part of the big-city criminal element. If you wanted a rush instead of the heroin "down," you took amphetamines, the mass-manufactured synthetic "speed" brought onto the market in 1932. Cocaine was shunted off to the social fringes of the upper classes and bohemia, a commodity that, like illegitimacy in a Dickens novel, spanned the class chasm in America, bridging the worlds of Cole Porter and the crazed, angry, brilliant young Harlem hipster nicknamed "Red," later famous as Malcolm X.

By Monday, June 23, State Attorney Arthur Marshall has made up his mind. No one is cooperating with the police. He decides to convene a grand jury.

"If the University of Maryland and their officials," says Marshall today, "had turned around and said right off the bat, 'This is what we know, this is what happened,' that would have been that . . . [and we] never would have gotten involved with this long, protracted, endless foolishness. . . . A young man died who was a very popular figure. I can understand in the beginning why they wanted to protect the good name of Bias and didn't want to tell his family. I can understand why they wanted to protect the good name of the University of Maryland. I can understand why Mr. Driesell wanted to protect his own name. But when a person dies, then there's trouble and I still don't understand why it took them six weeks . . . to cooperate."

The morning of June 23 he holds the first of what will be many press conferences. His statement is comprehensive, dramatic, foreboding. He reports that "cocaine was involved in the death of Len Bias"; that for the last two years he had been concerned about allegations of cocaine use on campus, including by members of the basketball team; that Gregg and Long may be offered immunity because "it appears that [they] didn't bring drugs into the room" and that the room was sanitized, "even the paramedics' materials were cleaned up." He says that the University of Maryland has been uncooperative with law enforcement authorities and that they should "self-examine themselves" because the "public is entitled to take a look at their university and see what's happening." He adds that Driesell acted improperly by meeting with the players, and that he thinks he knows "what Tribble does for a living."

In theory a grand jury safeguards citizens from being capriciously dragged into court. It is a fact-finding body. The Prince George's County grand jury is composed of twenty-three citizens, selected at random from voting polls, who are paid fifteen dollars a day for six months to meet every Tuesday and hear the prosecutor present subjects for possible investigation. The jurors and not the officer of the state are empowered to determine the direction of the inquiry. They have a singular power: witnesses appear before them without benefit of counsel and under the threat of contempt charges if they refuse to answer questions. At the end of the process, the jurors decide whether enough information has been presented to justify bringing charges of criminal conduct by voting to issue an indictment. Theoretically it is the perfect instrument for the sort of case presented by the Bias death: the commission of a crime, the sale and distribution of cocaine, was being obscured by uncooperative witnesses, in this instance men of importance and power.

In practice, however, a grand jury can be an engine of legal mischief, a bureaucrat's dream and paranoid's nightmare. Responsible to no one, threatening everybody, it can create rather than dismiss criminal charges and can inadvertently replace the presumption of innocence—one of the chief glories of the legal process—with the all-too-common public assumption that an indictment means guilt.

Probably Marshall's original motive in calling the grand jury was nothing more complicated than to get the truth out of Lefty Driesell; but in the two months it met—July and August—the Bias grand jury fell victim to all these possible failings. It became a "fishing expedition," as defense attorneys like to say. The inquiry was aimless and vast, casting wide suspicions—at one point the Terrapin basketball team was charged with throwing games—without ever offering a shred of evidence. Responsibility for these casual slanders was never fixed, and Marshall to this day hides behind the claim of the grand jury's autonomy, swearing that the citizens told him what to pursue, and not that they followed his suggestions. And, perhaps most important of all, the grand jury irrevocably fixed the attitude that was to frame all investigation into Bias's death. From then on, what mattered wasn't an inquiry into the truth, a commitment to discover what had happened, but a crusade against wrongdoers that wouldn't stop until the villain (or villains) came to trial.

Marshall's character partly accounted for the strictly prosecutorial cast to the inquiry. "Prosecutors," explains Alan Goldstein, "think of an investigation in terms of getting an indictment."

But the temper of the moment was also responsible for the

inquisitional nature of the whole proceeding. Leonard was so well liked, so "substantial" a person, as Sally Jenkins says, that his death seemed inconceivable as an accident you could only mourn and not revenge. No one wanted to let his loss pass without someone paying a price. And, too, people were reluctant to admit that Leonard might have been culpable in his own death. Only his closest friends, such as Johnny Walker, and his family loved him purely enough to accept this fault.

Furthermore, an extreme confusion surrounded the events of his death. Nothing was clear. Even the autopsy reports kept changing. At first, the medical examiner, a Dr. Smialek, suggested the evening was Bias's introduction to cocaine, that perhaps the star died on his first toot. Several days later he reversed himself, saying microscopic examination of tissue revealed Bias could have had previous experience with the drug. Shortly after that another state medical examiner said the evidence indicated that Bias was freebasing. Finally, a month or so later, another medical examiner claimed that Bias had taken three to five grams of the drug; he believed the victim drank the drug, suggesting that someone spiked Leonard's beer. And this confusion was coming from the normally reliable, straightforward state officials compared to whom the other sources—basketball people, the University of Maryland bureaucracy, citizens of black Washington, druggies—presented an impenetrable swamp of rumor-haunted unreliability.

Faced with these difficulties, the instinct of the investigators was to forget about the hard-to-conquer territory of the truth and head for more familiar turf, where good and bad were easily identified. Not only was the search ill-conceived, but cultural misunderstandings misled the investigators from the first. The most mundane events were read as ominous, the comings and goings around Leonard's death were seen as parts of an intrigue, rather than spur-of-the-moment attempts by beleaguered individuals to respond to a completely unexpected tragedy. "An armed robbery in Bladensburg less than an hour after Bias collapsed has intensified a county police investigation into ties between two of Bias's friends, one of whom is a D.C. police officer, according to informed sources," goes a *Washington Post* account of July 3. "Authorities have become increasingly interested in the association between policeman Johnnie B. Walker of the 1st District and Brian Lee

Tribble. . . . Walker and Tribble are acquainted and also are longtime friends of Bias, sources said. One of the victims of the robbery is related to Walker, sources said, and police believe that a safe taken in the robbery belongs to Tribble. Recently investigators have looked into the activities of Walker. . . . Lt. William White III, the D.C. police spokesman, said yesterday that the D.C. police internal affairs unit is investigating Walker's possible ties to the Bias case because 'allegations and innuendos have surfaced that could possibly involve misconduct.' . . . Police have not directly linked the robbery to Bias's death, but their interest intensified because one of the victims, identified as Julie Walker, is a friend of Tribble and is a relative of Walker, sources say. Investigators are attempting to find out what was in the safe taken from the apartment, sources said." The implications are clear. Walker and Tribble are in cahoots together, a cop tied to a dealer through a romantic involvement of his sister. The proportions of misunderstanding would be comic if the event that produced them and their consequences hadn't been so serious.

Conveniently, there was one figure—a phantom figure of evil from urban life—who could satisfy both the need to punish and explain: the pusher-man, otherwise known as a "big-time" dealer.

"There was one meeting I remember," Sally Jenkins says, reflecting on the way the *Post* proceeded with the story. "I think it was three or four days down the line. We all of a sudden decided we needed to take at least a minute to catch our breath. [Sue Anne Pressley, a *Post* reporter] had done a wonderful reconstruction of the events that went on that night as far as we could tell—some of the stops he'd made and so on and so forth. Then we were sitting there. We were just trying to figure where to go next. It seemed like the obvious question was—at first—*who* killed Len Bias?"

The answer was a dealer. And coincidentally there was one person involved with Leonard's death who seemed to fit that part perfectly: Brian Lee Tribble.

"It was a sexy file," says Alan Goldstein of the information the police were gathering about Tribble. "The more down-and-dirty stuff they were finding out that linked Tribble with drug dealing—and I think they were getting some snitch testimony from downtown and from drug dealers . . . the farther from their mind it was that they weren't going to bring criminal charges."

The day after Marshall gives his press conference, the state makes its first official announcement regarding the cause of Leonard's death. At a midday news conference, Dr. Smialek, the state medical examiner, states that Bias died of "cocaine intoxication." Noting that Bias was a healthy individual, he reports that there was "no evidence that Bias was a long-term user of cocaine and that it was 'possible' the fatal ingestion was the All-America player's first encounter with the drug." At the same time, Howard Silverman, the acting head of the state Drug Abuse Administration, states the cocaine taken by Bias was "unadulterated," and "dealer-level quality." "You're not going to stop on the street corner and get that quality," Silverman says, now contradicting the earlier reports of Bias's midnight journey to Montana Terrace. "You'd have to be pretty well connected."

The implication is clear: since Bias had never—or rarely—taken coke himself, whoever brought him the fatal dose was a dealer.

"Our opinion [was that Tribble was a lieutenant] while we were covering the story," says Sally Jenkins. "We were trying to figure out what could be going on—because how does cocaine of [such good] quality get into a [college dorm] room, that's the question, right? Because according to Smialek's report it was extraordinarily good cocaine. . . . Tribble was the one person we didn't know anything about—the mystery man. One question leads to another, and you start saying, well, could it have been this guy?"

The day after the autopsy report is made public, the *Post* publishes an article Jenkins has written on the mystery man's background.

"Tribble's link to Bias is not as well defined" as Gregg and Long's, the story says. "From interviews with friends of Bias and Tribble, a picture emerges of a relationship based on an attraction to each other's talents and possessions. . . . Tribble, for example was the proud owner of a silvery Mercedes Benz 450SL—the type of car Bias often told reporters he wanted to own. Bias's brilliant basketball accomplishments were out of reach for the shorter, stockier Tribble. . . ." In addition, "Tribble, 24, lived in a luxury apartment near campus on Cherry Hill Road. . . ." The story also says that Tribble "listed himself as president of Interior Services, Inc.," giving the company's address as his parents', that "D.C. Corporate records" show no such firm registered, that Tribble still owed thirteen thousand dollars on the car, and that Tribble and Bias were seen frequently at a dancing club called Chapter III in the southwest section of the District.

This remains the portrait of Tribble displayed to the public—the mistranslations of facts that make Mrs. Tribble feel she's going crazy when she reads them. "Tribble's two bedroom apartment is furnished with a rust-colored corduroy couch and chairs, tables of blonde wood and glass, a color television set with remote control and a stereo with equalizer and two-and-a-half-foot-speakers," reads one *Washington Post* report. Useless to explain the items are on loan from his older brother and that Brian is storing the furniture. The equipment makes up the good-time home entertainment section of a dealer's pad. And nothing can be done to dislodge the false characterization. The unlisted company, the Cherry Hill apartment, the fact that his corporate address is his parents' house—all this is no longer the rickety structure of her son's new adult life, but the impressive outlines of a hustler's scam, the proof that Brian leads a fine bachelor's life, makes all his money illegally, and uses his mother and father's home as a front.

Besides all this there is the car. For the press the car is no longer the piece of conspicuous, youthful consumption Mrs. Tribble imagined would get him over the hurt of his failed playing career, for which she wrote the monthly checks, feeding him at home because the boy earned too little to sustain himself. For the press the car is the smoking gun, the sure proof that Tribble had money to burn and that he had to be a dealer. And though Mrs. Tribble corrects the reporters' versions of things, they keep painting the same portrait of her son. A month after Bias dies—when reporters have had lots of opportunities to check the facts—the *Post* reports, "In the early morning of June 19, investigators have said, Bias stopped by Tribble's fashionable apartment, which is adorned with pictures of Mercedes-Benz autos, weightlifting equipment and stylish modern furniture."

Meanwhile the police work with the prosecution to build this case: Tribble is the dealer. The basis for this is the charge of distribution. Legally this simply means providing drugs. But on the street and to the public, the charge of distribution leads quickly to the term "dealer," which carries greater weight—someone who lives by selling drugs, the pusher-man. The moral and criminal difference between the two is immense, but the prosecution does nothing to maintain it. They use the accordion quality of the term "dealer" to suit their purposes, implying the worst case, even if the proof doesn't exist to confirm it.

Thus, today State Attorney Marshall argues of Tribble, "I'm not saying he's a big dealer. I never thought he was. I don't think anybody thought he was a big dealer. I don't think he was hardly anything more than a friend of Len Bias who was providing Bias with drugs. I don't think anybody came up and said, 'He's been selling a lot around the campus,' because I don't think he ever had. I'm satisfied based on the information that I had that he was the person that was a good friend of Bias's and I believe was a good friend of Bias's."

But at the same time, Marshall says the information he was receiving back then implied the opposite. "Everybody by that time knew that Brian Tribble was there [in Bias's room], Brian Tribble was clearly an outsider, Brian Tribble was clearly a person who ran with Len Bias, and Brian Tribble—according to everybody—was involved in the drug trade. . . ."

The fact that this information is third-hand, rumor, hearsay, and inadmissible in a court of law doesn't shake his conclusions about Brian Tribble. "[Police] started going [around the campus] and saying, 'Well, who is this guy Brian Tribble?' Someone said he played basketball. [Another said] no he didn't. Why does he hang around the school? He hangs around with Len Bias, he's a friend of Len Bias. Where does he travel? He travels with such and such. What does he do? I don't know if he works, but I know he's involved with coke. Things like that. These are the sort of statements that obviously aren't admissible in a court room but are admissible in my mind."

And are also seemingly admissible in the grand jury room. Robert Nevins is a twenty-four-year-old native of Bowie, Maryland, who served on the Bias grand jury.

"It seemed like [Marshall] had a personal thing against Brian

Tribble," Nevins says today. Marshall "would continuously bring up . . . how can this guy be making so much money a year and owning this car and . . . staying in an apartment that cost this much. . . . Because it didn't work out [with] the money. Every time we'd go in he would have something to say about Brian Tribble. He'd bring a witness in [who would] say Brian Tribble wasn't guilty. When the guy left, [Marshall would] . . . just shake his head and laugh. . . . [He] may have seen [Tribble] as some kind of big-time drug dealer. But, you know, I'm twenty-four years old and I went to Bowie High, and . . . I don't think he was selling it like Arthur Marshall thought he was. . . . not to the extent where Marshall wanted to get him for. . . . It seemed like he had a personal thing about Brian Tribble. I'll be blunt: To me he sounded like he was trying to nail Tribble because, I guess, it was election year that year—just to get publicity. In my eyes."

A large part of the information on which Marshall bases his conclusions comes from police interrogations. Reading the shakily written, ungrammatical question-and-answer forms, one can imagine the prosecutors putting together their case as these pieces of evidence, rumor, and prejudice come in.

On June 19 the police conduct their first interview with Ron Thomas, an athlete and bodybuilder who was a friend of Tribble's and was present at his house the night of Leonard's death.

"Thomas stated," a detective writes, "that he had met Tribble through his older brother, and when his brother died Tribble took over in the big brother role." Thomas fills out a Prince George's County Police Department "Statement of Victim/Witness/Suspect" form, describing Bias on the last night of the player's life: "On June 19 1986 Len called and I answered the phone he wanted to talk to Brain Tribble when Brain hung up the phone He said Lenny was coming over at 12:30 but he did not get there till about 12:45 or so. he came in smilen and shaken our hands. Then he ask me are those Patrick Ewing new Adidas i said yes. Then he maid a Few Phone calls to some girls why Brain was in The Room getting dress. Len Then said Lets go out its still early and They left thats all i know."

In a subsequent interview, Thomas gives a few extra details.

He met Bias with Brian about two and a half months earlier at Chapter III, a nightspot that becomes notorious in the press. On June 19, Bias made several telephone calls to some girls from Brian's apartment, looked "in good shape and healthy" and "very excited." Thomas knows nothing about possible drug use by Bias—"I have not been around him that much"—or by Tribble and his roommate, Mark Fobbs. "They drink a little beer and wine, but they don't use any drugs." The rest is unilluminating. Leonard came to the apartment, collected Brian and a girl, said they were taking the girl home and left. Later that morning, "the phone kept ringing at Brian's at about 0700 hours and I answered it and people that I don't know kept asking me if it was true. I don't know what was going on but I knew something was going because the phone kept ringing."

A few weeks later, when the heat is on Tribble, Thomas meets again with a detective and a sergeant at the Criminal Investigation Division.

"Thomas was asked," writes the detective, "if Bias or anyone else in the apartment had freebased Cocaine on the night in question and he stated that no one had. Thomas was then advised that we had information that individuals in the apartment had been freebasing on that night and Thomas became very nervous and evasive with his answers. This writer and [the sergeant] feel that Thomas was lying about his knowledge of Tribble's drug activities. Thomas asked if he could speak with this writer [and the sergeant] in a location other than a police station and he was advised that we would meet him any time or place he wanted and was then informed how to reach us."

Other witnesses don't need coaching. They simply state their assumptions, and their words, as recorded in their statements to the police, reveal a world of tantalizing social, moral, and emotional confusion. Witnesses say that they have heard that Tribble deals drugs; but none, when pressed, provide any firsthand evidence to back up the claim.

Nineteen years old, Dorothea Stripling has grown up in the Vista Street neighborhood and claims to have known Tribble since he was "young."

"Have you ever seen Brian Tribble deal drugs?" the investigator asks her in the Hyattsville Police Station.

"No."

"Does Brian Tribble deal drugs?"

"Yes. Just from hearing talk around the Vista Street neighborhood."

"Who does he deal to?"

"I don't know."

"Have you heard what he deals?"

"Cocaine."

After some intervening questions, the interviewer asks how long Brian has been dealing.

"Recently I heard he was."

"Did talk about Brian dealing drugs start before the Bias death?"

"Yes."

". . . Is it common knowledge in your old neighborhood that Brian Tribble deals drugs?"

"Yes, that's all they talk about."

"Could you tell me one person that Brian has sold drugs to?"

"No, I've never seen him personally do it."

". . . Who do you know that has personal knowledge of Tribble's drug dealing?"

"I wouldn't know, he has two sisters and one brother, one sister lives with his mother. I don't know where the other two live."

Wendell Harvey, a University of Maryland student who hung out with Leonard and the other players, fills out thumbnail sketches of the main characters. Jeff Baxter is a "class act . . . does not drink or smoke, or any type of drugs. Jeff and I are close like brothers." Keith Gatlin is a "good person, does not drink or smoke. Country boy sort of speak." Leonard is "like my big brother." About Tribble, the portraitist writes: "I don't know much about Brian Tribble, except that he supposedly sells cocaine, and that comes from what people tell me. He and Lenny were together pretty much. I have never gotten into a conversation other than a Hi what's up type of conversation or a conversation that was very short. He had a Mercedes Benz 450SL that he has just gotten. The day he bought the car he drove over to Lenny's apartment and showed it to us. Then he and Lenny went for a drive."

Finally there's the statement of Brian Bradford Hubbard. Hubbard is asked about the robbery at Julie Walker's. He says he suspects two guys from the Vista Street neighborhood.

"What makes you think they were involved?" asks the detective.

"They had the most at stake," Hubbard replied.

"What do you mean by that?"

"Worried about going to jail over the cocaine."

"Do they supply Brian Tribble with cocaine?"

"I don't know, Tribble could be getting it from them or they could all be getting it from the same guy."

"Where do they store their drugs?"

"I think out in Maryland."

"Did you hear where they were storing their drugs?"

"No, that's just a guess."

"How do you know that [the three of them] sell drugs?"

"I was asked by one to be a runner."

"Who asked you?"

Hubbard supplies the name—it's not Brian.

"What did he say to you?"

"This was last winter, he asked if I wanted some work, that might not be exactly what he said, he said for coke running. I refused."

"Has Tribble sold coke to anyone you know?"

"I guess, it's just common knowledge that he deals."

"Do you know if [they] keep their drugs at [the] same place?"

"I don't know."

"Do you know anyone who ran coke for any of these three people?"

"My sister ran coke for [one of them—again not Brian], she owes him $250."

A little later, Hubbard says that all three buy drugs from a guy who lived in a New York Avenue hotel. Then he relates what he knows about the night Bias died.

"I heard Bias was with [one of them] on Montana Avenue. I guesstimate they were picking up coke. Then they went to the dorm. It's all hearsay on the street."

"What else have you heard?"

"That Bias was selling coke."

"Is this statement true?"

"Yes."

"Do you have anything to add?"

"Your source," he says, in a sort of accidental poetry, "is wrong."

Hubbard's statement points to two elements that spur the investigation: the safe and Leonard's character. After Walker and Diamond reported the robbery and inventoried the apartment, Julie Walker found the robbers had taken the portable safe Brian had stored in her closet. Brian had given Julie the combination, and Gail Diamond had once opened the safe, finding only some rings inside. Still, as the investigation continued, the safe became the most significant item contributing to suspicions about Tribble. Even if you granted that Tribble's Mercedes was (somehow) a piece of juvenile self-indulgence, what was he doing with a safe hidden in someone else's house that is, coincidentally, stolen a short hour after Bias is stricken? The safe is the equivalent of Nixon's erased tape. There is simply no explanation for it unless Tribble is a dealer, and not just a dealer, but a big-time dealer.

Or so the police try to prove.

"Between 7:15 and 7:30," reads the statement taken from Sabah Allah Ali, Walker and Diamond's next-door neighbor, "I heard somebody screaming, they were weird screaming then I didn't hear anything, I opened my door after a few minutes and looked around, didn't see anything. Then about twenty minutes later they knocked at the door, they were in shock, they were crying and screaming, they couldn't stop crying, especially the tall girl."

"Did [the two women] ask you to call the police?"

"I just automatically called Bladensburg Police."

"How long were the girls present before you called the police?"

"Couple minutes."

"Did you mention that you were going to call the police?"

"No, I just automatically called."

"Were you present when the police interviewed the girls?"

"Yes."

"Was their story consistent?"

"Yes."

The investigator notes that the "girls" were wearing jewelry and asks whether they were fully dressed.

"Yes," responds Ali, "wasn't like their clothes were torn or messed up or anything, they were neat in appearance."

"Were the girls aware that you were calling the police?"

"Yes."

"What exactly did they tell you before you called?"

"They said they were robbed and they were forced back into a room at gunpoint by two guys, that's when I called the police."

"Did the girls tell you what was taken?"

"No."

"Does anyone lives in the apartment with the girls?"

"I don't know, I see a lot of people in and out, guys, tall black guys."

"Do you know if these girls keep or sell drugs in the apartment?"

"I don't know."

The investigator asks about Tribble's behavior. Tribble, Ali states, entered with another guy (Mark Fobbs), but Ali told him to stay out of the ransacked apartment. Tribble came into Ali's apartment and mentioned Bias. "He said he was with Len Bias and tried to give him CPR he said he had no pulse, he said he went to the hospital but had to leave and came home, he then talked about the Bias contract with Reebok shoes, he said I'm a close friend of Julia and if I tell her about Len she will get even more upset."

"Is there anything else you recall him saying?"

"He just said he gave Bias CPR, he went into a seizure and said he had a history of seizure, the ambulance came and took him to the hospital, he didn't know if Bias was alive or dead, he said he just left the hospital."

Two days later the police interview Gail Diamond, Julie's roommate.

"Was there a safe in that apartment that was taken in that robbery?"

"Yes."

"Where was the safe kept?"

"In Julie's bedroom closet."

"Who does the safe belong to?"

"I think it belongs to Brian Tribble."

"Why wasn't the safe reported to the police?"

"The police asked each of us to inventory our rooms. Julie mentioned it after looking."

"How long has the safe been in the apartment?"

"I don't know. A few months ago Brian Tribble called the house and asked for Julie. She wasn't home so he said he wanted some of his jewelry and that it was in a safe in her closet. He gave me the combination and I opened it up and took out the three rings that were in the safe."

"What does the safe look like?"

She draws the answer: silver in color; maybe a foot or so tall; maybe a foot or so wide; combination on front.

"Did it have any compartments on the inside?"

"I can't remember."

"Were there any books or anything else in the safe that you remember?"

"No."

"How often would Brian Tribble come to that apartment?"

"I have lived there since March of eighty-five and he has only been there about seven times. I work late."

"Do you have any idea of what may have been in that safe when it was stolen?"

"No. If he hadn't called that night I would have never known it was there."

"Have you ever met Mark before?"

"Julie and I rode by Brian's apartment just after he moved and I met Mark there."

"Do you know Brian's girlfriend?"

"No."

"Do you know what kind of work Brian does?"

"No."

"Do you know if Brian Tribble deals cocaine?"

"No, I don't know."

The innuendo concerning Tribble quickly spreads to Bias. After writing that Bias was "like my big brother," Wendell Harvey, the student portraitist, adds: "He has smoked [pot] in Terry's room and in my apartment on occasions."

Barrette Palmer adds to the story. She is a student basketball player at the university; Leonard, she claims, adopted her as his "little sister" before the two of them slept together. She details marijuana use on the basketball team as common.

"Have you ever seen anyone in 1103 Washington Hall [Bias's dorm suite] use drugs?"

"Yes, David Gregg and Terry Long."

"How many times have you been to Washington Hall and seen drugs being used?"

"Fifteen times at the Leonardtown apartments [where the team once lived] and about five times at 1103 Washington Hall."

Palmer tells the investigator that Leonard never used drugs; then, a week later, before the grand jury, she reverses her testimony, saying Leonard smoked pot with her, but had gotten paranoid about drug tests and stopped around Christmas. (Tribble tells a similar tale.)

The most damaging statement is from Gloria Jeannette Barber, an unemployed twenty-three-year-old student from North Carolina.

"What can you tell me about Len Bias?"

"I knew him and he knew me. I met him at the Capitol Heights subway station."

"Have you ever witnessed Len Bias purchasing cocaine or any other drug?"

"Yes, it was cold during the time I saw him on Montana Avenue behind the Rec Center."

"Did you talk with Bias that time you saw him get the drugs?"

"Yes I spoke to him and he called me Gloria."

"Who was with him that time you saw him?"

"He was light-skin guy. I asked Bias if he played ball too and he said that he went to school with him."

"What kind of car were they in?"

"They were in a small dark sports car."

"Did you hear Bias talking to the dealer about the quality of the cocaine?"

"Yes, he asked him how is it going to come back?"

"What do you mean by come back?"

"After you prepare it for freebasing."

"How many times have you see Len Bias purchase cocaine?"

"I only saw him twice."

"Did Bias ever say anything about people seeing him getting cocaine in the area?"

"He said he would really rather not want to come up here. The dude said, 'Take my beeper number and I will meet you somewhere else.' "

"Did many people up there know who he was?"

"Yes almost everybody knew and spoke to him just to say his name."

. . .

A theory emerges. Brian is not a protected manchild, still eating at home, a still not fully formed creature caught between giving up dreams and accepting the realities of his life. Instead, all the adopted symbols of the high, street life are taken for real and he's declared a dealer; and not a penny-ante seller who perhaps sometimes holds drugs for Bias, but an officer in an established criminal organization—a lieutenant. Bob Wagner, Bias's high-school coach, says that "lieutenant" was the word that came up when he asked people on the street about Tribble. There is even presumably a Mister Big in the cartel, a man named Cornell Jones. "That was the name that came up," says Wagner. "He was apparently one of the big dealers that was busted or they got him for something else." Even though he's in jail, Jones is still masterminding the operation, a sign of his power in the underworld.

Brian and Leonard begin a mutually beneficial friendship. A pretty straight kid, Leonard is under pressure now, enticed and confused by the money, women, and celebrity coming his way. Maybe precisely because he's been such a good kid he's drawn even more than usual to the nightlife. Anyway, he likes hanging out at the clubs with Brian. He likes drinking champagne. He likes taking the drugs. One witness gives a description of him standing at the front door of Chapter III, charming the females as he asks them for ID's. Meanwhile Bias is an important catch for the up-and-coming Tribble. Bias is a path into the big-time world of the NBA, a stellar client who will impress his boss. Tribble supplies Bias with only the highest-quality dope—maybe he even gives Bias freebies, lures to hook him. But the scheme backfires, the unexpected disaster happens. Even though he warns Bias not to lean back—Tribble knows this piece of arcana because Tribble's a dealer—the brother doesn't listen. He taunts him, and the seizures start.

From this point on two theories emerge. In the first, Tribble is a mastermind. He acts with the fabled decisiveness of a CEO. He makes sure to get the remaining cocaine, goes to the hospital, calls up some people and within minutes arranges for them to stage a fake robbery of Julie Walker. Then he leaves the hospital, goes home just long enough to act disturbed by the event and to create the alibi of needing to be alone, drives over to Walker's, *knowing* the police will be there and having arranged this whole exercise—and unmoved by the only hour-past death of his friend—coolly walks in and pretends to be surprised by the robbery.

Or Tribble is scared, a punk. Even as Leonard is dying, all he worries about is whether or not he'll be in trouble—he's as scared of his associates as of the police. After all—goes this theory—he has dope, money, and a telephone book of client names stashed in the safe at Julie's house. And he has the dope, a fifteen-hundred-dollar wad that belongs to his boss, not him. He wants to ditch the stuff, of course, but he's afraid. He wants to stay with Leonard, of course, but he's afraid. He panics. He calls his mother, calls 911. He makes sure he gets the dope, but doesn't know what to do with it. Then he arranges to drive to the hospital in Leonard's car with Jeff Baxter and positions himself on the passenger side so he can stash the stuff. At the hospital he calls his associates. He realizes he must leave the hospital before there is any actual, final word that Leonard has died. Arranging an alibi, he calls his mother to say Leonard is going to be okay, conveniently letting his comment be overheard by Baxter. Then he goes home and asks Mark to drive him to Julie's—not to see her, but to collect the safe; he is even prescient enough to take his gym bag, a clever way to hide the safe as he carries it from the building. When he arrives he finds another shock. Julie has already been robbed. The organization has acted without him. The consequence of what he has done overwhelms him. He walks downstairs to his car, speechless and drained, not knowing what the hell he's going to do, suddenly no longer a hotshot, but a young, frightened guy realizing he's in way over his head, terrified for himself—and with reason: these guys mean business.

Nothing counters this image. One of the prime pieces of evidence concerning Brian's presence in the room with Bias is a tape of Tribble's call to 911. The recorded exchange is pitiful. Tribble's voice sounds drugged and lost, his normal masked huskiness now a deep-throated, scratchy, fearful hush, certainly far from the cool, calculated emotions of a pusher-man who would be worried about being identified by the police.

Emergency Operator: P.G. County Emergency

Brian Tribble: Yes. I'd like to have an ambulance come, what, what room? What room?

Background Voice: Washington Hall.

Tribble: What, eleven-oh-three Washington Hall. It's an emergency. It's Len Bias and he just went to Boston and he needs some assistance.

Operator: What are you talkin' about?

Tribble: Huh?

Operator: What are you talkin' about?

Tribble: I'm talkin' about, uh, someone needs, Len Bias needs help.

Operator: Well, it doesn't matter what his name is, what's the problem?

Tribble: He's not breathing right.

Operator: What's the address?

Tribble: Eleven-oh-three Washington Hall on Maryland University's campus.

Operator: Washington Hall?

Tribble: Yes sir.

Operator: What's your name?

Tribble: My name is Brian.

Operator: Brian what?

Tribble: Tribble.

Operator: Tribble?

Tribble: Yes sir.

Operator: What's your phone number, Brian?

Tribble: I'm, I'm in Len Bias's room, I don't know the phone number there.

Operator: What's the room number?

Tribble: Eleven-oh-three.

Operator: Eleven-oh-three?

Tribble: Yes sir.

Operator: Okay. What's, it's just Washington Hall, what the address of Washington Hall?

Tribble: Its uh, I don't know, it's no address, its just Washington Hall. Come up by Hun—Hungry Herman's and go straight up there and its on the right-hand side, so please come soon as you can. It's no joke.

Operator: Okay, Washington Hall, apartment number eleven-oh-three?

Tribble: Yes, they're givin' 'im mouth to mouth. You

can hear it now. Hear 'em? (*Background noise*) This is Len Bias. You have to get him back to life. There's no way he can die. Seriously, sir. Please come quick.

Operator: Okay, Washington Hall and apartment, um room number eleven-oh-three, right?

Tribble: Uh-huh.

Operator: That's one thousand one hundred and three?

Tribble: Uh-huh. Eleven-oh-three, one thousand one hundred and three.

Operator: All right, we'll have an ambulance out, arright?

Tribble: 'Cuse me?

Operator: We'll have an ambulance out.

Tribble: Okay.

Operator: Thank you.

Tribble: Yeah.

On July 25, after a week of hearing thirty-five witnesses, the grand jury votes to indict Brian Tribble, David Gregg, and Terry Long. The two players are charged with possession of cocaine and obstruction of justice. Tribble faces four counts: possession with intent to distribute cocaine, possession with intent to distribute PCP, possession of cocaine, and possession of PCP. Long and Gregg are living on campus; no warrant is issued for their arrest.

Although Tribble's lawyer is in touch with the state attorney's office, the press reports that a manhunt for him has begun, sheriff's deputies looking for the fugitive for whom a quarter-million-dollar bail has been set. "Tribble's whereabouts in recent weeks," reports the *Post* ominously on July 25, "have become something of a mystery."

The next day Tribble surrenders. Prosecutor Jeffrey Harding argues in court that the high bail should be kept. " 'He drives a late-model Mercedes Benz, has a nice apartment, owns his own company. . . .' " he is quoted as telling the judge. "He would be able to come up with it. . . . Our investigation has revealed he could make the bond." The judge asks what the investigation has revealed, but Harding "refused to answer." The *Baltimore Sun* reports, "Judge Woods not only rejected Mr. Harding's arguments but was clearly irritated when the prosecutor said that the prosecution had good reasons why Mr. Tribble's bond should not be reduced, but could not share those reasons with the court." He reduces the bond to $75,000. After putting their house up as bond, the Tribbles post the bail; but a shackled and hobbled Tribble—irons are a Maryland custom—spends the night in jail. "What kills me," his father is quoted in the *Sun* as saying, "is things like yesterday. He walked in there on his own and he came back out in chains. Things like that go right through you."

The next day, as though to spite the lax judge in public, the *Washington Post* reports that "investigators . . . have located a safe, stolen during an armed robbery of a Bladensburg apartment, that police believe belonged to Brian Lee Tribble, who was indicted last week on drug charges stemming from the Bias case. . . ." The story states that the police had found the empty safe the week before near Patuxent River Park in southern Prince George's County "after receiving information from an anonymous tipster, sources said. Investigators have received statements that the safe had contained $60,000 in cash and about $100,000 worth of cocaine, according to sources." Later that week the *Post* reveals that Tribble's name has come up in the investigation of a mysterious death, the slaying of a man named Karl Lance Joyner who was found murdered earlier that month. The third-hand allegations about the safe, its contents, and the dead man give additional weight to the assumption in the public mind that Tribble is a dealer.

Arthur Marshall himself comes to share in the opinion. "When they rolled out the safe and the dead body down in the schoolyard, I thought [the case] was much more serious then," he says today. . . . I felt he [Tribble] was really tied in to some type of much more serious crime. . . . at the time they were pushing the safe back and forth into the courtroom—I mean the grand jury—I really thought Tribble was a bad guy, a really bad guy."

〰〰〰

In the mid-1970's cocaine became popular again. Ignored by the Mafia, coke was introduced by independent entrepreneurs of the drug world to a new and potentially wide market of young, white professionals. Following the lead of rock singers and entertainers, they adopted cocaine as their drug of choice. Between 1976 and 1977—the *annus mirabilis* of the drug's revival in America—there was a reported 50 percent increase in the number of Americans who had taken the drug.

Cocaine's return coincided with a new acceptance of drugs. "Drug abuse has become an emotional term that connotes society's disapproval and elicits a sense of uneasiness and disquiet," cautioned a commission appointed by no less a conservative than President Nixon in 1972. "It is a term that changes meaning depending on time and place. According to one's society, his place on the continuum of human history, and his reason for using a particular drug, such use is regarded as either socially desirable or undesirable."

The new attitude challenged the drug laws. Why were drugs illegal? The reasons usually cited, public health and social welfare, were clearly self-serving rationalizations because the laws were inconsistent. Why be jailed for possession of relatively harmless marijuana when alcohol and cigarettes, responsible for hundreds of thousands of deaths annually, were available to everyone? The fact was that some drugs were declared illegal not for reasons of public health, but because of profit, privilege, and puritanism. This was true even for a drug such as heroin. "By far the most serious, deleterious effects of being a narcotics addict in the U.S. today," argued the *Consumers Union 1973 Report on Licit and Illicit Drugs*, "are the risk of arrest and imprisonment, infectious disease . . . and impoverishment—all traceable to the narcotics laws, to vigorous enforcement of those laws and to the resulting excessive black-market prices for narcotics."

Cocaine was a natural example of the indefensible bias of the drug laws. In *Cocaine*, Drs. Grinspoon and Bakalar, two Harvard researchers, state, in the unfortunately obscure language common to the subject, "Cocaine provides one of the best examples on a small scale of how the morally ambiguous properties of a psychoactive drug, under the weight of the institutional and conceptual requirements of a society at a given historical stage, are molded into a public 'moral image' that has the typically ideological characteristic of revealing and concealing at the same time." Cocaine's effects were salutary; unlike the opium-derivatives, cocaine enlivened rather than deadened the user. At the same time, unlike the hallucinogens, it didn't space you out. Besides this, the drug, if taken in moderation, seemed virtually harmless. A 1975 White House white paper on drugs reported that "cocaine as it is currently used does not result in serious social consequences such as crime, hospital emergency room admissions, or death." Three years later another government commission declared that cocaine "does not seem to present a serious health threat to the individual when nasally inhaled in small amounts."

Crucial to this argument was a frequently asserted notion: cocaine is not addictive. Addiction, and the threat of addiction, is the imperative behind the drug laws. The whole thrust of the legislation is that these chemicals lead inevitably to the body needing the drug beyond moral or social suasions, a loss of self-control that ends in lawlessness and the state's intervention. Even today this belief colors the whole debate on addiction. "You can't legalize the drugs," explains Ed Jurith, "because people will continue to go out and get them." To claim cocaine was not addictive knocked out in one blow all the props of the drug laws—as though one suddenly proved it was not the fear of mutually assured destruction that had kept the superpowers from blowing each other up the last forty years. If people could take the drug without the body developing an uncontrollable craving, then the dominoes of social and personal cost—crime, health hazards, personal and communal deterioration—would not automatically tumble.

Two elements contributed to this assertion. At the time, the model of addiction was largely derived from opiates. Opiates cause the body to develop a physical craving for the substance and to experience psychological and physical withdrawal symptoms when deprived of a fix. This doesn't occur with cocaine, even though the craving for the drug and its effects if taken without restriction can be far worse than those of heroin. Thus, even though the laboratory monkeys had died from the cocaine and had never demonstrated a desire to abstain from its use, they showed no bad physical effects with abstinence. The experiment might have made them fiends; but they weren't addicts. "The results of these interesting experiments," write Grinspoon and Bakalar in *Cocaine*, "are too ambiguous to serve as a measure of 'dependence liability' in a conceptually precise sense."

There was also confusion about the drug's self-reinforcement mechanism. Cocaine grows in power with its availability. In the early seventies, when the pool of users was smaller and use was limited by cost, one did not find the severe effects from reinforcement one could observe among laboratory monkeys and rats given large doses.

Such scientific confusion and equivocation surrounded the drug with an aura of harmlessness. For example, Grinspoon and Bakalar advance only the wariest judgments of cocaine's negative effects. Noting case studies of violent behavior in cocaine takers, they refer to a 1974 cocaine mob called the Company, "described in the *Miami Herald* as 'the most vicious underworld gang to ever cast a shadow of brutality and lawlessness across South Florida.' " Commenting on thirty-odd sadistic murders the group was alleged to have committed, the authors say, "The drug can obviously exacerbate tendencies toward paranoia and violence that are already present in its users or encouraged by a criminal milieu. But most violence in the illicit cocaine trade, like the violence in the illicit heroin traffic today and in the alcohol business during Prohibition, is of course not necessarily related to the psychopharmacological properties of the drug."

Grinspoon and Bakalar exhibit the same circumspection toward the hallucinations, paranoid episodes, and seizures reported from the early part of the century. Doubtlessly these events happened. But since the drug was not addictive none of them *had* to happen. One could take the drug for pleasure and escape bad consequences. Cocaine's quirky, idiosyncratic effects proved in practice what the anti–drug law argument contended in theory: judging drugs was a relative matter, dependent on individual response and not normative, scientific proof. "Dependence, stripped to its essentials, is a matter of who is likely to use the drug and how; any more elaborate definition tends to dissolve under analysis. Too many statements about cocaine dependence appear to have a pharmacological or psychiatric basis but in fact are of dubious relevance to either the pharmacological nature of the drug or the needs of the drug user and society," assert Grinspoon and Bakalar.

The rationale for such caution was that the empirical evidence for the drug's destructive effects did not exist. Because the drug's use was restricted, instances of cocaine psychosis, violent behavior, or cocaine-related seizures were hard to find. "We searched all Boston for a case of cocaine psychosis," Lester Grinspoon states today, "but we just couldn't find one." They weren't the only ones. A government paper notes, "The Strategy Council on Drug Abuse stated that morbidity associated with cocaine use did not appear to be great. They further stated there were virtually no confirmed cocaine overdose deaths and that a negligible number seek medical help. . . ." In addition, the statistical record reflected a built-in class bias, because of the drug's cost. A suffering wealthy user was more likely to enter a private hospital than a public ward, his case unlikely ever to appear in the public record. The statistical numbers only exploded when the user population expanded to include teenagers, blacks, and the poor who could not afford private doctors.

What occurred next repeated the irony of a hundred years before. The drug found larger and larger markets throughout the late seventies and early eighties. ("What started the cocaine craze?" mused one Washington politician. "Wasn't it Hamilton Jordan in that bar?") More individuals also began taking it on a regular basis because the supply was more steady—they became cocaine "fiends" instead of erratic casual users. The pool of users began to resemble that of the 1880's, the victims of the horror stories that were now being looked on as old-wives' tales. Soon the symptoms of the earlier users began to be observed in the present ones. From the late seventies on there was a steady rise in cocaine-related medical emergencies, deaths from cocaine-induced seizures, and patients suffering from cocaine psychosis.

But this development wasn't analyzed—a possibility precluded by the political emotionalism surrounding the issue. Scientists didn't stress the social conditions that produce a drug epidemic; instead the debate remained fixed on the beneficial or demonic effects of the drug. As the National Institute of Drug Abuse compiled more and more statistics demonstrating cocaine's harmful effects, the transformation that cocaine had undergone a hundred years before happened again: nature's gift, the perfect drug, became (to use the old phrase) "the third scourge of mankind."

An instance of this demonology is the work of Mark Gold. A distinguished graduate of the Yale School of Medicine, Gold runs a "toll-free" hotline supplying callers with referrals to private doctors and drug-abuse programs (including ones run by Gold). (The market for such expensive clinics has expanded enormously over the last five years; in California ads for them run as frequently as ones for kitchen gadgets on late-night television.) In 1984—still before the cocaine fear went into high gear—Gold published *800-Cocaine*, an informational paperback. In the book, his individual judgments manage to straddle the issues and his crusade against drug use is principled: he points out the Reagan administration's hypocritical response to the cocaine epidemic. But his argument is simple: cocaine is a killer drug that threatens to destroy our society.

Gold's judgments are as strict and inflammatory as his earlier colleagues' were calming and ambiguous. Is cocaine addictive? "My answer . . . is an unequivocal yes—if by addiction is meant an irresistible compulsion to use the drug at increasing doses and frequency even in the face of serious physical and/or psychological side effects and the extreme disruption of the user's personal relationships and system of values." Can anyone escape? "What is most important, however is that *many* who start by using moderate amounts once in a while escalate their doses, begin to binge, and move swiftly to the most dangerous route by far—freebasing." Can cocaine kill? "At this point the reader might say to himself or herself, 'Okay, snorting doesn't kill.' Doesn't it? Here's an account given at a national conference on cocaine of a *snorting-related* death by someone with firsthand experience—Dr. Charles V. Wetli, Deputy Medical Examiner of the Dade County Medical Examiner's Office in Miami, Florida." Gold then quotes the report: "A typical cocaine death *might* be *similar* to that of a young girl's (aged 15) I autopsied who used cocaine rather infrequently. She went out one particular night to a disco party. She drank, snorted some cocaine, and then told her friends she wanted to lie down. She did that, had a small seizure, got up, snorted some more cocaine, and then lay down again. She soon went into violent seizures which literally threw her off the water bed." (Italics added.) The book warns that recent studies show the occasional user follows a short road to addiction and once hooked carries the cross throughout life.

The judgments expressed by Gold's carefully phrased self-promoting alarmism are highly debatable—reading his book one wonders why every North American boy and girl isn't spending his or her days in a round of urine samples and group therapy sessions. The terrible effects of which cocaine is capable notwithstanding, the fact remains that the scientific record of cocaine's addictive properties—however loosely you define the term—is equivocal. While Charles Raab, head of Customs under Reagan, claims cocaine causes addiction in 90 percent of those who use it, the figures contradict him: Edgar Adams of NIDA figures that out of the over 20 million Americans who have used cocaine at least once, approximately 1.5 million can be said to be addicted. "It's true that there are a lot of people who use cocaine and don't become addicts," says Sue Weiss. "It's not clear why this is so." A contributor to a 1985 government-sponsored pamphlet on the drug writes, "Knowledge about the consequences of use is limited. . . . Many questions about the relationship between use and consequences remain unanswered." Three scientists who have surveyed drug use among high-school seniors for the last twelve years state: "The main point . . . is that there is no clear evidence that there is an inevitable progression in cocaine use. Use on a few occasions does not seem to produce any necessary increase at a later period." The crucial point is not the power of the drug, but the conditions under which the drug is used: who takes it and for what reasons.

One of Gold's most egregious errors is that for him—as, indeed, for his opponents—the only people using the drug are the middle class. His only subjects and his only audience are yuppies. Unintentionally his book provides a view of the frighteningly self-satisfied, self-referential sensibility that sets the tone of popular social thought in the Reagan Era. The aura of money and privilege, the *Bright Lights, Big City* world of cocaine, shines over each case history he cites. One patient "was no deprived street kid looking to forget his ugly world . . . [but] a typical American, brought up in an intact, church-going family, with father earning an adequate and steady living as a department supervisor in a mail-order house; his mother a homemaker and conscientious PTA member." Another is a "tall and quite handsome man of 31" who, upon entering his father's business, "proved to be a brilliant businessman" and was earning—before the hell-hound struck—"well-over $100,000 a year," besides being married to a "pretty and intelligent woman" and driving both a Mercedes and a Triumph. Another is a "woman of the 80s with everything going for her" who works as an executive in a "major publishing house . . . lunch[es] at the Four Seasons with well-known authors and edit[s] best-sellers," and whose daily schedule includes "a life-style of weekend vacation houses, designer clothing, and an apartment with a dazzling view of Central Park." As if more proof were needed, Gold also includes the results of a 1983 sample of five hundred Hotline callers. Noting that one in three were women and that 85 percent were white, Gold writes, "They were well educated. . . . Within the group there were college graduates, men and women with M.D. and legal degrees, business people. . . . Given this background, it is hardly surprising that these callers were, on the whole, among the top earners in the country."

His meaning is clear. If *these* people succumb to cocaine, no one is safe. *Society*, not just the "deprived street kid," is threatened.

At the start of August everyone is waiting. State Attorney Marshall claims to have proof of Tribble's guilt, but so far no witnesses have testified to Tribble's buying the dope and bringing it into the room, even actually to his being in the room with the cocaine—much less linking him to the purloined safe, the frequently mentioned sixty thousand in dope and one hundred thousand in cash, and the murder victim the PGC police believe might be a part of the case. Still, everyone thinks it's just a matter of time before the case breaks and the pusher-man is exposed. At least one reporter spends late nights at the clubs where Tribble and Bias hung out, the bartender coaching the journalist in the verbal cues and finger gestures hustlers use to negotiate deals as they work the floor.

Then everything stops. Nothing new about Tribble surfaces. The leads dry up. The rumors simply get repeated. The sources can't produce anything but the same allegations. Marshall says that after the police officer pushed "the safe out of the courthouse, I never heard another word about it. . . . That was the end of it, the end of everything as far as Tribble and everything else went. The rest of the trial was spent on the University of Maryland. . . ."

The University of Maryland means the basketball team and Lefty Driesell. Since Bias's funeral, both have been under a steady attack. The day after the service the academic counselor of the team quits, telling the *Washington Post* she left "because she felt . . . Lefty Driesell did not place enough priority on his players' education." Then the *Baltimore Sun* reports that unnamed school officials claim several university athletes—not just basketball players—tested positive for drugs the previous year. The following day the *Post* runs its second editorial about Bias's death. "It's time that Mr. Slaughter and the trustees take a long and thoughtful look at the university's whole relationship with its student athletes," the *Post* writes. "Five of the twelve players on the Maryland basketball team flunked out of school last semester. One was Len Bias, down twenty-one credits from graduating. One in ten Maryland athletes flunks out every semester. . . . There is history here. The university has seen former players Adrian Branch and Steve Rivers convicted of drug possessions. It has watched former player John Lucas's cocaine addiction ruin his professional career. It has seen other players accused of sexual misconduct and breaking and entering. It made a lot of money on each of these players." In an interview two days later, athletic director Dick Dull says, "Being a manager of an athletic program while being an educator is a conflicting issue." Dull then blames preparatory schools for the academic failure of college athletes. The same day the mother of a young player on the team says she and other parents had written two letters to Driesell before Leonard's death about their sons' academic performances. "We weren't upset with Coach Driesell," she explains, "we just thought if we all got together we could express some of our concerns." The following day the academic coordinator of the basketball team announces "he now realizes there is potential for an athlete to substitute a different urine sample," and "from now on athletes taking tests would either have to strip while taking the test or be observed." The *Post* publishes a poll showing that 50 percent of Maryland adults think there is widespread use of drugs such as cocaine among Terrapin athletes.

Once the police investigation proper gets under way these themes swell. A player is found to have copied a classmate's answers in a speech course final exam. Marshall says Driesell knew of another player who had a drug problem, and that others cheated drug tests by "putting a common plumbing chemical into their . . . samples." The next day a report surfaces that players had used an assistant coach's telephone credit card, running up bills, one television reporter announces excitedly, of over twelve hundred dollars! This is followed by a revelation from Steve Rivers, an ex-player who was caught one night several years earlier with marijuana while driving around with Adrian Branch, that both Driesell and Dick Dull knew he "experimented" with marijuana. His allegation contradicts the two administrators' frequent assertions that neither knew about a drug problem on the team. Consequently the *Post* interviews Dull again. Trapped, Dull admits his dishonesty with a disarming ease worthy of Lefty Driesell: "Steve is correct. He indicated that in the past he had experimented with marijuana. . . . My previous statement needs to be amended."

In their details—a star short twenty-one credits, a twelve-hundred-dollar phone bill—these stories are hardly unique to the University of Maryland. Corruption of some sort accompanies all big-time college sports. But the allegations at the University of Maryland point to a larger failing: the university administration's surrender of control to Lefty Driesell.

Terry Long becomes the unfortunate example that proves the case. The story of Long's admission into Maryland highlights two troubles with the program: Driesell's acceptance of unqualified students and the university administration's agreement to let the coach fudge standards.

"The story . . . is that Lefty wanted to bring in [Keith Gatlin and Terry Long]," says the *Sun's* Molly Dunham. "He went to the admissions department. They said, 'We don't think we should bring either of them in, but we'll give you one.' So Lefty said, 'I'm going to take Keith because he's a better player.' So then he goes back a little bit later and says, 'You guys took Gatlin, Terry Long here has better SAT scores, you got to let him in too.' So he got Terry Long in too. The admissions department fought him tooth and nail the whole way on both of those kids. And [Chancellor] Slaughter intervened and helped Terry Long in . . . and then reinstated him twice, after he'd been actively dismissed."

Long is also a prime example of Driesell's questionable attitude toward his players.

Barrette Palmer, the young woman basketball player who claims she had a love affair with Bias and calls herself the player's "little sister," begins the story. She and Terry smoked pot regularly, she tells a police investigator, buying the stuff at 5 Fraternity Row, a stately crescent of distinguished-looking buildings directly off of Highway 1, from a contact in the frat house named Bowser.

"How long has Terry Long been using drugs?"

"As long as I have known him, since 1984."

"Does he use drugs on a regular basis?"

"Maybe once a week."

"Has Long ever explained the procedure used when he and members of the team have the urine tests for drugs?"

"No, the most he ever told was how they did the test."

"Do you know of any players on the team who have been disciplined by Coach Driesell for any drug problems?"

"Yes, Terry Long."

"Do you know when this was?"

"I think it was last year, 84–85 school season, sometime in that year . . . [during] the spring semester."

"Can you tell me what you know about that?"

"Well . . . he just said I think they had detected marijuana in his system and I think it was if he had it again he would be suspended or something like that. It was a pretty harsh punishment, I don't quite remember everything, but it seemed like he would be put off the team."

"Do you know if he tested positive the next time he took the test?"

"No."

"Do you know if any disciplinary action was taken?"

"No."

"Do you think Coach Driesell used any discipline with the team as far as them going to classes, studying, and the use of drugs?"

"Well, I'll say it like this. He tried his best but he couldn't be around all the time as there were times when you know they did things he told them not to do, they did it anyway."

The general belief is that these failings represent only a fraction of the real story. In the same way the press and prosecutors try puzzling out some grand design in the comings and goings of Bias's friends, so they now seek a pattern to explain the behavior of Driesell, high-school coach Bob Wagner, and Lee Fentress of Advantage. They want to find out if the three men acted to hinder the investigation.

The refusal of the athletic department to talk to the press and the basketball team's seeming reluctance to participate in the investigation of Bias's death inflame these suspicions. Believing a major scandal waits to be discovered, the press examine everything they can about the University of Maryland athletic department.

"The best [the administration] could have done was have a daily briefing and say; 'This is what we know, if you care to come to this briefing, we'll tell you what we know, if you don't, fine,' " says Mark Hyman. "Instead, access to people and information was horrible. . . ." Their behavior "produced friction, and I don't care what any reporter tells you, the more resistance there is from official sources, the more you think, 'Well, there's got to be something there worth knowing if they don't want to tell me.' And access was so poor to the people who should have been most accessible that I think it really drove the story for months and months and months."

The competition for a good juicy story is heightened by the already existing rivalry between the *Sun* and the *Post*, a contest the *Post* wins for the first several weeks with its long series on athletics at Maryland.

"There *was* pressure to come up with something a little bit different every day," says Hyman, who spends that summer hanging out at Cole Field House trying to track down leads. "The attitude here was pretty obvious. They [the editors] said, 'Go down to College Park every day. Stand in Cole Field House, talk to the people who will talk to you and trust you, and try to figure out which way this thing is going.' Some days that resulted in a story about Lefty. For example, one day . . . I found out Lefty had polled his players and physically handed each player a ballot and asked them to vote secretly whether they wanted him to remain as coach."

In time the *Sun* catches up: Slaughter's intervention in the Terry Long affair is broken by the paper. But the desire for news, to keep the story going, is never slaked. A symbiotic relationship develops. The media want stories. The state investigation supplies the media with the stories the reporters want: the investigation receives publicity, and the newspeople get copy.

The most notorious instance is the point-shaving charges. In point-shaving, the classic form of corruption in college basketball, a player or team controls by how many points it wins so gamblers can collect on bets. The most famous point-shaving scandal was at City College in the early fifties. The players were representative sons of the New York working class, blacks and Jews enticed by an Italian gambler. The boys came away with less than ten thousand dollars total—one guilt-racked player never taking the tainted money out of the shoebox where he stored it. Today point-shaving is an anachronism. Given the enormous earnings possible in the NBA, no gambler could offer an amount sufficient to lure a promising college star—the sort of player one needs to make the scheme work—to jeopardize his future. Yet on July 17 an AP story quotes Marshall: "Among some of the other rumors [we have] specific allegations involving the fact that at least one person, Brian Tribble, may have traveled with the team or at least been at the scene of a couple of the out-of-state games, and as a result of that there have been some statements made that maybe point-shaving was involved."

On July 18 Marshall clarifies his statement, saying the gambling is *not* point-shaving. "We've had allegations brought to our attention regarding potential gambling. It comes from a reasonably reliable source, so we're looking into that possibility, perhaps not this week in the grand jury, but perhaps a little bit further down the line."

Today Marshall dismisses the whole incident. "We had one person make such a representation," he says about the point-shaving. "Absolutely nothing substantial in it."

Prosecutor Jeffrey Harding's account is more informative. "I had in my hand one day . . . a Maryland [basketball] schedule. The schedule had the point-spreads and the points, plus or minus. . . . That just happened to be on the schedule I procured. We were looking at the schedule for dates. [A local television journalist] was in our office doing an interview . . . He saw that in my hand. That's where [the point-shaving story] came from. . . . That's the type of reporting that was going on at that time. Had I walked down the hallway and said, 'Heroin,' it would have been in the front page of the paper."

Leaks plague the grand jury investigation. Grand juries are supposed to be conducted in absolute secrecy to protect the people under investigation in case there is no indictment. But during the Bias investigation the media reports every detail of the proceedings.

"We had judges coming in that courtroom on three occasions, bitching at us, actually sitting there yelling at us not to say anything to the media," says jury member Robert Nevins. "But yet, by the time I got from the room to my car, a quarter-mile away, and turned on the radio and drove home, I heard every damn thing that went on in that courtroom."

Nevins believes the information came from the state attorney's office because the press received the privileged information so quickly. "I don't know where everybody—everyone in the courtroom, or the jury members—went after they left there. Most of the time they walked to their cars. But it just seemed like it was awful quick. . . ."

Alan Goldstein, an expert witness on the vagaries of the PGC legal world, believes that prosecutor Jeffrey Harding was the source and that Marshall was "ruefully aware" of Harding's jabbering.

Harding has another story.

"My phone rang until two in the morning. Constantly. And I didn't have an answering machine. ABC, NBC, CBS, Channel Four, Five, Nine, Seven, Eleven, and Two in Baltimore. AP, UPI. Every night. Ask my wife about that. Drove us nuts. Here's the usual call. "Jeff, this is Joe Blow from the UPI. You had investigations. It's leaked that somebody said this." Or "You've learned this today, I need to confirm it or I'm going to lose my job, everybody else has got it." Sob stories. All night long. Can't you give us something? Off-the-record. We won't quote you. Just give us anything. That was the intensity of it. . . . And let's talk about reporters for a minute. . . . In the average situation, people are *thrilled* to talk to [reporters]. They want to see their name in the paper. . . . When you tell a reporter, 'I'm not commenting,' that fires him up. Now he's doing what he's getting paid to do. . . . It got really, really ugly. There was stuff printed, as I proved in motions, that was unconfirmed by the *Baltimore Sun*. . . . The reporting was so competitive . . . that people . . . [were] making stuff up to get in the paper and be ahead of the next stuff. . . . I *didn't* do anything. I would not. I mean, they tried every trick in the book . . . never once did I comment to the press. . . . When I'm quoted in the paper, it's something I said in open court, or as a press release. . . . I was well ahead of the game. I saw where this was coming. I saw that it was going to be blown up out of proportion. I was far-sighted with this. And I never once did it. And if you can find me a place, show it to me and I'll kiss your ass right there."

Harding speculates that the leaks came from numerous sources. "I couldn't pinpoint it. . . . Sometimes Channel Seven would have it, and sometimes the *Post* would have it. Sometimes Four, sometimes the *Sun*. You know, it didn't seem to be a real consistent leak. . . . I think it was just all these high-paid reporters going after everything they can. Working twenty hours a day, being everywhere. Every time I went to a function or a party there were seven or eight of them there, vying to buy me drinks. Standing behind me when I'm in the bathroom. *Waiting* for me to say something. [They'd] . . . buy, beg, borrow, steal to get information."

One afternoon Harding even imagines the state attorney's office is the target of a surveillance à la *Mission Impossible* (or *Get Smart*).

Information "came out for a few days that was close to being accurate. We were concerned about it. [Until then] the information was very general. . . . Now we were getting quotes. . . . To me it was immediately apparent when it was a good source and when it wasn't. Because I knew what was said. Because I interviewed everybody before they went in there and I wrote down little questions on a folder for Mr. Marshall to ask them. . . . We were sitting in my office which is one floor above the grand jury and looking out at one of these 'Live at Five' antenna dishes that was pointing at the grand jury window. Normally they are pointing up in the air. And I guess . . . they were shutting it down. But I looked at it and somebody pointed it out and said: What are they doing there? Are they listening in to the grand jury room or something? We never substantiated it, but that's . . . how whacked out we were getting. . . ."

Another frequent rumor holds that Marshall is springing the leaks, hoping his campaign to clean up the campus will attract votes. To this day, Marshall denies this, claiming his investigation aroused voter hostility. But it's unclear whether this was a risk Marshall took knowingly or not. The common assumption about the Bias investigation at first *was* that people wanted drugs out of the university. Only later, when the consequences of the investigation began to be clear, did popular opinion change; and by then Marshall would have seemed a hypocrite to call off the inquiry.

Yet when the grand jury starts to hear actual witnesses, the word from the closed sessions is that the talk of scandal is grossly exaggerated. "One of the jurors," reports the *Post* on August 12, "who asked not to be identified, said that 'the team, as a whole, looks pretty clean. . . . A lot of this stuff about drug use among team members seems to have been blown out of proportion."

Marshall is in trouble. As the election nears, his two-month-long widely publicized, heavily criticized investigation has resulted in nothing more substantial than unproven charges against one defendant and empty allegations against the favorite institution of the state. And his bête noire, Driesell, the troublemaker who started the whole thing, is going to get off. He needs a miracle.

"When I went to the grand jury," relates Bob Wagner, ". . . if I was asked one hundred questions, twenty-five or thirty of them had nothing to do with Leonard Bias. They had to do with stuff about the school, how our athletic program was run, about the teachers who might have changed grades, about some guys on the football team that were dealing. I said, 'What the hell does this have to do with Leonard's death?' "

Then, for a moment, it seems like Marshall's fabled luck will strike again. The grand jury reconvenes on August 15. In the middle of their sessions assistant coach Oliver Purnell testifies that Driesell ordered him to clean up Bias's room—the command that Purnell ultimately refused to obey. At the time, people know about Driesell's meeting with the players, but not his directions to Purnell. Not even Marshall knows the details of the whole story.

"We had a file on each witness," says Marshall. "We used one room to bring the witnesses into, where we sat down and they were interviewed by a police officer from the University of Maryland or someone from my office. . . . And they sat in one room, and then they would bring in all the material, and I'd go over that and read it and then bring them in. . . . Basically all he [the witness] was doing was repeating what he told the police at that time. . . . Purnell was a surprise. I don't think we knew exactly what he was going to say until he walked in the door."

Purnell's testimony is followed by a bigger shock. On Wednesday, August 20, Lefty Driesell waives his right to immunity from prosecution, takes the stand and tells his story for four hours.

The appearance is a dramatic gamble on Driesell's part. Waiving immunity demonstrates his belief in his own integrity. The drastic action may help convince the jury, in the courtroom and the larger jury of the public, of his innocence. If they declare him guiltless he will be exonerated as a victim of the press and prosecution; if he fails to persuade the jury the testimony compelled under oath can be used against him in a trial.

Marshall also takes a gamble letting the coach appear. A grand jury interrogation is "not really the kind of examination that you can structure like a courtroom examination," explains Alan Goldstein. "It's informal. There's no judge. Marshall can ask Driesell questions, but Driesell doesn't have to answer it, and nobody's going to say to him, 'Answer the question.' Driesell could get into hearsay, he could say whatever he wanted. There's no rules of evidence. . . . Driesell [could have] said, hypothetically, . . . that his only desire was to help the kids, when he sent . . . Purnell over to clean out the room—that [his only intention was] to prevent the kids from getting charged with a crime because they destroyed the evidence. . . ."

Besides this, Marshall agrees to let Driesell's lawyer, the legendary Edward Bennett Williams, EBW, address the grand jury before Driesell's appearance.

Williams said "something along the lines of just bringing [Driesell] in here and talking to him was going to discredit him," says Robert Nevins. "He was trying to point out that what we decided in here was going to settle his life in a certain way. If we were to convict him of obstruction of justice, how was he going to look in everybody's eyes? Are you *sure* it's an obstruction of justice. He was just trying to make the guy look like a normal citizen. And letting us know that we had the power to hurt his life, ruin his life."

Williams's efforts aren't in vain. "When they dragged Lefty Driesell in there," says Nevins, "everybody just was shaking their head . . . because they didn't think he—he had to be in there."

Driesell of course has his own reasons for appearing. Obviously he wants to clear his name. But he also hopes that testifying will help him keep his job.

"Lefty was cast in a very unfavorable light immediately for several reasons," says Mark Hyman. "One of which was that it was alleged that he had perhaps committed a crime by instructing one of his assistant coaches to clean up the room. So immediately there was a suggestion that Lefty could be indicted. And that's not a real good thing to have on your résumé. In that sense he fell out of favor very quickly. . . . Slaughter also was very embarrassed by the academic revelations. And it wasn't so much that the kids were failing. It was that Lefty didn't seem [to make] any extraordinary effort to get them the help that they needed."

But Driesell still has the remaining nine years of a ten-year contract with the university.

"No one who knows Lefty [would] *ever*, for a minute suspect that he would walk away from the contract," says Mark Hyman. "For two reasons. Number one, he likes money. And number two, the admission of guilt in a sense."

His reluctance to retire puts the university administration in the embarrassing situation of paying a large amount of taxpayers' money to a man they had determined wasn't performing his job well. An indictment would have resolved the difficulty.

"This is a theory that has been advanced," says Hyman, "that very early on Slaughter became convinced that Driesell should not continue as basketball coach. From that point . . . the simplest solution would have been—from the university's standpoint—that

Lefty could have been indicted. If he had been indicted then that would have put into question . . . his contract—because he had some sort of morals clause in the contract. That would have voided the contract and the university could have taken action against him without any fear of repercussion."

Deploying his full talent for self-presentation and all his good-old-country-boy sincerity, Driesell marshals his reserves of conviction and piety and talks for four hours without a slip. The atmosphere is friendly. One juror even waves, calling the coach by his nickname.

"They liked him," says Marshall. "[He was] very personable . . . a very likable, God-fearing country boy. . . . Bobby Knight probably would have been indicted."

"He was very outspoken," remembers Robert Nevins. "He brought in facts [about] how many kids graduated in his programs in all these past years. He was more or less defending his program at Maryland. . . . It seemed like he was telling everything as truthful as it was, and like he had nothing to hide. . . . This is how it is. He knows there is a drug problem at the University of Maryland, just like every other campus. . . . He didn't sit there and try to make up anything. . . . He just came out and whatever questions they asked he tried to answer."

Nevins's recollection of Marshall's behavior toward the coach is surprising. Marshall had accused Driesell publicly of suspicious activity and of betraying his responsibility as a university official; privately he blamed the coach for the whole investigation—"this endless foolishness" as he now calls it. One would imagine he would have shown his displeasure with the coach, the same way he showed contempt when he dismissed other witnesses. Instead, says Nevins, Marshall "didn't treat him like a criminal, if you will. . . . He was very polite to him and everything. . . . he treated Lefty like he was wasn't really that involved" in Bias's death. Nevins also says Marshall didn't share with the jurors his belief that the entire investigation had been caused by Driesell's behavior, or that the University of Maryland had been uncooperative, the sort of judgments he indicated to them concerning other witnesses.

"I have a theory," says Alan Goldstein. (Goldstein may wear a Mickey Mouse watch, but he is considered one of the county's top lawyers because of his ingenious theories.) "My impression [was] that a lot of people just dumped all over Lefty the minute they got in the grand jury. So, by the time Bud got around to Lefty, he hated Lefty, based on what everybody was saying about him. And these were people that he'd had before the grand jury. So—and this is just Goldstein's theory—Bud had to get Lefty to go before the grand jury because [Bud] thought if he got [Driesell] before the grand jury he'd have him nailed on a perjury charge. He figured Lefty would lie . . . [and that] he had enough meat on Lefty that if he lied about anything, he had him, he'd have a perjury charge. And I think the price for getting Lefty to go before the grand jury and waive his immunity was that Williams got to go in after him. . . . And Bud thought he was probably getting the better of the deal because he figured that after Lefty lied in front of the grand jury Williams couldn't save him . . . [and that] the jury wasn't going to buy what Driesell said."

A week later the jury votes on whether to indict Driesell, Fentress, and Wagner on the obstruction of justice charges.

"The vote was taken by a show of hands," says Robert Nevins. "All in favor of indicting Lefty Driesell and so and so, raise your hand."

Only one person votes to indict.

According to Marshall, the grand jury found that there was "no ill will, evil motives, or corruptness" on the part of the three men.

The judgment is a direct repudiation of Marshall. When Marshall comes back in after the vote, Nevins remembers, "He just sort of like—Lord, you know—acted like he was [mad] . . . he got all businesslike and quick to hurry things along and get out of there."

~~~

The exclusive focus of the cocaine debate on the problems of white, middle-class Americans resulted in a domestic Vietnam. This lengthy, exhausting, emotional inquiry, which employed the full arsenal of modern American social and physical science, first failed
~~~

to predict and then completely ignored the most important long-term consequence of its subject: the mutation of cocaine into crack and the infestation by the drug of the black community.

The following are citations from the June 1987 proceedings of the National Institute of Drug Abuse Community Epidemiology Work Group:

- In New York, "the ethnic distribution shows increasing trends among blacks and declining trends among whites and Hispanics."
- In Denver "the proportion of blacks in treatment has more than doubled."
- In Los Angeles, the "death data . . . show that in 1986 blacks 'caught up with' whites for the first time."

These local trends are reflected nationally. All national information on drugs is tabulated and generated by the National Institute on Drug Abuse. NIDA uses three surveys to chart drug trends. By their account, black American use of cocaine has exploded in the last eight years. Hospital records (the Drug Abuse Warning Network—DAWN—reports) show this rise in particular. In 1981, the start of the Reagan administration, blacks made up approximately 35 percent of all cocaine emergencies. By 1987, for which the latest figures are available, blacks made up 55 percent of all such emergencies, and this proportion was still on the rise. Black use of cocaine is so widespread that cocaine has replaced heroin as the drug of choice, more blacks now dying from cocaine than from heroin.

These numbers probably minimize the extent of the drug "problem." Drug statistics are notoriously unreliable. A recent national sampling, for instance, reported a total of almost four hundred thousand children who had used cocaine; yet a New York State study begun in 1985 "before the crack epidemic began" estimated "at least 97,000 people under the age of 16 who are heavy drug abusers in the state."

Drug statistics are also severely distorted by race and class biases. In 1985, for instance, for the first time NIDA "oversampled" black and Hispanic populations to determine "whether or not there is a disproportionate amount of drug abuse in any specific minority group." The sample was restricted to "households." The definition excludes "persons living in group quarters or institutions such as military installations, dormitories, hotels, hospitals and jails and transient populations such as the homeless." But these places are the very lodgings of the "underclass," the locations where one could confidently expect to find "overrepresentation." The official explanation for this oversight is that NIDA can't afford the million and a half dollars it would have cost to include "non-household" participants. This amount is slightly less than what New York City pays about every three days on drug-related problems. The result of such budgeting is to wipe out a larger and larger section of the population: to declare them *statistically* nonexistent is to distort the factual basis upon which official programs are predicated. Public funds don't reach troubled areas, and social conditions deteriorate exponentially—thus the effect of *statistical* nonexistence is quite simply death, *actual* nonexistence.

But even correct numbers don't suggest the full scope of the problem. The reason cocaine is a plague in the black community is not because of the number of black Americans who use the drug, but because of the drug's effect on the life of the black community. Cocaine has become omnipresent for black Americans. One hears reference to the drug and its disastrous consequences even in the most casual conversations. A mother of four grown children ticks off victims as though she were numbering war casualties. A young black professional mentions offhand a high-school friend hitting the pipe and says in six months dealers have transformed his once lower-class D.C. residential neighborhood into a drive-in, stop-and-shop drug bazaar. A social worker exclaims that her six-year-old daughter is taught about drugs in her private school. "I mean it's crazy. She's *six years old!* It's needed, but its crazy." The crack-cocaine plague has undermined basic economic, social, and moral underpinnings of the black community. In its worst instances the epidemic has even altered the biological balance of the community: since the introduction of crack the national rate of black life expectancy has *declined* and the infant mortality rates in many black areas have shot up. A black social worker whose beat is Bias's own Northeast says, "They call drugs a problem. For white people drugs are a problem. For blacks drugs effect every aspect of our lives—health, education, the family, the whole way of life of the community. It's not a problem. It's the subjugation of a people."

Even mentioning the seemingly obvious difference between drugs in the black and white communities breaks a powerful taboo. Everyone resists admitting the distinction. Whites prefer to believe the color line has been abolished in society. Meanwhile blacks are afraid the national political will to fight the cocaine plague will disappear if whites think drug abuse is primarily a black disease, just as gays fear government support for AIDS research will disappear if the heterosexual community thinks itself immune.

Yet race is at the heart of the "drug problem." It is the violence in black communities, the appalling rates of criminal activity, poverty, and disease associated with drugs, the wholesale attacks drugs commit on every communal institution that make the majority of the national population concerned about drugs. The drug plague both reflects and magnifies the color line of the society. "It is the civil rights revolution that makes poverty a great issue in America, not merely poverty," the sociologist Nathan Glazer wrote in 1965. Now, after years of refusing to recognize race as a cause of continuing conflict in our society, the focus of the equation is reversed. Race doesn't make drugs an issue; the crack-cocaine plague makes race an issue. The "drug problem" is the latest expression of the effects of institutionalized inequality in our society and has become the focus of whites fears and hatred as, say, a small black child entering an all white school was twenty years ago.

The destructive effects of the drug are endless. No one can afford the drugs on a regular basis—especially those dependent on them. This increases the crime rate, which in turn accelerates the deterioration of community life. Meanwhile media stories contribute to the stigmatization of the black community by chronicling one grisly crime after another until unspeakable brutality comes to seem a given rather than a symptom of the plague—a genetic defect, not a disease. And the coverage contributes to the disorder. Speaking about Dennis Hopper's presumably socially conscious movie *Colors*, one black social worker says, "Things like [that] don't help the situation at all. . . . Someone doesn't think about drugs at all. Then they see a black teen and they think he's dealing. And [the movie] affects the kids. They start to dress a certain way. It becomes a style." The ceaseless human-interest portraits of crack addicts mixed with the reports of decimated and frightened communities paint a picture of a fratricidal people. The old racist dream of blacks killing blacks—the expression of the idea that somehow life means less to blacks—is made horrifying real in the tabloids with daily stories of gangland murders and child abuse. The public mind begins to see the black community as a social bedlam, a domestic Beirut or Belfast, where the causes of civil violence are psychological—"crazy niggers"—rather than social. White sympathy for blacks diminishes and concern for law and order replaces social programs. The immiserization of the community increases. As conditions worsen the drug business infects and distorts every aspect of black life. Simultaneously, the unequal conditions of black life—the quantitative documented difference in average wages, level of employment, general health, education, and so on between blacks and whites that are inexplicable unless one takes race into account—exaggerate every power of the drug. One of cocaine's most powerful effects, for example, is to enhance one's self-confidence and sense of mastery. This quality surely heightens the drug's attraction for teenagers already feeling disenfranchised, insecure, and neglected. How much more enticing is this power to black youths for whom the possibility of going to jail is twice as likely as attending college?

The tornado-like spiral wastes every aspect of black communal life. Take health. Studies report that pregnancies in mothers using cocaine (and especially crack) result in an "increased incidence" of spontaneous abortions, ruptured placentas, premature labors, growth retardation of the fetus, and also Sudden Infant Death Syndrome. Yet in New York it was only in city hospitals used by black populations that these dangers resulted in a rising infant mortality rate. "In Central Harlem," reports *Newsday* on August 31, 1987, "the number of deaths rose from 16 per 1,000 in 1984 to 27.6 per 1,000 in 1986," of which a "disproportionate number"—what a way to represent human reality!—"of the mothers are cocaine users."

But the most visible effects of cocaine are in the area the black population is already most sensitive about: crime. The exact number of ripoffs caused by drugs is of course impossible to count. A national survey conducted by the National Institute of Justice claims 13 percent of all inmates were in prison because of crimes committed to support their cocaine habits. This estimate is undoubtedly low. Present surveys suggest that perhaps as much as two-thirds of the inmate population of urban areas is drug dependent, largely on cocaine. The *New York Times* reports that 50 percent of all those serving sentences for robbery, burglary, theft, or a drug offense in the metropolitan area were daily users of an illegal drug—significant numbers when you consider that twelve thousand people were arrested in New York alone simply for dealing or possessing cocaine in just one six-month period. But even these crimes represent only a fraction of all illegal activity committed because of drug use. Drug users don't break the law only once; they live as outlaws.

A 1985 study of Harlem heroin users found that addicts performed 1,075 illegal acts each per annum, including victimless crimes, such as running the drugs. As the Detroit chief of police told the Select Committee on Narcotics Abuse, "crack cocaine which is not an exorbitant habit, costs $18,250 a year, 365 days to support. Where is a ninth-grade dropout getting $18,250 a year from?"

Crime is the raw nerve of black-white relations; it charges the white view of blacks—as interracial marriage once did. Every report of a ripoff, every neighbor's tale of having been held up, every newspaper report of a crazy hostage situation, confirms the worst white stereotype of blacks as both dangerous and inferior. In this regard cocaine is doubly vicious. The drug necessitates law-breaking; but because cocaine exaggerates paranoid traits, cocaine fiends have a tendency to commit particularly ghastly crimes, the sort chronicled in the Company gang. In Queens, New York, for instance, where gangs set up a powerful crack distribution center, the murder rate rose 25 percent in one year, unmooring a once stable working-class community.

The daily criminal activity not only adds to a general sense of social disorder; it also contributes to the breakdown of the criminal justice system. In New York State one-third of a $1.5 billion yearly crime-fighting budget is spent on drug related crimes—about one-twelfth of what the entire Federal government allocates for criminal justice expenses for the entire country. Taxpayers resent this expense because all that money still fails to provide them with a safe environment. In May 1988, the *New York Times* reported that "the police say the type of robbery that has become the most common—one committed by a crack addict who reaps a few dollars—is still almost impossible to prevent. The police complain that, while they are making more arrests, drug-related robberies are rising so fast that they cannot bring the overall robbery rate down more."

One of the most dramatic examples of the communal breakdown caused by the crack-cocaine plague is in Bias's hometown, Washington, D.C. In 1986, the assistant chief of police there complained to the Select Committee, "If you look back at 1981 in the District of Columbia, we made over 6,800 arrests. In 1985 we made over 11,000 arrests, and the problem of drugs goes unabated. There are more drugs on the street now than there have ever been. There is more cocaine on the street now than there has ever been. . . ." The trend escalated. Shortly after his testimony, crack invaded the city. By April, 65 percent of all persons appearing in D.C. superior court tested positive for cocaine use. The murder rate jumped, averaging a killing a day for 1988; juvenile drug-abuse violations reached almost two thousand by January 1988. Meanwhile an increasing number of babies at D.C. General were being born with severe cocaine dependencies. The newspapers were filled with the daily casualties of the crack wars: a young ball player, a fan of Bias, swallowed six chunks of crack and died; a heavy crack user strangled to death her two children, one eight, the other three years old. By summer 1988, the crack trade had traumatized the entire metropolis. If you cruised the city—not the official hub of manicured embassy lawns and government buildings or the ritzy strip of Connecticut Avenue, but Bias's Washington, D.C., the District—every other street corner seemed a vision of teenage hustlers wearing gold chains and scooting around in "Beamers" (BMW's), four-by-fours, and customized Jettas with gold-framed license plates. At one point the police in desperation simply blocked off streets that were known to be drug malls, and rap groups put out a song pleading that "D.C." not come to mean "Dodge City."

The response to such crime waves is, of course, to make more arrests. "Drug arrests number 69,200 last year, with felony narcotics busts up 123.2 percent," said the *New York Post* in one 1988 editorial, commenting that this was "all good news." Not really. Criminal courts exist to determine cases of individual justice. Called upon to grapple with a social problem of immense proportions, they fail, breaking down like a machine suddenly compelled to produce twice as much but with half the power. In the summer of '86, Robert Morgenthau, the Manhattan district attorney, testified before the Select Committee, "We are tremendously overburdened. . . . Last year, we sent five thousand people to prison or jail from . . . New York County. That is still a very small percentage of the total number of people being arrested. I think that what that shows is that we cannot effectively deal with the flood of drugs that is coming into this country. When the amount of drugs in this country goes up from 25 tons in 1980 to 125 tons in 1985, we can't deal with the volume of drugs that are coming in here." Recent figures indicate that in New York one-half of one percent of the approximately 25,000 drug misdemeanor cases—and the Select Committee heard testimony that 75 percent of crack sales are considered misdemeanors—go to trial, the statistical representation of the conservatives' accusation that liberal judges let criminals walk free. Meanwhile ballooning drug arrests have resulted in a dangerous and inhuman overcrowding of federal jails and a precipitous rise in the black percentage of the national inmate population. The ultimate consequence of the spiral of seemingly unmanageable social problems is hopelessness and heartlessness. In 1986 New York City mayor Ed Koch argued quite casually before the Select Committee that the federal government should site jails in deserts and the Alaskan tundra. "Not a concentration camp," he explained. "They are not going to be tortured. They are not going to be killed. But they are going to be incarcerated and there is nowhere to run, because there is a desert out there, or if it is in Alaska, on the tundra, there is nowhere to run, because it is snowing out there."

This proposal for an American Siberia reflects more than the mayor of New York's social macho. Koch's proposal expresses the current public view of the addict as a moral and spiritual weakling. "If we conceive of drug addiction as a spiritual disorder," writes Norman Podhoretz in a newspaper column published after two years of crack epidemic, "we immediately begin seeing it as a freely chosen condition. The addict . . . [is] . . . someone who in pursuit of pleasurable feelings (or to avoid pain) repeatedly gives in to temptation."

This demonization of the addict has accompanied a class change in the drug-using population. The first large group of drug addicts in America were Civil War veterans who had become hooked by treatment for injuries suffered during the conflict and women who had been prescribed the drug by doctors. These people were seen as victims. "The psychology of the drug addict," wrote a public health reformer in the twenties, "is the psychology of the average human being. It is the psychology of you and me when in pain, of you and me when desiring relief. . . ." As the next large group of addicts appeared—young, male urban heroin takers—this sympathy vanished. "When the young tough snorting heroin in the street corner was perceived as the dominant addict type, new and more radical theories of addiction were in order," writes historian David Courtwright. "Psychopathy connoted irresponsible, deviant, and often criminal behavior, which fit the hustling style of the emerging nonmedical majority."

Demands for institutionalization, rather than treatment, of the addict grew. The head of the Federal Narcotics Bureau wrote in 1928 that "most drug addicts . . . were 'mentally deficient or psychopathic characters.' " In the late twenties, the surgeon general said addicts should be divided into two categories, those who used drugs because of "disease, injury, or the infirmities of age," and " 'drug addicts' or dissipators, or persons who habitually use narcotics for other than medical reasons. These are the real addicts, and include psychopaths, neurotics, and criminals." The drug user was increasingly cast as someone beyond the pale of normal behavior or understanding, a vision confirmed as the laws themselves created the need of the addict to live an outlaw's existence.

Even this attitude seems compassionate compared to today's view. Until the Vietnam War drug users were still simply marginal members of society, Johnny Machines, losers and dreamers. Though drugs might be associated with blacks, drug use did not characterize the entire race. The last twenty years have changed that. Now the specter of drugs haunts black Americans. In the public view blacks are irrevocably tied to drug use and the crime it produces. And the user is characterized as morally and personally deficient, the person who can't say no, the latest embodiment of the classic stereotypes of blacks as shiftless, amoral sensualists.

Yet the black community, in its behavior or ideas, bears as much responsibility for this social trauma as a Third World village does, say, for being wiped out by an earthquake.

Drug epidemics are diseases. The drug is the pathogen, the causative agent of the illness. It is carried by the drug merchants who, whether they are legal (as in the 1890's) or not, search for a host for the illness, a mass market for their goods. Inevitably the avenues of infection they come upon are communities with weak resistance: turn-of-the-century middle-class housewives, displaced young urban males of the 1920's, today's ghetto dweller. In each case, the community has less internal strength to combat the disease; each new outbreak is more virulent, its symptoms—violence, communal and personal degradation—increasingly severe.

Presumably the black community in the late seventies would have been resistant to such an attack. In the popular mind an unprecedented granting of privileges had flowed to blacks from the Civil Rights movement and they were now full partners in the society. But although the Civil Rights movement brought significant political gains for black Americans, the social and economic advances of the struggle were largely confined to the black middle class. In 1988, on the twentieth anniversary of the Kerner Commission, a number of newspapers and state commissions examined the condition of black America. What they found was not an upwardly mobile population, but a deeply fractured society within the society. There was a small but successful middle class and a growing, increasingly disenfranchised, desperate, and—except for their attacks on white society—all but forgotten "underclass" for whom, in the words of black sociologist William Julius Wilson in his book *The Truly Disadvantaged*, "the past three decades have been a time of regression, not progress."

This regression was caused by a combination of factors—overdetermined, as the Freudians say about a symptom produced by a multiplicity of causes.

Throughout the late seventies there was a contraction of the American economy. Wilson, who summarizes these findings in his book, cites reports that some 700,000 manufacturing jobs, jobs substantial enough to support an entire family, were lost in industrial states during the seventies. Blacks relied on this employment. In Illinois blacks composed only 14 percent of the total work force, but held 20 percent of the jobs with over 2,000 firms that left central cities to relocate to the suburbs between 1975 and 1978. Most of these laid-off workers lacked the educational skills needed to work in the new, high-tech industries replacing the vanishing manufacturing jobs. Wilson writes, "If one examines recent data on central-city educational attainment by race, the extent to which inner-city blacks are poorly matched for these employment trends is readily apparent." One statistic is particularly eloquent. In 1930, 80 percent of the entire black male population was employed, but few were professionals. Now one out of every four black working males is a professional; but only about one out of every two black males is employed.

This relatively sudden disappearance of steady work followed an equally sudden spurt of the youth population in the central cities in the late sixties. The growing number of young people created a new, intolerable demand upon the already strained resources of the community. "Age correlates with many things," Wilson writes. "For example, the higher the median age of a group, the higher its incomes; the lower the median age, the higher the unemployment rate and the higher the crime rate (more than half of those arrested in 1980 for violent and property crimes in American cities were under twenty-one). The younger a woman is, the more likely she is to bear a child out of wedlock, head up a new household, and depend on welfare."

But what whites saw was blacks living better. They pointed to a rise in the number of black professionals and black homeowners. They observed young, well-dressed black professionals driving expensive cars and populating the new glitter bars of yuppie America, a vision that anyone who travels, especially to the new boomtowns of the South and West, can attest to. Any sympathy among whites for government programs disappeared. Federal and state interventions seemed unnecessary. An extreme conservatism became the ruling ideology. Poverty was no longer seen as a social problem, but as an individual failing. The conditions of ghetto life were not viewed as symptoms but as a "pathology" that an individual could conquer with strong doses of moral fortitude and willpower. From this vantage point, government programs (to paraphrase William Wilson) contributed to rather than combated the social ills of the ghetto: constitutional safeguards resulted in greater crime, government programs promoted unemployment and moral sloth, affirmative action decreased self-esteem. And whites weren't the only ones advancing these arguments. The black movement had been fractured by past government repression and the growing split within the black community between haves and have-nots. Now, in the absence of a large, vital black movement, black authoritarians castigated white paternalism as the cause of black suffering. The Reagan administration selected Joe Clark, the black Paterson, New Jersey, high-school principal known for his bullying tactics, as a moral exemplar.

Abandoned by society, the urban poor found themselves in a hall of mirrors separating them from the rest of society. Sixty-eight percent of the white poor lived in what Wilson calls "non-poverty" areas—heterogenous communities—but this is true of only 15 percent of blacks. The rest, 85 percent, or almost all, lived in the unrelieved squalor of late-twentieth-century American poverty. "In a neighborhood with a paucity of regularly employed families and with the overwhelming majority of families having spells of long-term joblessness, people experience a social isolation that excludes them from the job network system that permeates other neighborhoods. . . . And as the prospects for employment diminish, other alternatives such as welfare and the underground economy are not only increasingly relied on, they come to be seen as a way of life. . . . Thus in such neighborhoods the chances are overwhelming that children will seldom interact on a sustained basis with people who are employed. . . . The net effect is that joblessness, as a way of life, takes on a different social meaning; the relationship between school and postschool employment takes on a different meaning. The development of cognitive, linguistic, and other educational and job-related skills necessary for the world of work in the mainstream economy is thereby adversely affected. In such neighborhoods, therefore, teachers become frustrated and do not teach and children do not learn."

These were the areas first conquered by crack: communities without the inner resources to resist the disease, communities living on an ever contracting base of health—to use Oliver Sacks's phrase. "Income . . . intact famil[ies] . . . feeling that change and hope is possible—those things, I think, tend to retard how fast [addiction] progresses," says Peter Bell of the Minnesota Institute for Black Chemical Abuse. He compares the crack plague to cancer: "If you have cancer and I have it, how fast [the disease] will metastasize through our bodies is determined by how much either of us smoke, our diets, do we get any exercise, what's our emotional state. I think that's true with addiction, and with black people it progresses faster."

The odds favor that the rate of addiction will increase, not diminish. NIDA keeps long-term records of the high-school seniors in their surveys, tracking the kids as they grow older. "Every class—even in the stabilized years—increased its use subsequent to graduation," says Edgar Adams, NIDA's head epidemiologist. "There has to be a topping out somewhere. But this clearly shows that each class increased its use." NIDA's studies also predict increasing use of the drug; the institute's surveys show that use of alcohol, marijuana, or cigarettes makes one a probable candidate for cocaine use, and that the younger a person is when first trying the drug, the more likely he or she will be to continue and increase use. "If you took your first drink when you were eighteen, then only 7 percent go on to try cocaine. But if you took it at thirteen, 40 percent went on," Adams explains. "A very similar pattern is seen for cigarettes. . . . [Among those] using marijuana at ten or twelve, seventy percent or more have tried cocaine." These statistics represent a desperate reality: if, say, after tomorrow, no one new ever took crack again, the society could still count on a sizable and growing population of thus-far untreatable addicts—exactly how large is uncertain since so many people are systematically excluded from the surveys.

The effect is to produce a desolate Third World country in the midst of American society. Descriptions of the cocaine boom in South American producing countries mirror the miseries crack causes in black American communities. The drug has overtaken whatever fragile local economy existed, driving out other agricultural activities in South America while closing down local businesses in black communities at home. It has created a class of drifters—*flotantes*, as they are called in South America—who can earn more from the drug than anything else. It produces a state of constant anarchy in the community, empowering fascist cliques there, giving rise to cocaine gangs here. What one sees is a distorted underground imperialism in which the colonized entrepeneurs cannibalize each other: South American peasants grow a drug sold by North American blacks who use their profits to buy hundred-dollar sneakers manufactured by sub-minimum-wage workers in Taiwan.

The suicide is not simply physical, but spiritual; the destruction is not only of individuals and communities, but of a heritage of many generations. In discussing the effects of the crack-cocaine plague, a black Washington drug counselor compares his civil-rights activist father to today's hustlers. "My father told the white sheriff of the town, 'You have a problem with me, you meet me after sundown and we can throw down, man to man.' And they must have thought he was crazy. But for any black male to self-determine his own behavior in this country he has to be a little crazy. That's what this drug behavior is—a little madness. The dope dealers are the ones who are admired. They are the new leaders. When the kids come to the agency we ask them to draw something. They draw a Mercedes Benz with a guy standing outside with a cane or an Adidas sweatsuit. We ask them, 'What do you want in life?' 'Oh, I want a big mansion, I want some nice clothes.' They're not born that way. They're taught that. The kids see the guys driving around and they say, 'Hey I want to be like him because he's successful and he's doing what this country says you must do to be successful: have a lot of money.' "

~~~

The day after the jury votes not to indict Driesell, the *Washington Post* attacks Marshall. "No one has ever accused Prince George's County prosecutor Arthur A. Marshall of being a wallflower," says an editorial, "but his latest misbehavior in the Len Bias grand jury investigation has surpassed all his other showboat performances. Mr. Marshall . . . has seized the moment to run a serious closed-door criminal proceeding into a highly injudicious public smearing of University of Maryland basketball coach Lefty Driesell. . . . From the outset, Mr. Marshall has been using his important as-
~~~

signment as an excuse for a running series of attempts to grab center stage and front page at the expense of what many other prosecutors consider the normal bounds of correct prosecutorial conduct. . . . Alex Williams [Marshall's opponent for state attorney] . . . has called" the grand jury investigation " 'nothing more than a witch hunt, a fishing expedition.' If enough Prince George's County voters agree, they have a grand opportunity a week from Tuesday to support Mr. Williams and ring down the curtain on Mr. Marshall's bad show."

Ten days later they do. On September 9, a little less than two weeks after the grand jury vote, Marshall loses the election, though by a slender 2,000-vote margin. Goldstein's analysis has proved correct. Notably, though, the bigotry contributing to Williams's victory is overlooked by the latter's supporters. "Williams overwhelmed Marshall in the county's predominantly black voter precincts," writes the *Post*, "and also did well with white voters, prompting his supporters to conclude that the county electorate is growing more racially tolerant. 'It's a testament to the political maturation and the sophistication of our voters,' says one." Perhaps—though white voters might also have imagined a black state attorney would never dare to risk their support by attacking the university.

Marshall is bitter and proud in his defeat. More than ever he now has reason to pursue the investigation that is being blamed for costing him his job and win the Bias case. But winning the case presents a problem. He can't pursue Driesell anymore. He has an indictment against Tribble, but the promise of a major case has evaporated with the disappearing leads of August. An August 28 story, buried on page 22 of the *Post*, reports that "sources" now say that investigators doubt parts of the information given to the grand jury about the infamous safe, and think that "the death . . . may not involve Tribble. Another source said that the grand jury has heard testimony that the safe recovered by police, which was twice hauled into the grand jury room, was not the one taken from the Bladensburg apartment of Julie Walker, a longtime friend of Tribble's."

Marshall doesn't only lack evidence to prove Tribble a big-time dealer. He lacks evidence to prove Tribble guilty of anything. "My honest opinion is that we don't know anything more today than we did when this case started," the *Baltimore Sun* quotes one grand juror on October 1. "It's all circumstantial. We've only returned a few indictments, and the few we have won't hold up in court. Take the one on Brian Lee Tribble. . . . It can't hold up: there's just not evidence. He'll probably get probation. And the same thing goes for Long and Gregg. There's just not enough there."

Faced with losing perhaps the most important case of his career, Marshall does what he has steadfastly shunned. He approaches Gregg and Long's lawyer, Alan Goldstein, to talk about their testimony and to ask them to waive their immunity before the grand jury.

Marshall will not—and does not ever—certify an agreement or a deal. He is afraid that Tribble's attorney will argue Gregg and Long concocted a story to save themselves.

"Marshall was very, very concerned about making a deal," explains Alan Goldstein. "He didn't want to make a deal that would then come back to haunt him in the trial. . . . I made a decision that I could certainly trust Marshall and that it was in the best interest of my clients to go before a grand jury. That I thought that would end the case. And I thought it would end it very favorably."

Goldstein enjoys this confidence for a good reason, other than his own infectious self-assurance. He believes the case against Tribble is so weak that Marshall would never pursue indictments against the two witnesses who could help him. "Marshall was desperate enough that he had to get rid of their cases against them. Marshall didn't know where he was going to get the evidence to prosecute Tribble. . . . There was no place else to go."

Goldstein has been waiting for this moment since his first involvement with the case—the morning Gregg and Long left Wagner's house so early that the high-school coach didn't even hear them go.

"They got to me through [the lawyer] who was the Student Legal Aid attorney at the University of Maryland," who "evidently had seen them at the request of either Driesell or one of the assistant coaches. . . . He called my office and indicated that he had this case. And I didn't get the message till that evening, and I think we met with them the following morning, early in the morning, before court."

Goldstein immediately set up a list of priorities: keeping Gregg and Long out of jail, in school, and on the basketball team. He also advised the boys to keep their mouths shut: "Nobody could really predict how carried away the media would get or where Marshall was going to go, or what . . . so we had to treat this thing very conservatively."

Still, from the first he believed that sooner or later the state would have to deal with the boys.

"I felt—right or wrong—all along that they couldn't possibly indict these kids because they had to use them. They *had* to use them. The equation was simple. . . . You got a dead guy everybody *wants* to have somebody blamed for. You got the perfect candidate for the blame. And you got two guys that you need to get to him. Now you don't indict all three because you deprive yourself of the very testimony you need. . . . We were the only guys that could get them into the room" where Bias died. "So I honestly felt the whole time that they would never indict these guys, that they would *have* to deal with us."

Early on he got in touch with Marshall. "I think in the first conversation I just . . . congratulated him on getting a wonderful case that should bring him lots of publicity . . . I said we'll be in touch. . . . Bud is, if anything, indefatigable. And I felt that he would bulldog this thing to wherever it led him."

As the investigation proceeded into the summer, Goldstein waited for the call proposing a deal. "We kept waiting for an invitation to the party . . . the immunity ticket."

Conversations with Marshall—Goldstein ignored Harding, wanting to psyche the ex-Marine in case the assistant argued the case in court—proved useless. "Maybe you'll get a subpoena, maybe you *won't* get a subpoena. . . . I think they didn't know what they were going to do."

When Gregg and Long were indicted, Goldstein was surprised.

"I couldn't figure out what [Marshall] had, where [he was] coming from. And I was looking forward to trying the case. You don't want your client to get indicted, but if he's going to get indicted you want to have a case you can defend. And *we* had a marvelous case. . . . Who was going to testify that they possessed [cocaine]? Tribble? Not going to happen. . . . We had an eminently triable case. . . ."

Goldstein and Gregg and Long waited. It wasn't an easy time for the two ball players. Campus was an isolation chamber. Goldstein had ordered them not to talk to any of their teammates about Leonard's death and their silence distanced them from their buddies. Driesell had also separated himself from them.

"Driesell . . . cut them loose," says Goldstein. Driesell wouldn't even talk to these kids. . . . They were playing in pickup games and, you know, Driesell could have said something at any time to them, just a word of encouragement or something. But the word I was getting was Driesell was very hostile to them in his attitude, [his] demeanor."

There were other worries also.

"A couple of times during the investigation Marshall would call me and say that he couldn't tell me why or how, but that it would be a good idea if my guys left town," says Goldstein. "Supposedly the threat was coming from somebody higher than Tribble. That's what we were given to believe. But we were not being told the down-and-dirty scoop. Things were vague by the time they got to us."

The first time the experience was a nightmare. "I wanted to get them out of that dorm. [I got] an operator on the phone [who] said that line is disconnected. [I was] almost dying. . . . I had these visions of assassins cutting the phone lines. It was just awful. We drove over there and we didn't know exactly what dorm they were in! Because every time we would drop them off after we'd meet with them we would see them walk up a hill where there were three or four dorms. So there I was. The phone wasn't working. I was sitting in the car with my associate saying, 'Which fucking dorm are they in?' " Finally they saw "some tall kid and he points it out and we get them and they come down to the car, and we brought them over [to] David's house, and then put them on a bus that night to get the hell" to Terry's grandmother's farm in Virginia. Goldstein "kept them there for about a week. . . . [Gregg and Long] were very frightened. Terry said that he remembered somebody getting killed in a drug case in Richmond, right on the streets."

. . .

Now, with Driesell in the clear and the case against Tribble so tenuous, Goldstein commands the field.

"Marshall basically came and said, 'Well, would you trust me?' " says Goldstein. "I said, 'Sure, I'll trust you.' And he says, 'I want your boys to go before the grand jury.' "

The first step is a meeting between Gregg and Long and Marshall. Goldstein has explained to his clients that now he wants them to tell the truth.

"Because at this point the deal's cut. Or the nondeal is cut. Whatever-you-call-it is cut. At this point lying . . . is the only risk they've got. Now [they] are protected, unlike before when the premium is on silence and keeping [their] mouth shut, *now* the premium is on confessing all [their] sins."

But the scenario doesn't go as planned. After hearing Gregg's and Long's testimony, Marshall becomes enraged.

"[They] came in with Alan Goldstein and just flat-out lied," says Arthur Marshall. "[They] sat there and tried to give me this story and waste my time. I left the two of them. . . . I don't like to be lied to. Lawyers coming up and telling you they're telling the truth and they're still bullshitting you. I didn't want to waste my time with it, didn't need it."

"What they were lying about were tangential things," says Goldstein. "Whether Bias had ever done cocaine before, whether they had ever done anything before. . . . I think they said they didn't know what happened to the cocaine or something like that, when in fact David had cleaned it up and had given it to Tribble. . . . Marshall felt that was a lie and told them he thought it was a lie and kicked them out of the office, which was really funny. We had no place to go."

Still Goldstein doesn't panic.

"I was a little pissed off that I hadn't gotten the whole story straight. But Marshall didn't have anyplace to go. Where was Marshall going to go? He was going to go with other witnesses? All of a sudden because *my* kids weren't telling him the truth, did that mean he was going to drop the charges against Tribble?"

So Goldstein questions Gregg and Long again. This time he is accompanied by James Wiseman, a retired policeman used by

Marshall to investigate the case. Wiseman is "one of the great bullshitters of history," says Goldstein, explaining why he brought the investigator along. "He could talk Eskimos into buying ice cubes."

Goldstein and Wiseman go into a room alone with Gregg and Long, debrief the clients, and return to Marshall's office.

"They go back in, Marshall says 'You're now ready to tell the story?' The kids say we are. And they tell the story. And now it's acceptable to Marshall. And so we walked into the grand jury and they testified to the grand jury."

On October 16, the players appear before the grand jury. On October 20, Marshall drops the charges against the two "because," reports the *Post*, "they had testified 'honestly and truthfully' and had 'expressed remorse over the tragedy that took place.' " Two days after this the gist of Gregg and Long's secret testimony before the grand jury appears in the *Post*. On October 22 the *Sun* gives the same details and adds important perspective on the case. (In its modest way, the Baltimore paper's reporting often upstages the *Post*'s, concentrating on aspects of the case the Washington paper overlooks.) "Neither Gregg nor Long was able to tell the grand jury that he saw Tribble bring the cocaine into the College Park room or that he had positive knowledge [Tribble] owned it. But the source said jurors were satisfied by Gregg and Long's testimony that Tribble had acted in such a manner, through remarks and actions, to indicate the cocaine was his. . . ."

On October 30, the grand jury perform their last act in the "endless foolishness": they charge Tribble with the "obstruction of justice," the indictment Marshall had so eagerly hoped to win against Driesell.

~~~

It is futile to argue that the Reagan administration could have stopped the cocaine epidemic. The point is, it never tried. The president trumpeted his administration as antidrug. Yet in its international and domestic policy and in its ideology, the Reagan people did everything possible—short of actually *selling* the
~~~

drug—to *potentiate* the epidemic of the drug in urban, poor America.

One needn't look for secret conspiracies to prove this assertion. Like earlier heroin epidemics, the cocaine plague accompanied an anticommunist crusade; a growing literature shows the administration's cynical partnership with dope dealers. But the search to find a "smoking gun," the piece of paper or tape that proves George Bush was in league with Noriega, is beside the point. The Reagan policies were as lethal as any kilos smuggled into the country by CIA-sponsored drug runners. "The existence of a smoking-gun memo is a bit of Washington mythology," writes Jefferson Morley in an article in the *Nation*, "cherished by high-level miscreants and investigative journalists. . . . Journalists, because it relieves them of the burden of thinking historically. . . . Wrongdoers, because it relieves them of responsibility in all but the most heinous crimes." The "smoking-gun" in the crack epidemic is the public historical record itself.

In international affairs, the Reagan administration showed little interest in the cocaine problem except to use it as a propaganda ploy. In late 1984, for instance, the Reagan administration made much of the testimony of a dope dealer who claimed the Sandinista government was exporting cocaine into the United States. "I know that every American parent concerned about the drug problem will be outraged to learn that top Nicaraguan government officials are deeply involved in drug trafficking," the president said in a nationally broadcast appeal for the Contra aid package on March 16, 1985. He then displayed a photograph, claiming the secretly taken picture showed a top aide "to one of the nine commandants who rule Nicaragua, loading an aircraft with illegal narcotics bound for the United States."

The facts turn out to be different. The airfield where the photo was taken was a civilian airstrip, not one run by the Nicaraguan government; the identity of the aide is currently disputed by Washington officials; and the drug shipment, the Drug Enforcement Administration says, was the only one they could trace through Nicaragua. Furthermore, the man who made the charges against the Sandinistas had brought the cocaine there himself. This man, a coke dealer named Adler Barriman Seal, was accused by four pilots of transporting arms from America to the Contras and running cocaine back. Seal produced the story about the Sandinistas after contacting vice-president George Bush's drug task force in an attempt to work out a deal; he wanted to trade his testimony for a reduction of a long prison term he was facing on drug charges. (The deal did Seal little good: he was gunned down one morning while leaving the shelter where he stayed during his probation.)

Similarly meretricious were the Reaganites' attempts at international control. Throughout the Reagan years, more and more agricultural land in South America was converted into coca plantations. Ballyhooed campaigns such as Operation Blast Furnace, intended to wipe out cocaine laboratories in Bolivia, were almost immediate failures. Countries long innocent of any dealing with cocaine, including Equador, Venezuela, and Brazil, began to produce or distribute the drug. Unable to reduce the importation of drugs, the Reaganites simply fudged the failure. Thus an administration bureaucrat, Mr. Westrate, testified before the Select Committee that 25 to 30 percent of all the drugs coming into the country had been interdicted the year before. His testimony amazed Congressman James Scheurer. "Now you are not suggesting to us here that you have picked up anywhere near 30 percent or 25 percent or 20 percent or 15 percent or 10 percent of the narcotic drugs that are coming across our borders. . . . You must be the Dr. Pangloss of the day if you can take any encouragement at what is happening in South America as far as drug trafficking is concerned." Two years later the administration's efforts to stop the growth of coca continued to be worse than futile. About the U.S.-sponsored attempts to curb cocaine husbandry in Peru's Huallaga Valley, one expert said: "The ironic and tragic consequence of the government's drug enforcement operations has been the dramatic spread of coca cultivation in recent years."

The Reagan domestic policy was equally toothless. Reagan's massive military programs armed America against the theoretical possibility of nuclear attack; his domestic policies, by omission and commission, disarmed the country against the real threat of drugs.

These policies were not specific to the drug problem; they were part of the general Reagan social ideology. Through the cuts of the first Stockman budgets and the huge government investment in defense, the Reagan administration effectively ended numerous social programs. In the period 1981 to 1986 drug program funds shrank from $154 million to $117 million per year.

The severity of the cuts surprised even those who were anticipating a reduction in funds. "Who ever thought [the Reaganites] would turn their back on law enforcement?" asks Ed Jurith of the Select Committee. "Even when Congress proposed money for law enforcement they tried to budget it out—and this was just law enforcement, lock-them-up-and-put-them-in-jail kind of stuff. They didn't even want the state and locals on that."

The cuts eliminated the federal role in fighting drugs and left it to the states. But the states were mandated to allocate the money in particular ways. "So by the time they got the money they were looking at less money and more mandates that they had to perform," explains the chief legal counsel for the Select Committee.

For a state like New York the results were catastrophic. One expert estimated that there had been a 40 percent cutback in federal funds to New York state between 1980 and 1986, and that New York City and State expenditures combined matched the total "federal response to the drug crisis dollar for dollar," the New York City Police Department spending twice as much as the DEA, and the city's five DA's seven times more than the Justice Department's Criminal Division.

By the time right before Bias's death, when the crack crisis was about to explode on the national scene, there simply was no coordinated effort to counter the spread of drugs. NIDA's role had changed from leading the attack on drugs to being a passive clearing house for scientific data and literature about drug abuse. The number of federal narcotics agents had declined by half. Money for drug treatments had been severely cut back. The federal government spent less than 20 percent of the $1.3 billion allocated nationally for treatment and prevention, the rest coming from local and state resources that were often the most strapped financially. As Elsie L. Scott, the executive director of the National Organization of Black Law Enforcement Executives, told the Select Committee, cutbacks in funding are "a big concern of our organization. Many chiefs of police, especially big-city chiefs of police, are from cities that are pretty much bankrupt. Most of the chiefs are in cities where you have black mayors. Usually we don't get black mayors until the city is pretty much bankrupt."

The final shock came in the fall of 1986. After Bias's death, Reagan's advisers decided drugs was a profitable issue for the president to exploit in the fall congressional elections. Reagan gave his support to the comprehensive drug bill that had been prompted partly by Bias's death and that was passed by an overwhelming majority. But when Reagan submitted his budget he asked for a billion less that was called for in the bipartisan legislation.

"Rangel was astounded," says Ed Wiener, the press information man for the committee. "Shocked. He really believes—and he tells the story—that when he was standing there at the signing and the president said, 'We're going to declare a war on drugs,' and turned around and was handing the pen—he went around Rangel and handed the pen to Nancy—he thought that with the president's commitment to his wife that this meant we were really going to fight a war on drugs."

Only ideologically were the Reaganites completely truthful. They presented their view of drug use as a matter of individual evil without hesitation. Fighting drug abuse was a new, domestic cold war in which the reasons for drug use were unimportant—even a distraction—and the only line of resistance was the individual, the individual saying no and also enjoining others to participate in his or her campaign.

Thus shortly after Bias died, Nancy Reagan published an oped piece in the *Washington Post*. She explained that for her, Bias's death was just one of many "stories of grief" that she had heard "for many years now." Now, she continued, most Americans knew about the dangers of drugs, but didn't know how to combat them. The answer was for each of us to reject the "stigma against speaking out against drugs" and to be intolerant of drug use—anywhere, anytime. "Schools owe our children a drug-free environment in which to grow and learn," she wrote. "There are schools that haven't made this commitment because they believe that drug abuse is *society's problem*. Yet schools today can be made clean with a no-nonsense approach that simply says drugs will not be tolerated. . . . An atmosphere of intolerance has to be created. . . . It's too late to save Len Bias, but it's not too late to save the young kids who idolized him. For their sake, I implore you to be unyielding and inflexible and outspoken in your opposition to drugs."

How did the administration put these principles into practice? Coincidentally, the Bush administration's new drug czar was the most forceful spokesman for the Reagan policy. A year before Bias died, William Bennett, then secretary of education, testified to the Select Committee about the administration's policy toward drug education programs. All drug experts had testified that education programs were vital to an attack on drugs. The committee called upon Bennett to explain why, out of a total education budget of $15.7 billion, the department had set aside only $3 million for drug education and alcohol abuse.

Bennett presented himself with his usual belligerent feistiness. "I have to point out," he began, ". . . that whether mandated or not, almost every school district in this country has drug education programs and we are still awash in drugs. . . . We need to get tough, and we need to get tough as hell, and we need to do it now."

Bennett cited examples of schools that promoted stiff punishments and where, Bennett claimed, there is "no drug problem today," including an Atlanta high school where the principal called parents, "saying eloquently and simply, 'If I catch your child with drugs, I will make two phone calls. The second will be to you.' "

But these examples of tough talk and daring action weren't enough. Bennett introduced a "work sheet of an 18-year-old student who is probably a graduate of a drug education program." The work sheet detailed the kid's drug operations. "He talks about profit, leads, half-leads, very well drawn maps," Bennett said, savoring his irony. "This kid is good on his basic intellectual skills." Then he got to his point. "He is a graduate of a drug education program. He may even have gotten the message that drugs are bad because he doesn't use them. He just sells them for a profit of about $20,000 a month or maybe $10,000 a month."

Bennett's cavalier abuse of facts—forget the ten-thousand-dollar difference; Bennett promotes the kid from a probable graduate of drug education programs to a definite one in less than a paragraph—obscures the focus of his argument. For him this child is evil. What needed to be taught was not facts about drug abuse, but moral lessons such as the ones given by Joe Clark. Instead of giving more money to educational institutions, Bennett argued, federal funds should be withheld from "any school or school district or college or university that does not have a serious commitment to ridding its school of drugs."

Rangel was appalled. "For years this committee has been dealing with the law enforcement people," Rangel began his response to Bennett. "FBI, U.S. Attorney's office, Customs, everything. They tell us what we have to do is to deal in the areas of education and prevention because unless we do this, they will have a job that they cannot truly perform. So, we go to the secretary of education and ask what programs, you know, would you have us to support in terms of preventive teaching, telling the kids how to keep their minds and bodies straight, to get treatment. You tell us we should enforce the law. . . ."

Bennett's response was characteristically belligerent. "I said more than that, Mr. Chairman."

Rangel stood his ground. "You said enforce the law and zero tolerance. Then you said expulsion. Then you said that forty percent of the kids are scared to death of drugs. We are going to say we agree with you. We are going to say you are one hundred percent correct. Kick out the traffickers; kick out the abusers. . . . But for God's sake you are going to have to help us besides telling us that the secretary of education is recommending that we identify effective educational programs. . . . You are not going to say the only way to get rid of the drug problem with kids in education is to close the school and kick out the abusers and the traffickers. What do you do with these people? . . . Kicking them out is an easy thing to do. Now that they are kicked out, what do we do? Where is the education?"

Bennett was adamant. "I am sorry. I believe that is education. I believe that is a very effective form of education. . . . You have taught a profound and important lesson to the children in that school: We are not going to have someone in this school who is trying to destroy you. That is a good educational lesson, Mr. Chairman. We ought to have more teaching of it more regularly. . . . As a former professor of philosophy, I would note that it has long been the hope of philosophers that a course in ethics will make human beings better. It never has. There has never been one. It may give them encouragement, justification, argument for being better, understanding of why they should be better. When human beings become better, it is because there are a whole host of activities to encourage them to become better, like their parents, the law, their government, their neighbors."

This is intellectual snake oil. Even by his own standards Bennett failed: the "host of activities" his administration provided was an environment of thoughtless, ultimately deadly, social cruelty. After two and a half years of Bennett's self-aggrandizing moral toughness, the only change in the drug problem was that crack was available in high schools across the country and Bennett was calling for the military to take charge of the problem.

"Look how ridiculous this administration is," said Ed Jurith several months before Bennett was given his new post in the Bush administration. The secretary of education "calls for the military and the secretary of defense calls for education. It's a circular firing squad!"

~~~

The day after the grand jury returns its final indictment against Tribble, Driesell finally resolves his status with the University of Maryland. He resigns to become an assistant athletic director with vaguely defined duties to promote, market, and fund-raise for the athletic department. His deal is reported to include his regular annual salary for eight years, $200,000 a year in television money whether or not he takes part in any show, and an allowance to continue to run his basketball camp for two weeks every summer.

The deal ends a five-month struggle. After the grand jury refused to indict Driesell, Chancellor John Slaughter began his own investigation of the coach. The *Baltimore Sun*'s Mark Hyman claims the effort was very secretive and that its motive was to discover a pretext to void Driesell's contract.

"The contract became *the* issue," says Hyman. "I think [the administration] just said, 'Look, we made a huge mistake signing this guy to a ten-year contract, he's obviously not the kind of person we want representing the university. We care about academics and he doesn't share the kind of concerns we have. He's not the
~~~

right person. Let's get him. Now, how are we going to do it?' "

The first victim of the purge was athletic director Dick Dull.

"As the story progressed, it became apparent," says Hyman, "that Dick hadn't done a very good job of policing the department. The ten-year contract he gave Lefty was just the mistake of all mistakes."

Lacking the armature of Driesell's self-assurance, Dull suffered from the criticisms.

Dull "was just the opposite of Lefty," says Hyman. "While Lefty was in Bethany [Beach, his summer house] having a wine cooler, Dull was holding his head and saying, 'Why me?' " Dull felt he was left holding the bag, argues Hyman, that Driesell's behavior "was acceptable to the chancellor of the university, it was acceptable to everybody who knew what was going on in Maryland basketball. They knew the kind of kids that were coming in, they knew what kind of person Lefty was, what his priorities were, what he valued, what he didn't value. And suddenly Len Bias died, and now Dick Dull is a horrible man for allowing this to go on."

As the summer dragged on, he had to endure a public chastisement.

"There were all sorts of task forces out there evaluating the athletic department and coming out with reports on what had been done wrong and the mismanagement and it was humiliating. Here he was sitting on some of these task-force committees and professors of mathematics were making judgments about the way he set up travel schedules for the basketball team. . . . It was like a public hanging . . . and rather than subject himself to that indefinitely it was simpler to opt out."

Dull resigned on October 7. By then the possibility of forcing Driesell out of his contract had vanished. But the university was under pressure to make a decision: unless Driesell's status was settled, the season would begin with Lefty walking out from the locker room with his hand in the air acknowledging the cheers of the crowd.

"Then began a period of negotiation between the university and Edward Bennett Williams," says Hyman. "Under what terms would he be willing to step down as coach? Initially, Lefty was not willing to step down under any circumstances. . . . [He] said, 'I've done nothing wrong, why should I be negotiating my own dismissal or reassignment, when I've done nothing wrong?' That was his attitude. How do you reason with a guy like that?' " The university and he "were talking at completely different levels. And the way it was explained to me was that EBW finally explained to Driesell that these people don't want you here. They don't want you in this job. You're not serving your own best interests by remaining in this job if they choose not to have you here." Then the university offered him their last deal "if he wanted to remain as coach. He could [coach] for one year, but [then] . . . they would be free to dismiss him if they chose. . . . [So] Williams used his influence to tell [Driesell], It's over, and the best thing you can do is step aside graciously, cut the best deal you can for yourself, and if you're determined to coach again wait it out for the next good coaching opportunity."

With Driesell's resignation, the story starts to fade from the media.

The files from the *Washington Post* reflect the change. On one Thursday in late August the paper runs five full stories related to the Bias death: 943 words on the first page about the university decision to keep Driesell; another 1,211 front-page words on critical attitudes toward Marshall's handling of the case; 369 words on page 23 of the first section about Driesell urging drug testing in 1984; another 930 words on the opposite page reporting that Tribble's lawyer had filed an indictment to dismiss charges against Tribble because of Marshall's misconduct; and finally a 972-word column by Ken Denlinger, one of the paper's sports journalists, saying Driesell has outlived his effectiveness, but that he doubts the coach will actually be fired. A month or so later, this constant buzz has ended. The case drops from view.

"I guess there was a sense somewhere along the line people were no longer interested in reading about it as much," says the *Post*'s Sally Jenkins, "because there wasn't as much news coming out about it. I'm not sure how much we did, but I would say between the end of the grand jury process and the Tribble trial, I would say there would certainly have to be a steep dropoff . . . and the fact is I think we were probably becoming weary of it during the grand jury process."

For all the work that the reporters have done, they have proved as unsuccessful as Marshall.

"I think we may have undercovered the story," says Jenkins. "There are a few avenues I would have liked us to pursue. . . . I've always felt like we didn't quite get at the heart of the story. Maybe it's a question of perspective and not number or volume of stories. . . . [Information] about what happened in that room is so thin. Veteran reporters tell me that with stories a lot of times you never know the whole truth. I suppose there's a little bit of that here."

The prosecutors share similar doubts. Their last surprise witness, Adrian James, is a retired D.C. cop who has promised to blow the whistle on Tribble, but his testimony turns out to be a fiasco of press publicity. When Jeffrey Harding recalls the events surrounding James's testimony, he can't even get the facts straight about the witness's appearance. "What I heard was that [James] called Gary Reals [a local television journalist] and Gary Reals says, 'I want to talk to you . . . we've heard your name has come up in the investigation,' [James] said, 'Yes, it has, and I'll meet you.' And Gary Reals says, 'Come to Prince George's County and meet me.' . . . Then he called us and said, 'I'm going to be in Prince George's County.' So when we got to him we didn't know that Channel Seven was going to be there. Maybe that's a bad example, but that's how involved the press was. That's how close the press was at our heels. But on that occasion they were in front of us."

Instead of being resolved, the investigation simply peters out. In discussing the case, Harding says he never thought much about where the inquiry was heading or how it was proceeding. "I was just too swamped and too busy to worry about that. I mean I would reflect on it, when I got home after twelve or sixteen hours' worth of brutal work, for a couple of minutes and fall asleep and get up and do it again the next day." Still, at the time, he could sense something was not right. "If you want my personal opinion, it was getting to the point where . . . maybe it was getting counterproductive. Maybe the press was getting too feverish about it and maybe it was turning into something that it shouldn't be."

Although everyone talks about drug addiction and abuse as a sickness, this phrase is generally meant metaphorically, to indicate something out of control or bad, as when we say we have a "sick" society or that something someone does is "really sick."

But if one follows the metaphor more precisely the notion ends up illuminating and challenging many of the most basic ideas about drug abuse.

Central to many misconceptions about drug abuse is the idea that somehow drugs and those who use them are separate from the rest of society—scourges, plagues, the work of God or the devil, ruining our lives, beyond our control.

But no sickness creates itself. "There is no specific disease," wrote Florence Nightingale, "there are only conditions for specific diseases." Pasteur, Oliver Sacks reports, concluded the same, saying on his deathbed, "The pathogen is nothing, the *terrain* is everything."

The same is true for drug addiction. "It is the variety of social factors within the community that make it susceptible," says NIDA's Edgar Adams, "much the way that poor sanitation used to make communities susceptible to a host of infectious diseases in earlier centuries."

Imagine society as a body, an organism. Then the plague of drugs in the black community is not happening to others, but is our sickness, no more capable of being distinguished from the "healthy" sectors of society than, say, a congested chest or broken arm can be separated from the body of which it is a part.

And if the plague is a sickness of the whole body, it can't be cured simply with a corrective device. When Sacks's patients responded wildly to L-DOPA, one therapeutic response was to perfect the dosage. "We see from their responses to the continued and continual administration of L-DOPA . . . that these patients have needs over and above their need for [brain] dopamine; and that beyond a certain point . . . no mere *substance* . . . can compensate . . . these other needs. . . . These considerations are passed over in the current insistence that patients can be 'titrated' with L-DOPA indefinitely, in a perfect commensuration of supply and demand. They can be 'titrated' with L-DOPA at first, as eroded ground can be watered, or a depressed area given money; but sooner or later, complications occur; and they occur because there is a complex trouble in the first place—not merely a parching or depletion of one substance, but a defect or disorder of *organization* itself. . . ."

For Sacks's patients, of course, that defect or disorder of organization was incurable, a physical fact of life that became an intractable aspect of the spirit. With society the disorganization is a matter of the spirit: the lack of human solidarity between white and black that has and continues to affect every aspect of our national life. This is the *terrain* in which the disease thrives; in the cocaine plague that "defect or disorder of organization," that conflict within the organism of society, becomes a physical fact of life. Of the pitiless conditions of his patients, Oliver Sacks writes, "Expressed in their sickness . . . is the living imagination of nature itself." The crack addict is the living imagination of our society. The mother who strangles her own children, the strutting teenage runners, the gold-bedecked hustlers, the emaciated wretch on the corner who asks you for a dollar each night—the cases of individual terror and misery are the symptoms of *our* disease, the pains and fevers of *our* illness.

There is an element of volition here. These victims suicidally embrace the sickness. This is part of the overall disease, as, say, a group's superstition precludes their ever getting healthy. "Health is infinite and expansive in mode and searches out to be filled by the fullness of the world," writes Sacks. "Disease is finite and reductive in mode and endeavors to reduce the world to itself." But no kid takes or deals cocaine simply to perform evil; they are going along, getting over, entering the *terrain* of pleasure and greed surrounding them. "In essence," says a black drug counselor in Washington, "the drug trade today is a new kind of slavery because Afro-Americans are enslaved to material things. Now the shackles have moved from the chain around the ankles to the gold chain around the neck. We are trying to attain a standard which is being set for us. And our kids—this generation—have learned that lesson better than any generation before." Innocent and aggressive, self-deluded and deluded, they embrace—like their famous, tragic brother, Len Bias—the sickness of Reaganite America. And like Leonard, but unlike everyone else, they pay the price: they die.

By winter, the only one left is Tribble. He remains, not paid off, not excused, as isolated and vulnerable in his notoriety as Bias was in his celebrity. The whole society's infatuation with cocaine ends up a devastation for the young black population; the need for a villain results in the trial of a twenty-four-year-old as a pusherman.

Mrs. Tribble never asks him what happened. She just offers shelter, as she did that first morning. To her the notion that Brian is a dealer is a joke. Man, she questions the reporters, if he was such a big-time dealer then how come his apartment wasn't hooked? But to the press his pad *is* hooked. And as soon as she explains away one troubling item, another pops up to take its place—down goes the television and up come the nightclubs, down go the nightclubs and up comes the car.

Even the court doesn't want to listen. Mrs. Tribble goes to the grand jury with all of her check stubs to show the monthly payments for the car and to explain her son's living situation. But State Attorney Marshall listens with an ironic smile, letting her and the jury know he thinks she's lying, asking her how it was possible she didn't know her son was a dealer.

Throughout the winter she waits for the trial. When she climbs into bed next to Priscilla, she goes to sleep immediately. Unconsciousness is her only relief. "I never minded the nights. Because then you could sleep. It was the mornings that killed me. I'd open my eyes and face the nightmare all over again."

TRIAL

On the morning of May 25, 1987, almost a year after Leonard's death, Loretta and Brian Tribble prepare to go to his trial. The mother and son look as though they're about to attend a college graduation. She wears a summery coffee-colored dress, the soft curls of her hair framing the round sweetness of her face. Brian has exchanged his usual T-shirt and running shorts for a conservative double-breasted charcoal-gray suit and burgundy tie—not the splashy, in-your-face fashion statement Leonard would have made, but an outfit that dresses him with an appropriately grave and handsome dignity. Believe his story and he is a diligent young man who will repay responsibility with effort; doubt his tale and he's the "player" depicted by the prosecution, hoping, like any mobster, to fool the jury with his somber attire.

With the defense attorneys they drive the twenty-five miles to the county seat. At the turnoff to Upper Marlboro they enter a Colonial landscape of brick houses and stone walls, chestnut bays and mint-green lawns; alongside the road, black field hands trudge with packs of grain on their backs, hats shading them from the sun, characters from etchings of the Old South. The car weaves past the Civil War Monument, passes the tobacco auction house, and turns onto the main street. It's a Cotswold village with red-brick sidewalks and wooden shingles announcing law partnerships and sub shoppes. In the quiet freshness of the morning it seems impossible that anything to do with disaster, the life and death of one young man, the fate of another, can happen here.

Down the street, a pack of reporters and camera crews are already camped outside the colonnaded courthouse. News vans line the side street, their transponders tipped to the sky, their wires snaking over the green fronting the building; the picnic table on the courthouse lawn (a courthouse with a picnic table?) serves as a dumping ground for camera equipment. The journalists represent every local network and paper, and several national ones. As the defense team nears, the newsmen marshal their crews. Cameras poised bazookalike on their shoulders, the cameramen rush by the historical markers and follow the silent Tribbles to the courthouse door.

This is the moment Mrs. Tribble has waited for—her day in court, when the prosecution will have to prove its case instead of just making up lies. Only today the *Washington Post* has once again referred to Brian's "fashionable high-rise apartment."

But as she approaches the building, she loses all confidence in a flood of dread. She imagines Brian going to jail and thinks, *I am not going to survive this, this is going to kill me.*

Then she reminds herself of the hospital. Shortly after giving birth to Priscilla, she stayed with her aunt in Fall River. Weak from the delivery, she didn't treat a developing pneumonia; by the time she entered the hospital she had suffered a heart attack. For three weeks she lay in an oxygen tent, the doctors believing she was dying.

"Everybody was saying you're dying. I'm saying inside myself, 'No I'm not.' They sent to call the priest and he gave me the last rites and threw holy water on me. I'm saying to myself, 'Christ, I'm not ready to die, this is a joke.' But I couldn't talk, I was so weak, I couldn't say anything. . . . Finally a whole bunch of them come in my room. I said to myself, 'Well, this must be the day I'm going to die.' But I didn't feel like I was dying. How do you feel when you're dying? How did I know? I'd never died before. . . . I'll never forget one time when I was asleep and I heard the doctor say, 'Did you check her?' and I opened my eyes and I saw him take a breath, and I said to myself, 'God, do they want me to die?' "

Who were they anyway to say she should die? God decided that. When she was due to go nobody would have to tap her on the shoulder. Slowly, the tide of her sickness reversed; instead of a statistic, she made a recovery so remarkable that her case was written up in the *New England Journal of Medicine.*

Well, she thinks at the courthouse entrance, you didn't die then. You ain't gonna die now.

She gathers her breath, smiles once at the reporters, and walks into the courthouse.

Inside they meet security, a woman cop standing guard at the metal-detecting gates that have served as the welcome mat for government buildings since the early seventies. Outside the town is a mini-Williamsburg, but inside the Colonial courthouse is a microcosm of city life. Furious black kids stalk the halls, their rage simmering in miserable silence or boiling over in sudden explosions to harried lawyers, besieged mothers, scared codefendants. Lawyers scuttle around, plea-bargaining, explaining incomprehensible distinctions to clients who only want to know the simplest answers: How much is the fine? Can my son get off without serving time? The only ones who seem at ease are the cops. Large country boys, they ramble down the echoing halls, their pistols angled prominently on their hips, exchanging gossip and small talk with each other.

Their courtroom is upstairs, the largest one available. Outside there is another security gate. The precaution is unique for the Tribble case, though what danger threatens is unclear: fear that someone will bust him out or try to kill him? Journalists already queue outside the chamber. The presiding judge, an old-time Marlborian named Magruder Rea, has indicated displeasure with the extensive press coverage given to the case and has said several times the trial is nothing more than a normal drug case. The rumor is that he plans to bar the press. No one believes this, but the gossip heightens the drama of the anticipatory moment, and the security guards are ordering the reporters to calm down, treating them with bullying contempt. The noise and nervousness alert every passerby that something special is going on here.

The Tribbles pass the reporters, empty their pockets, and go through the gates. The room is large and unfriendly. Harsh, blank light pours through the windows. At the front a smiling red-headed court clerk named Mr. Luckett introduces himself to the counsels. Mrs. Tribble takes a seat in the front row. Brian sits in the stiff-backed bentwood chair at the defendant's desk, pad and pencil ready for notes before him. His face sets into the somber, eyebrow-cocked, dramatic cast it won't break for the next two weeks. Both sides ready themselves, emptying their formidably large, special legal briefcases, piling their case-law books on the long tables. All they're waiting for now is the judge, his empty chair set magisterially in the triangle created by the crossing of U.S. and Maryland flags. In this improbable setting, with its unlikely mix of past and present, ideal and real America, beneficent middle-class life and enraged poor, country lawyers and city dope dealers, the final act of the tragedy of Len Bias is about to begin.

~~~

Tribble's defense lawyer is Tom Morrow. "That's all I had on my side," Mrs. Tribble is fond of saying, "God, the truth, and Thomas Morrow."

He is an unlikely-looking savior. Morrow is an ex-Marine like Harding; unlike his opponent, Morrow looks the part. His body has the heft and power of a boxer's; he carries himself in a military posture, and his short hair is clipped in a straight line above the starched collar and pressed jacket of his standard-issue courtroom suit. His voice is raspy, direct, skeptical—the nasty sound of Jack Nicholson; his narrow hazel eyes burn with an impatient, anxious energy; a jagged scar dents the casing of one eyebrow. He strikes one more as a drill instructor from Central Casting—a tough heavy from a B picture—than a latter-day Clarence Darrow. If you were a defendant passing him in court you would pick him as the hard-assed prosecutor you prayed wasn't assigned your case.

Morrow is a native of Baltimore. He first worked in the DA's office there while attending night school; after graduating, he spent many years as a prosecutor, bumping up the ladder from street crimes to white-collar cases. "I like prosecuting," he says. "You always win. If you lose a case you blame it on the jury or a crooked judge." But the pay was minimal: Morrow has three children. Besides, defense work is always more challenging; for all his experience and straight-arrow appearance, Morrow masks a renegade intelligence: he's attracted to the off-key, the rebellious or defiant.

The attraction isn't entirely a matter of principle. Morrow com-
~~~

bines two male influences: the stern rigor of his stepfather, a war hero whose wounds left him in a wheelchair, and the free spirit of his father, a tobacco buyer. (Morrow visited him in Cuba as a boy. The journey infected him with a love of warm weather and lazy days—another weakness completely contrary to the stony rectitude he exhibits in court.) He is sympathetic to people's failings. Every Sunday Morrow leaves his roomy, suburban home and takes his kids to the local Episcopal church. Twenty-four hours later he is deciding to handle the case of, for instance, a disc jockey accused by a sixteen-year-old of sexual abuse. "It's a bullshit case," he says, his thin lips smacking with his usual nervous energy as he gathers his ideas, the thick shoulders and powerful arms and legs of his fighter's frame extending over the couch in his law firm. "She slapped some skull on him and her boyfriend found out." His search to find the legal loophole or right angle toward the case comes from a passion simpler than a love of civil liberties. Defending the undefendable is one of the few exercises that can sap his seemingly endless energy, defeat the monster of middle-class boredom that threatens to overwhelm him.

In theory the Tribble case was supposed to have been a minor item on Morrow's calendar. But by now the once ordinary cocaine case has escalated into the most important courtroom battle of his life, a crusade against what Morrow sees as a misguided and malevolent prosecution.

He didn't pick the case; Tribble was assigned to him. The day after Leonard died, Tribble called a Washington lawyer. The attorney suggested Tribble secure Baltimore counsel, since any legal proceedings would be held in Prince George's County; he recommended Weinberg and Green, a large, prestigious firm whose several floors of offices have views of the shops and restaurants of the city's refurbished inner harbor. The Washington lawyer contacted one of the managing partners; eventually Morrow—who was responsible for all of the firm's criminal cases—received the assignment.

At the time Morrow was preparing to go to the West Coast. A devoted amateur athlete, Morrow had agreed to pace a racer for a section of an "endurance run," a torturous hundred-mile trek into the mountains of eastern California. Morrow decided to meet Brian first and hear the story before postponing the trip.

"It was very difficult for [Brian]. . . . He was still in almost a period of shock and denial at that point. . . . He kept waiting to wake up and think this was all some terrible dream. . . . He would be talking and describing incidents, and he'd get to points where Lenny was lying on the floor and he would just stop. I would be waiting. I was taking very careful notes. I would stop and look and he would be shaking his head and saying, 'I can't believe it, I was just talking to him yesterday, I can't believe it. . . .'"

At the time, Morrow says, no one on the defense foresaw the magnitude of the coming case.

"We had no idea that this thing was going to be the national spectacle that it was. . . . We had Bud Marshall . . . attempting to get a lot of publicity over this investigation, and we figured it was all going to blow over. . . . [The] case was going to be a relatively straightforward, relatively simple case, . . . a couple of trips down to Prince George's County. We had no idea . . . that they were going to make this the case of the eighties or whatever. . . . What I saw as a worst-case scenario [was] if they [could] establish a link with the cocaine . . . [and] go after Long, Gregg, and Tribble for possession of cocaine. That's what I saw as the worst. You go in and you say, 'Okay, we screwed up.' You plead him and he serves eighteen months' probation and then that's the end of it."

The evaluation allowed Weinberg and Green to defend Tribble. The state attorney's office frequently referred to Tribble's representation by a "downtown Baltimore law firm"—yet another sign of profitable big-time drug dealing. Actually, the Tribbles had barely scraped together enough money for a binder, both they and Weinberg and Green thinking the legal fees would be minimal. As the case progressed, the Tribbles incurred serious debt, finally owing the firm a substantial amount. In addition, Tribble was the first drug client the firm had permitted Morrow to accept; the bulk of his work had been defending white-collar crimes.

"Weinberg and Green had a policy that they did not do anything that involved drug defense," Morrow explains. "They didn't want to be associated with drug lawyers . . . old Mr. Weinberg didn't want any of his bank presidents to have to sit in the same waiting room with a criminal. . . . I was getting increasingly frustrated because I was not able to take cases that were coming to me. . . . I felt that my primary reputation and my primary expertise, and, more important than either of those, my primary interest, lay in individuals and criminal cases. I think I had a lot of rapport with a lot of prosecutors and the system and so on. And I thought we were getting to a point that we were going to have to sit down and decide what my future as a criminal litigator in Weinberg and Green was going to be."

For Morrow the nub of the case was establishing one fact: who brought the drug into the room. "The only issue, from purely a legal, analytical perspective, is distribution. That's a serious offense. Ten years. How are they gonna establish distribution?" Morrow felt from his conversations with Brian that "from a legal perspective they were going to have a tough time establishing the proprietary ownership of the stuff . . . I spoke with Alan Goldstein early on and asked him what was going on. Are his clients making a deal? . . . What do your clients say? Are your clients going to say that . . . Brian brought it in. And he said, 'They're going to say that they don't know.' . . . And once I heard that, I felt that [I had confirmed] my original perception."

So Morrow kept his date in California.

"I kept my eye on the papers to see if anything was happening while I was gone. Nothing happened. I do my thirty-mile run or whatever . . . [and] come back. I start gearing up trying to get into the case and meet with Brian. Start to establish a little more rapport with Brian—to Brian, you know, we're this big fancy law office and Brian's associates are basically other black guys who play basketball. . . ."

It was now early July; Marshall was appearing almost daily at news conferences; the findings of the criminal investigation were being leaked to the press. The injudicious flood of information pleased Morrow. "I was picturing in my mind all the motions I was going to come up with if Brian was indicted. When he would make the statements about Brian Tribble, I had somebody clip the papers and I was putting them aside on the expectation that they were going to become exhibits in my motion to dismiss for prejudicial pretrial publicity. The fact that the prosecutor was, in my view, making certain statements about his opinion as to the guilt or innocence of my client—express opinions about the guilt or innocence of an individual who has yet to be tried: I mean *that* was a motion. Almost every night I would turn on the TV and look at the different stations and just start cataloguing the different motions that each one of Marshall's statements was going to trigger."

Morrow's first warning that he had seriously misgauged the publicity attached to the case and his opposition's determination came the morning Tribble turned himself in. The surrender had all been worked out with the PGC sheriff. Tribble met Morrow in Morrow's office to drive together to Upper Marlboro. Upon leaving the office, they ran into reporters and news teams. Morrow decided to duck them, but one group kept up a chase, even following him with their news van onto the highway out of town.

When they arrived in Upper Marlboro, Morrow checked Tribble in with the sheriff and went to arrange a bail hearing. Morrow imagined the bail would be low. ("I was stupid and naive," he says.) He confirmed with the judge's secretary that they could have a bail hearing that day and went up the street to type motions asking the court to release Brian on his own recognizance. But when he returned and spoke to Harding, the assistant state attorney told him that it was too late for a hearing that afternoon. Morrow went to check this with the judge's secretary; she confirmed what Harding had told him.

"So I started to get a little annoyed. I went back up to Harding. I said, 'Look, I'm starting to get the impression that I'm being set up down here. You, obviously, have no reason to object. I've been here all day. Why don't we just walk up to the judge and say, "You have no objection, I have no objection." We'll sit down and have an informal bail hearing before the judge.'

"[Harding] goes, 'Well, I don't want to treat this case in any way out of the ordinary.' He said, 'If the judge wants to have it tomorrow, I think we should just have it tomorrow.'

"I said, 'What are you doing? This is bullshit. You say that you don't want to treat this case any differently than any other case, and the first thing you do is tell me that my client's going to sit in jail overnight because of some stupid rule that the secretary lied to me about? This really smells!' I was pissed. [I felt] I had been set up and I [could] just picture the newspapers saying the next day that because Mr. Morrow failed to file the papers by two o'clock the client had to spend the night in jail.

"That was my first inclination that . . . this was not going to be like old Tom over in Baltimore County where I know all the prosecutors and . . . [everything] was pretty much handshakes and play fair. I definitely had the impression . . . that my client could expect to be treated a little differently than everybody else down there. . . . I started to have the perception that this isn't just an opportunistic politician going out and trying to make some political hay off of a case. They're really trying to get this guy."

The discovery of the safe confirmed his suspicions.

"I didn't hear about the safe until sometime in July when they recovered it. Then the next thing I heard on the news was that they were trying to attribute it in some way to Brian . . . and they were wheeling the safe back and forth outside in view of the cameras. And there were all these leaks in the grand jury. Everybody was talking about the safe, and all the leaks from the grand jury. . . . [I thought,] How in the world can [Brian] possibly get a fair trial when everything that happens, they're bringing out some new piece of evidence?"

His next meeting with the prosecution continued the pattern of harassment. In mid-August Mrs. Tribble went to testify at the grand jury armed with the personal ledgers and cashed checks she believed proved Brian to be her hardworking, perhaps foolishly suggestible son, and not a degenerate drug dealer.

Morrow continues: "I called up Harding"—he claims Marshall wouldn't speak to him—"and said, 'I have a busy trial schedule. Is there any possibility that you could accommodate me by getting us in and getting us out, because . . . I think [Mrs. Tribble's appearance] is going to be fairly quick because I don't think she has what you want.' He said, 'Fine, be down here at eight-thirty and you'll be a little early and I'll get you in first and you can get out.' I said fine. We went down there at eight-thirty—and for me to get down to PG County at eight-thirty is a real travail—and we sat there till about ten-thirty. Nobody even acknowledged our presence. . . . Finally at one point I stood up and said to Bud Marshall, 'Excuse me, Mr. Marshall. I don't think we've met. My name is Tom Morrow.' Marshall said,"—with his flair for acting,

Morrow mimics Marshall's contempt, his voice becoming a sneer of sarcasm—" 'I know who you are.' "

Morrow explained to Marshall his agreement with Harding.

Marshall answered, " 'You'll get in when we get you in.' Or words like that—very terse and hostile. . . . So I said, 'Well, I'm not asking for any special treatment, I just was asking for a little courtesy.' He says, 'If you want to move it along why don't you just tell them to take the Fifth Amendment.' Of course the press was all back there. I said, 'The Fifth Amendment? You mean the Fifth Amendment is recognized here in Prince George's County? That's fantastic! I'm really relieved to hear that!' And the conversation went downhill from there."

Added to Morrow's worries about the prosecution's vengeful attitude was a nagging fear that the state had some hidden surprise evidence. From the beginning Marshall had stated publicly he knew who brought the coke into the room; Morrow couldn't believe the prosecution was simply bluffing.

"I kept saying [to the state], 'Look, if you have evidence that he brought [the coke] into the room, tell me what it is. If you've got me cold, then obviously I don't have any choice but to go back to my client and say, 'They got us cold, just make a plea. So let me see it.' "

When Long and Gregg "flipped" in early October, Morrow, overestimating the state's case, was thrown.

"I got concerned again. Have they changed the testimony? What's the story? Why would Marshall give them a walk?"

Finally in November, the two sides met for a pretrial conference. The conference was Morrow's first encounter with Judge Rea.

"He seemed like a nice fellow . . . very friendly, very cordial. The first thing he said when we came in was"—Morrow breaks into Rea's slow, courtly drawl—" 'Lemme ask you something. I see "Sixty Minutes" out there and Dan Rather standing out there, I see this, I see that, but isn't this just a drug case?' I said, 'Your Honor, I could not have been more eloquent in summarizing this entire farce.' "

But the case had already become more than that. Most "drug

cases" don't even go to trial; they are pled out, the defense and prosecution agreeing on the punishment. If this weren't so, the criminal justice system would collapse altogether. But the possibility of any settlement between the two sides here had never existed. Morrow's only hope was that perhaps with the change in administration would come a change of heart.

"I thought, well, Bud Marshall is out of the picture. Harding is basically someone whom I perceive to be just doing what he was told so there wasn't any point in talking to [him]. I knew Alex Williams from a prior case in which I had been involved. He seemed like a very reasonable, decent guy. I thought, 'Well, I'll write him a letter.' "

~~~

Smiling, arms crossed over his chest, Bob Bonsib, the man Morrow finally contacted, now stands opposite, waiting for the preliminaries to begin. He was appointed in January by Alex Williams as the new chief legal administrator of Prince George's County. This is his first major case in his new office, and it may well be the single most publicized trial of his entire public career.

Bonsib—"It comes from the Alsace-Lorraine area, so you've got sort of almost an all-French name with a hard German end"—is Morrow's exact opposite. A native of Fort Wayne, Indiana, he has appealing, stereotypically farm-boy fresh looks. His apple-red cheeks radiate good health and a cheerful disposition. His thick, prematurely white hair balances an earnest, early Jimmy Stewart smile. His bright blue eyes sparkle. Instead of Morrow's driven push, he hums with a steady, even energy. This man is happy in the universe.

There is one more difference between the two. Bonsib is pure prosecutor—pursuing wrongdoers is not merely a job for him but part of his nature.

Bonsib started work in Marshall's office after graduating from Catholic University. He stayed in Maryland at least in part because the crimes he handled were more exciting than those he would have found back home.

"I would go back to visit my folks and I would read the local
~~~

papers and find out what the crimes were that were going on. You know, on one hand it's nice to live in a crime-free community, but if you're going to be a criminal lawyer, you look for the exciting cases and I just didn't see them there. There were burglaries and robbers. It would have been a very boring criminal practice."

Under Marshall he proceeded up the hierarchy of the office. The experience was revelatory.

"The typical way most law schools train lawyers, everybody [expects their] job is to protect the criminally accused, who is always being railroaded. And you get into the real world, and you see that ninety-five percent of the criminals who come in are guilty. And you find that there are some people who are simply evil, bad people. And over the course of doing some of that you find that being a prosecutor *does* give you the opportunity to—at least on an individualized basis—try to do some justice, to right some wrongs. You also come, of course, to the recognition that what you do isn't going to change very much."

Bonsib likes interrogating himself as well as others, and speaks easily, with a cool passion about the horrors that have affected him.

"Selected cases bother you. Cases that you prosecute where you get very involved with the victims or the survivors. Family members. That bothers you a lot. Why does this have to happen? I had a case of a young couple who lived in the county—twenty-eight-or-nine-year-old couple. As I recall, they were both schoolteachers. They were a perfect all-American-type family. The two of them. They had great plans for the future, and they got along very well together. Middle of the night. The woman is one of these women who's always hearing noises in the middle of the night. And she's always telling her husband to get up and check on the noises. Well, this one evening she's hearing noises. He's been up once. She hears noises again. 'All right, I'll get up, and I'll check.' He goes out in the hallway and there's a young kid—an eighteen-or-nineteen-year-old kid. He's got two butcher knives in his hands. Stabs the guy in the head. And I believe, as I recall, in the side of the neck. While the husband is there dying, the woman has the foresight to be calling 911. So she's on the telephone reporting this as [the] kid walks in the room with nothing but his underwear on, and she's yelling into the phone her address, somebody's breaking into my home, and we could hear the kid slap her. The phone jumps on the ground, and you could hear the phone rattling, and then it hangs up and there's silence. The police respond, and by that time she's been dragged out of the house and the guy's in the process of sexually assaulting her in a next-door neighbor's backyard."

Opposed to such victims are people who are—with only a little prodding the word comes easily enough to Bonsib—evil. "It's not a question of being products of broken homes," he explains, "but there are some people who . . . are just born to be bad."

In time he became more and more involved with drug cases. In those precocaine days, the local drug of choice was PCP, a hallucinogen used particularly in the District and Los Angeles. Bonsib saw a lot of what he calls "weird murder cases."

"We've had cases down here where people have cut their mothers' hearts out. . . . One case I remember, this kid—young kid, married, had a little infant in a crib—had been smoking PCP for a day or so. For some reason he gets in his mind the idea the child is now the devil, and he's got to kill the child. So he takes a shotgun and blows the baby's head off while it's in the crib. This is a kid whose background was not bad. He didn't have a series of criminal activities, but he had a history, or a problem, with drug usage. . . . And that's not an atypical situation. That's not everyday, but it happens often enough."

As he progressed in the office the scope of his effort widened from responding to crimes to preventing them. He is particularly proud of arresting and convicting a motorcycle gang that controlled PCP in the area.

"We did a wiretap on them. Took them out. . . . And when they went out of the business, to the extent you ever put them out of business . . . the cops were telling me, 'It's hard to get PCP on the street, people aren't getting it, prices are going up.' And we felt real good about that. Because we felt we'd had some impact."

In 1982 he got a position in the Baltimore Federal District Attorney's office, investigating and prosecuting dope cases. What he learned there illuminates his attitude toward the Tribble case. "If you decide to focus on a suspected drug dealer, nine times out of ten, if you do it right, you can make a case on it."

He first heard about the Bias case when he was still working for the federal DA. He and his wife were attending the bar association's annual conference. "My wife and I are sitting on the beach the morning after Len Bias died. People are talking: 'You hear Len Bias died!' I had absolutely no idea who this young man was, or why his particular unfortunate death was significant over anybody else who happened to die under similar circumstances. I became more intrigued and followed it as I would follow any criminal case that was getting a lot of publicity."

Three months later Marshall lost the election and Bonsib was approached by one of Alex Williams's campaign managers about working as the new state attorney's deputy. Despite his dislike of administrative work and his worry about offending his old boss, Marshall, he accepted.

When he entered the office the Tribble case was in limbo. Marshall was gone and Harding was too inexperienced to handle the court proceedings; the attorney who had been tracking it since the fall had run and lost against Alex Williams as the Republican candidate and was about to leave the office. For a variety of reasons, including his own interest in the case, Bonsib assigned the Tribble file to himself.

In retrospect, the moment was crucial in the history of the case. Until this point the evolution of the case had been a direct consequence of the confusion of the first days—the "endless foolishness" growing out of Driesell's silence, Marshall's anger and ambition, and the press's eagerness to plug a story. But now these factors had been stripped away; there was no political or social obligation to continue with the prosecution. Williams had no involvement with the Tribble indictment; he had criticized Marshall's handling of the grand jury, saying the longtime prosecutor had gone on a "fishing expedition." Bonsib had the perfect opportunity to plea a deal and end the case with a minimal amount of publicity.

Morrow eagerly offered him this opportunity. Tribble's defense had escalated considerably beyond his or Weinberg and Green's original notion of a simple case. Several partners were suggesting Morrow drop the whole thing. According to Morrow, a member of the executive committee said he "had been at an ABA meeting in New York and [a client] said: What is Weinberg and Green doing representing this drug dealer? . . . I said I don't believe he's a drug dealer. I think he's been *screwed*, I think he's a scapegoat, and I think that he basically was a victim of somebody's political ambition. I think this is the type of case that our law firm or any law firm should be involved in. . . . I let it be known . . . that as long as Brian Tribble wanted me to represent him, I was going to represent him. And that would be true if I was at Weinberg and Green, and if Weinberg and Green wasn't going to be representing him, then I was going to represent him somewhere else. . . . At that point he said, 'Well, it's an interesting perspective, and I understand that, and that clarifies it, but one perception is, why are we representing a drug dealer?' "

Under this pressure, Morrow tried to explore an out-of-court agreement with Bonsib. He "went down to meet with him in February. We had a very cordial meeting. I said that I felt this case had been *totally* blown out of proportion, that there was no way that I could see that he in any way could condone, nor was I holding him responsible for anything that had happened up to this point. It seemed to me that it was appropriate that we sit down and discuss this case rationally in the context of a college kid who is in a room in which maybe there is cocaine and somebody dies, unanticipatedly and so on. I mean that's what the case is. I said if you adopt it on those terms, what you have is a possession count, some period of probation, and we make this case go away. We call it what it is.

"While not specifically agreeing with me, Bonsib said, 'Maybe that's what the case is, maybe it isn't. But there's a reality here that you cannot disagree. The fact of the matter is, first of all someone died, which takes this out of the context of three or four college kids sitting around.'

"I said, 'I'm not so sure it does. The fact that the person died happens to be an unfortunate and unforeseen circumstance that was unintended from the beginning and was not a reasonably foreseeable or natural outcome from this. And therefore how could you hold someone responsible for something that was unforeseen? Why is this different, except the fact that it's a tragedy, from four kids sitting around and snorting coke in a dorm room?'

"He said, 'Well, I understand your rationale, but the fact of the matter is, it *is* different. The fact of the matter is, that somebody's dead. And a *further* reality is that everybody in the country knows about it, and everybody in the country is looking at *us* as to what's going to happen here. . . . The reality we have here is that this is a highly intensive, press-oriented case. . . . We take drugs seriously in this county, and we feel that anything less than a jail sentence in this case will unduly depreciate the seriousness of this case.'

"I said, 'Look, I'm not here as part of a pro-drug lobby. I understand drugs are serious. It seems to me that your credibility and your boss's credibility is saved by saying, 'We're going to go after drug dealers, and we're going to go after drugs in a serious way. I have made an independent evaluation of this particular case, and it is my conclusion that there is insufficient evidence as to the nature of the crime in this case, other than the fact it was a possession case. And this is how we're going to deal with possession cases, and I'm not going to be influenced by the media, and I'm not going to be influenced by the University of Maryland. I'm going to be influenced by the facts. And the facts of this case, and the only facts that I have, are four guys snorted coke in a room.'

"He said, 'Look, . . . we have evidence that your client is a drug dealer.'

"I said, 'Fine. . . . If you have it'—and understand that I'm paraphrasing the conversation—'then you're entirely right that you should not take a plea to possession. But tell me what it is.' "

Bonsib is considerably more reticent about this dialogue than Morrow—he doesn't want to divulge lawyer-to-lawyer conversations—but his account generally agrees.

"I don't recall ever seriously entertaining or offering anything in the possession range. If they wanted to plead to a distribution count, that was open to discussion. But always in the back of my mind were two things. Number one, this was a case that was being viewed by the public. Now normally that by itself isn't going to make any difference. But we view drug cases in this office . . . very seriously. I didn't want to make it appear that we were offering a disposition that was inappropriate, based upon the nature of the charge, which was a distribution of cocaine . . . [and not] a minor amount. And, secondly, somebody died as a result of it. So that even if it had been a very small amount of drugs, when you have a *death* that results from drugs, you've got to read it differently. There's sort of an assumption of the risk as a drug dealer. It's sort of like driving drunk, in one sense. You get behind the wheel of that car, maybe you're not a real bad person, but you've had too much to drink and you kill somebody. Drunk driving by itself is one crime, but when you kill somebody when you're driving drunk it's something else. And in this case, when you're dealing drugs and somebody dies as a result of it, even though you may not have intended that as the result, you're going to be held accountable for it."

Bonsib's unyielding position was based on the evidence in the case. But what was the evidence? This was what haunted Morrow. Was there something he didn't know? Something he hadn't been told? Under the rules of discovery the prosecution was bound to inform the defense of any exculpatory information and all physical evidence. Did the prosecution have something that was actually damning, a phantom witness who was going to prove their case?

"Obviously, the only possible reference that could have been made by the state at this point was that somebody was going to say [Tribble] was a drug dealer," says Morrow. "The only thing I could *think* of—and I thought about this ad nauseam—is that they had somebody who was going to say, 'I sold the drugs to Brian Tribble and I saw him take this big pile of drugs and get in the car with Lenny Bias.' Okay, that'd be pretty tough evidence. Now, that was a possibility, but I thought that doesn't make sense. Because if they had a witness, why would they be trading him for Tribble? *He'd* be the guy you'd want. . . . That brings to mind a statement Marshall made early on. . . . Someone had called the U.S. attorney's office and said, 'Would you like to find out about the Tribble case? If you can give me immunity, I'll come in and tell you from whom he got the drugs. . . . ' So we called Bud Marshall and said, 'Did somebody call you and offer to testify?' And he confirmed it with the comment, 'I'm not interested in your testimony. I deal up, I don't deal down.' Or some words to that effect. Meaning I make deals with people at the *lower* end of the hierarchy to get the higher end of the hierarchy, not vice versa. Which is only logical. . . . We used to sit and just brainstorm for hours—what could they have that they're not telling us about?"

At the time, actually, Bonsib was still acquainting himself with the case. By his own admission, he approached the case with some predispositions. His preliminary impressions had been formed by the papers. When asked if the stories he had read about Tribble in the newspapers detailing his supposed "high life"—the Mercedes, the "high-rise luxury apartment," the fancy interior decorating—had convinced him Tribble was probably a drug dealer, Bonsib answered unequivocally: "Yes. . . . When I read the paper? Yes. Usually when there's smoke there's fire. When there's *that* much smoke, you assume that there's some fire. And that's an assumption that I had at that time." When asked whether he might have changed the view he brought to the case if the newspaper accounts had focused on other aspects of Tribble's life—the family's average income, the lack of a day nurse for Priscilla, etc.—he again answered in the affirmative, though with a momentary hesitation: "That's—that's certainly possible."

With this impression he began his search for the same thing Morrow wanted: evidence.

"There were really two questions. One was putting the drugs in the room. The other one was who brought them there? And I wanted to see what kind of evidence [the grand jury] had about that. So, obviously, I was very interested in seeing what Gregg and Long had to say. . . . It's particularly difficult when you're picking up a case from somebody else that has had that much work gone into it. You don't always know what you have and what you don't have because different people put their cases together different ways. So the most important thing initially is to make sure that you've accumulated all the sources, all the information. So I wanted to get all the information we had, all the information that existed in the homicide squad, and all the information that existed in the vice squad. . . . You've got to remember, this case had a lot of angles to it. It was investigated by the homicide squad of the county police. The drug aspect of it was investigated by the vice section of the county police. Eventually the Maryland Police Department had a role in it because it occurred, at least in part, on campus. And so they had some files and information on it. And whenever you have a case that far apart—plus you have an extensive grand jury investigation, plus you're not there at the beginning—you've got to make sure that you're not missing things."

He conducted his review around the time he met with Morrow. His reaction to what he read was that the defense had "a lot of running room" on the distribution charge.

"My impression from the evidence at that point was that if they [the jury] believed Gregg and Long that we had a good circumstantial case for distribution. But that it wasn't, by any stretch of the [imagination] a concrete case, it wasn't an open-and-shut case. . . . There was a significant amount of running room on the distribution aspect of it for Tribble. . . . There was a lot of room for the defense. . . . I didn't think it was a lost case. . . . I wasn't worried about going in and losing. I was satisfied that we could go in and we could put on a respectable showing, and let the jury decide."

Bonsib says the evidence for distribution was the statement of Gregg and Long. But when asked why he didn't pursue any kind of plea arrangement with the defense, he alludes to evidence that convinced him Tribble was a drug dealer. Again, what was the evidence? Bonsib says at this time he was working from the files developed under Marshall. Yet Marshall says unequivocally that those files did not indicate Tribble was a drug dealer in the sense of someone who made a living selling drugs. When informed of Marshall's statement, Bonsib said, "Well, Bud and I had a different evaluation of the evidence."

But when pressed Bonsib also equivocates about his legal judgment of Tribble. "Strictly evaluating *this case*, based upon the *evidence* that we thought we could present at trial, the evidence in *my* mind at that time established that there was a dealer involved. . . . You don't come up with that quantity of that purity of cocaine if you're an average schmuck on the street. So the only *real* question was, who *was* the one responsible for producing that cocaine? Because the one who produces it is a dealer. Under the law, a dealer means somebody who distributes the drugs, whether it's for profit, for friendship, for favor, or for whatever. It is a *transfer* of drugs. So perhaps *dealer* is a different term.

"Now the question is, was there sufficient evidence to proceed on a possession with intent or a distribution of cocaine charge? It was *our* belief—and still my belief today—that there was more than ample evidence to proceed. Now when you say, 'Was Tribble a dealer in the sense, was he out there moving and shaking? Was he going, selling lots of cocaine for profit on the street?' . . . You have really two different evaluations here. One is, was there sufficient evidence to go forward on the charges that Bud sought indictment from the grand jury on the felony charges? And in our opinion, there was. But that doesn't *necessarily* mean that those charges would reflect that whoever provided the cocaine was a big—a high-roller dealer. It simply means that there was evidence to show that somebody was responsible—in this case they indict Tribble—for producing that cocaine, for distributing the coke."

In short, at the time he spoke to Morrow Bonsib lacked the admissible evidence to prove Tribble was a dealer: "The admissible evidence, in our opinion . . . could have supported a finding, if the jury believed the evidence, that Tribble was the supplier, in the sense of the *provider* of those drugs."

When he was asked if that meant the admissible evidence did not support the finding that Tribble "made a living selling drugs," he replied, "That's correct, that's correct."

So Morrow's phantom witness didn't exist. But Bonsib didn't conclude from this that there was no phantom witness. Instead, he decided that the investigation—an immensely complicated and multifaceted one that involved three different sectors of the Maryland State Police—had failed to uncover him. The investigation itself, he reasoned, had been flawed. It had pursued two goals: examining the University of Maryland and making a drug case. He wouldn't fall into the same trap; he would simply proceed to make a drug case, and following this route, would find the witness that had eluded everyone so far.

"With the background that I'd had in prosecuting drug cases, . . . that if you've got a person who's involved in distribution, generally there is information out there about what they're up to. And all you've got to do is find it. A person doesn't deal drugs to one person one time, if they're any kind of significant dealer. They've got to deal—they've got to put themselves out front. . . . Local dealers have contacts with all kinds of people, as they must to have their business, and the kind of people they're dealing with are also the kind of people that are likely to be talking. They're going to get in trouble and they're going to tell people who they're getting it from. So my next step was to survey the traditional sources of information for that sort of stuff. Police files and things like that. To see if there were some leads that had not been followed up, or if there was evidence that had been obtained that I thought we had to look into."

In his repeat of Marshall's search, Bonsib concentrated on a specific point. In their testimony before the grand jury, Gregg and Long had referred to an event that cast suspicion on Tribble. They had testified that one night in the middle of winter, after a game, Leonard had driven them to Tribble's. There the three players—Tribble didn't take part—snorted cocaine until early in the morning. Bonsib felt this incident was damning for Tribble. But since the event happened long before the night of June 18 the laws of evidence forbid it to be referred to in a trial on possession and distribution. A way out of this prohibition was to enter a conspiracy charge, citing the defendant with a plan that extended over a longer period of time. In this instance that would mean citing Tribble as dealing drugs for a year or so. But Bonsib had no witness to prove such a charge. His mission was to find one—a "live, available, and willing witness" who could give admissible testimony.

The ex-detective Jimmy Wiseman, Goldstein's "great bullshitter of all times," helped Bonsib in the task, pursuing a variety of leads.

"I'm not going to get into specifically what they were. But there were a number of things that I asked him to check out as a result of the file. Some of them had already been checked out by the police, some of them, perhaps we just had a little bit different angle on."

By March they still had nothing and they postponed the trial date for that month. At the last moment—in Bonsib's recollection three or four weeks before the trial began—the work paid off: Wiseman found the "live, available, and willing witness" Bonsib had been looking for—someone who claimed he had worked for Tribble.

The witness was Terrence Moore, sixteen, a short, thin kid who lived with his parents in Mount Pleasant, one of the Maryland suburbs on the way to Upper Marlboro—"not much of a drug user," Bonsib describes him, "just a young criminal."

From the age of twelve on Moore has lived in state institutions from which he has escaped or was relocated. The reformatories had failed to rehabilitate (or, given his age, habilitate) him. When Bonsib first contacted him, Moore faced a battery of charges, including some that could have resulted in lengthy sentences in adult prisons.

In the fall or early winter of 1986, Moore had been arrested for an outstanding warrant. While booking him, the police found a paper address and telephone book; inside was a number with Brian Tribble's name. The police forwarded a xerox of the page to the unit investigating Bias's death. But for some reason the lead wasn't followed until Bonsib (or Wiseman; Bonsib isn't sure who actually came across the scribble) discovered it while going through the files.

Bonsib's thinking was the same as that pursued by the journalists shortly after Bias's death: What was 88 percent pure cocaine doing in Bias's car? Clearly Bias must have known a dealer. Why did Terry Moore have Tribble's number? Clearly, Moore must have been working for him.

"There's no other logical connection. There's no indication that they're friends or that they run together. They don't live in the same area. . . . Why is [Tribble] in there? So it's a logical thing to go out and look . . . and among the other leads that Jimmy pursued, he pursued this one."

Wiseman conducted the first interview with Moore, and they decided he would make a credible witness. "One of the things you do is you let him talk. And you see if what he says is corroborated by other things that you know. And when Terry Moore talked, he said things that he had no business knowing if he wasn't there. He told us things about—and these are things that he testified to at trial—that he really shouldn't know about, they weren't things that were spread all over the papers. . . . They were little things."

So Bonsib accompanied Wiseman on the next visit. "We talked to him with his folks. Then we talked to him for one evening, for a very long period of time." The other interviews "lasted perhaps an hour or two. And I'll tell you, that these were very open-ended interviews we had with him."

Moore claimed he had worked for Brian Tribble for most of the last year, calling Tribble to buy packets of cocaine that he would sell out on the street. He said he had accompanied Tribble when Tribble did business at nightclubs and that he had met Len Bias through Tribble at Montana Terrace.

Bonsib decided Moore's testimony would convince a jury.

"I thought putting him together with the rest of the case would give them a good picture of what was going on. I didn't have any expectations that he was going to come across and be somebody that they felt sympathetic toward, or that they would like. In most of these drug cases I've had worse witnesses. I can remember one I had in Baltimore where he's on the stand and the defense attorney's asking him, 'Did you put a bomb under my client's car?' The guy says, 'Yeah, I did.' He says, 'Well, what if it would have blown up?' He said, 'What if it would have?' I mean just absolutely no concern. Now do you think the jury liked a guy like that? . . . Gregg and Long I thought would make very good, believable witnesses. They weren't criminals in the normal sense. They were people who liked to use cocaine, perhaps a little bit of marijuana. And that they would build the foundation and that Terry Moore could put in context some of the circumstances they set up . . . could show that Tribble's activity over a period of time—that what Gregg and Long testified to, was consistent with this overall pattern."

But Moore had still not agreed to testify. "He was scared to death . . . this wasn't something where he was, you know, *anxious* to come forward. We really had to sit down and talk with him and we had to talk with his folks, and I think it was really probably his—I don't remember if it was his mom or his dad—but one of them really was telling him, 'Look, you should come forward and do the right thing here, you shouldn't be involved with these guys, you should tell [Bonsib and Wiseman] what [you know].' And I think it was *that* that convinced him to come forward, more than anything *we* said. He was a very reluctant witness, for obvious reasons. Who wants to be labeled a snitch? . . . in a high-profile case like this, where everybody in the world is going to know about you." His parents "were very concerned, at the same time, for his safety. I mean it was sort of a mixed bag on their behalf. On one hand, they're very concerned about what does this mean for his safety, on the other hand . . . They wanted to know what we could do to protect him. And the answer that we gave them and what we give just about everybody is 'We can't make any guarantees.' We can't. We don't have a witness protection program on the local level and we really can't offer much in the way of protection. So that's a little bit of a risky proposition for witnesses."

But Bonsib did promise that the state would help Moore in his coming appearances in court. He said they "would go to bat for him, that we would tell the judge of the nature and extent of his cooperation. But there was no indication that we were going to recommend probation. . . . We just told him that if he did this, we recognized that it was a substantial step, that he was putting his safety in jeopardy, and that if he chose to do it and he testified truthfully, that we would go to the judge and we would explain to the judge that he took a big risk in doing it."

To Bonsib's satisfaction, Moore agreed. "I felt that we had gotten a link that took us from being a circumstantial case. [We were] in a position to have a witness testify that what happened in January and what happened in June were not isolated incidents, but that they represented *acts* that were part of a continuing course of conduct on the part of Tribble. And I thought we'd sort of completed the picture. [Moore] really sort of tied [things] up together."

~~~

The opening stage of Tribble's trial has three parts: the selection of the jury, the final motions—all Morrow's, offered strictly for the record—and the opening arguments. No one knows for sure how long the trial will take. The prosecution originally presented a list of seventy witnesses; when Morrow complained—"It makes a mockery of the discovery process if the state is entitled to throw balloons in the air to confuse you," he says—they whittled the list down to a slightly less unmanageable forty. Now everyone expects twenty or so. But neither side is sure of what the other is going
~~~

to do. Morrow *hopes* he knows what Gregg and Long will say. He remains unsure whether the prosecution will call Driesell. Finally he can't predict how much the state's mystery witness, Terrence Moore, will hurt his client. He has been told the name of the witness, but not what he's going to say. Tribble claims he has never heard of Moore. Meanwhile the state won't know until the last moment whether Tribble himself will take the stand.

At nine-thirty sharp Mr. Luckett's broad, country grin vanishes as he calls the court to rise. "I've worked with Judge Rea a lot," he says, in awe of his boss. "He doesn't tolerate any nonsense. He'll keep a trial moving."

Entering from the side door, Judge Rea hardly seems a hard taskmaster. Sleepy-faced, tousle-haired, the jurist shambles toward the bench, his black gown falling over his slightly slouching shoulders with no more solemnity than his morning robe. With his shabby-genteel, Southern-gentleman, patrician looks, he seems a more likely candidate to preside over a mint-julep tasting than the trial of a young black man for cocaine distribution.

"We've got to wait for the bell to ring thirteen times before we can begin," he explains. He gathers the loose folds of his robe around him, addressing the court as though everyone there were guests in his living room. "I don't know why. I think it's for the thirteen colonies. But I'm not sure. It's just the custom down here in Upper Marlboro."

The courtroom beneath him is packed with some 150 potential jurors. Morrow has fought to conduct an individual voir dire of each juror; not surprisingly, the motion hasn't been granted, but the judge has agreed to conduct a more wide-ranging examination of the panel than usual and will examine the full panel all together. Behind them, bunched against the back wall, notebooks at the ready, sit the press, representatives of all the local news media as well as national correspondents from CNN and ABC. Judge Rea has refused to partition a section of the courtroom for them: he wants to make it perfectly clear that with him, justice, not the media, comes first.

The bells—electronic of course—ring. Judge Rea becomes Thornton Wilder's Stage Manager, guiding us through the complexities of the action. Speaking with a placid, almost soporific calm, the long-voweled singsong of his voice informs the jurors of the charges and nature of the case, somehow reducing the drama while actually reminding the jurors of the unique mission they are about to perform.

Then he introduces the main actors to the audience. Tribble stares out, wary-eyed but self-possessed, Morrow and the defense team—a young black man and woman—surrounding him. They all look serious and worried. In comparison, Bonsib and Harding seem casual, Harding pulling at the edges of his walrus mustache, eager to get under way, Bonsib smiling and self-assured, arms crossed over his chest as he surveys the audience: the case will only be as good as the jury about to be picked, and he is concentrating on the task.

Both sides pursue the same strategy in the selection: what matters is not who's on, but who you keep off.

"The biggest thing . . ." says Bonsib, "is to avoid people who come with a prejudice against you . . . the weirdos and the people that are not going to give you a fair shot that come in either with no element of common sense, or who may be disposed against you before you even get started."

In his paternal drone, Judge Rea patiently explains he is going to ask questions of the jurors to see if there is anything that will prevent them from rendering a "fair and impartial verdict." This is what Morrow wants. He doesn't believe jurors follow the fine discriminations of criminal law. The judge may tell the jurors a defendant is presumed innocent—"cloaked in innocence"—but unless the point is brought continually to their attention they won't listen to the instruction. More important than winnowing out potentially damaging jurors, the voir dire allows the judge to remind the jurors a substantial number of times that Tribble is presumed innocent and that they are to disregard anything they have ever heard previously about the case.

Judge Rea leans over the desk and peers into the audience as he begins his first questions.

"Now, first, does anyone here know either Mr. Bonsib or Mr. Morrow?"

A middle-aged black woman toward the back stands up. Painstakingly, Rea establishes the connection: she has known Mr. Bonsib because she took a course with him.

Rea smiles; this is his meat. "Did he give you a grade in this course?"

Everyone laughs. This is the mood he wishes to establish. None of that big-city media distorting facts and truths, but the homespun reality of American justice: common sense, respect for the law, the in-gathering of the community to render its decision.

From the dock, Morrow looks on dubiously. He doesn't believe any potential juror will admit a prejudice; if he had conducted the voir dire, he would have pushed individuals to admit their presumptions. Rea asks if any jurors are involved in law enforcement. A large black man stands and introduces himself as a member of the Metropolitan Police. "Would that cause you to fail to render a fair and impartial verdict in this case?" Rea asks. "No sir," the man responds. He sits. Morrow will have to use one of his precious "strikes" to bar the man from the jury.

Still the questions offer valuable clues. Behind him, stands his associate, defense attorney Ava Lias; her looks are as exotic as her name, her face an Egyptian triangle with enormous black eyes and cheekbones Greta Garbo would have envied, and she scans the crowd in a pose of such intense concentration she seems like some beautiful alien mind-reading the audience.

The drama of the opening of the trial is replaced by the dull, domestic chore of justice. And yet, at the same time, there is nothing ordinary about the procedure or what is at stake. One look at Tribble—his eyes peering relentlessly into the crowd of onlookers—tells you that.

Slowly the most obviously prejudiced jurors are separated from the rest. Two middle-aged, proper women stand when Rea asks whether they know any of the notables; they attend the same church as Mrs. Bias. Another has heard Mrs. Bias lecture. They don't exclude themselves, saying they will be able to render a fair and impartial verdict, but Ava Lias strikes them down: these born-agains can hardly be expected to listen sympathetically to the trial of a man who lured their prince into darkness and death.

Rea asks for people who are associated with the University of Maryland to identify themselves. One-third of the courtroom rises.

"Do you have an opinion on the case?" Judge Rea asks a young white man, in the same ceremonial, dull tone.

The juror tenses. "I believe . . ." he starts.

"No, no—" Rea interrupts, charmed by the novice's misinterpretation of the question. "I don't want to *know* your opinion—"

But the juror has his agenda. "I believe," he continues, "Brian Tribble is not responsible for Len Bias dying."

The calm of the courtroom freezes. The newsmen suddenly are startled into activity: Who is this guy? What's going to happen next? The black courtroom guard—black guards, black defendants—moves to get the offender as Rea admonishes the juror to shut up. The juror is led out with a flourish, the staid authority of the court disrupted by this calculated piece of civil disobedience.

Thirty minutes go by as the jurors, to preclude another outburst, answer the question at the judge's desk. The legal process becomes a web of whispers. The defense team is hunched by the desk. Tribble stands with them, listening intently, his eyebrows knitted in intense concentration. Morrow's two instructions to him were about clothes and attitude. He wanted him to dress nicely, without calling attention to himself—a challenge for Tribble, with his looks. And he warned him not to make facial expressions—another instance of Morrow's distrust of juries. "I didn't want him to frown, or make facial expressions, telegraphing to the jury what he felt about the testimony or the judge's rulings or anything like that, because I'm of a firm belief that many jurors have no idea what is going on lots of the time and they watch for the Greek chorus to see if it was a good thing or a bad thing."

Two and a half hours after he began, Judge Rea asks his final question. The case might last several days. Will this produce a hardship?

One young black woman stands up and says she's still nursing.

"How old's your son?" the justice inquires.

When the woman tells him the boy is ten months, Rea is flabbergasted. "And you haven't weaned him yet?" Rea says, revealing the attitudes of old-time PGC. "Reminds me of a mare I got out in the field. We got to get her out to stud pretty soon!"

Now the first real contest between the two sides begins, each jockeying to gain an advantage with the jury's makeup. The jurors approach the bench in panels of twelve, the group filling the box then listening as the two sides seek to exclude for cause and then decide to employ strikes or not. Bonsib gets rid of younger women—he doesn't want Tribble's looks influencing the verdict—and those with some knowledge of drugs. The cops, the women who attend Mrs. Bias's church, some others associated with the University of Maryland, are struck from Morrow's side. White women, especially older ones, are definitely out.

Morrow queries Tribble about each selection. "It's his trial and it's his life," says Morrow. The young man exiles several Morrow would have taken, including an older black man whom Tribble decides is very authoritarian, one of those older, working-class fathers who could be James Bias himself.

With their last challenge, the defense must choose between an older white woman and a sad-looking white man wearing a polyester leisure suit and bifocals. Gambling, Morrow goes for the polyester. Shoulders hunched, the man takes the last chair. He joins an oddball collection: a long-haired kid whose eyebrows point right at the ceiling like a cartoon character's, several working-class black men, an engineer, a middle-aged black woman who listens to the judge with the unswerving attention of a model student.

The fight begins that afternoon. For the next week, battling is all Morrow will do. Nothing happens or threatens to happen that he doesn't object to; he can't make enough motions to dismiss, disqualify, instruct, reinstruct, and admonish. He loses them all, but he never complains. Thanking the judge for every ruling, including those that go against you, is a tenet of his: who knows, he figures, the jury might not be listening and think you've actually won a point. It is impossible to divine whether his embattled posture is genuine outrage or simply another legal tactic. "I figured, look, if [Brian's] gonna go down the tubes, then maybe I'm not going to be a great hero by keeping him from going down the tubes, but godammit, there's not anybody who's going to say that he didn't get every ounce of a vigorous defense and that we didn't go down fighting every lick of the way."

. . .

Behind every interruption is the issue of a fair trial. Morrow believes Tribble is innocent—he wants to believe this and the facts indicate to him that he should. He's been bamboozled by clients before and by now he thinks he knows when he's being lied to. Besides, he had jeopardized his standing at the firm with his defense of Tribble; to contemplate the possibility that Tribble betrayed his trust would be self-destructive. But about one thing he is unequivocally sure: Arthur Marshall tried and convicted Tribble in the press before the case ever came to court. And Morrow takes every opportunity to remind the jury of the rules of evidence and the presumption of innocence, the profound influence of the state attorney's office in the case, and the enormous amount of publicity the case has already received. Judge Rea's comment that the case is an "ordinary dope case" is correct. The courtroom presents the classic confrontation of television drama: the prosecutor protecting the community and the defense using the law to get his client off.

This afternoon Morrow argues that the jury should be sequestered. Morrow has heard that Rea agrees, but that Rea's boss has vetoed the idea because of its prohibitive expense. "It would require a suspension of disbelief to think the jury can hide from the publicity," he tells Rea. But the judge rules against him. The jury can go home every night—but not without a warning. The paterfamilias has already divided the court into three sons. The press are the bad boys, beloved, but always trying to put one by you. The attorneys are the clever, older siblings, vying for his approval. The jury is his favorite, the recipient of all his patience, protection, and guidance. He admonishes each in order. He complains that during the lunch recess Tribble was the victim of a "riot scene." (The description betrays a certain parochialism: not more than twenty reporters bothered the family, barely minimum coverage for a major trial in New York or Los Angeles.) Don't interfere with the legal process, Rea warns the journalists, and don't bother the jury. Next he instructs the attorneys not to talk to the press. And finally he elaborates on the theme of how the jury may escape the malign effect of the press. Do they have VCR's? They can use the editing device to wipe out the news broadcast. Don't listen to those all-news channels on the car radios going home. And if they get the paper at their front door in the morning make sure a family member first cuts out the stories about the trial before they peruse it over their bowl of oatmeal or eggs.

Then the jury is dismissed. At the bench the two sides argue the talmudic distinctions of conspiracy law, struggling over the admissibility of Terrence Moore's testimony. Morrow knows he has already lost his motion before proposing it; his objective is to enter Moore's name, until now the privileged information of the court, in the public record. With the Tribbles strapped for money he can't hire an investigator and he can't charge the expense to Weinberg and Green—he has already gypped the firm by not marking down weekend work on the case or charging the family the usual twenty cents a mile for every trip he's taken. But he needs some information on the state's witness: he hopes that if the press gets hold of the co-conspirator's name, the reporters will find out damaging information about the man. Brian has acted tough about Moore so far—"I can't wait to see this guy," he's told Morrow, "I can't wait to find out who he is"—but Morrow has no idea what the witness will say, and it would be better to attack his testimony with a stockpile of ammunition and not just with whatever he can steal from the prosecution. He succeeds in entering the name into the public record, but the judge dismisses his motion. Even though expected, the ruling is a blow. Morrow leaves coming to the conclusion he has always dreaded: Brian is going to have to take the stand.

The next morning the legal arguments continue. Rea listens, leaning back in his chair, head resting on his palm, a teacher listening to his students perform. Occasionally he interrupts the counsels, restating their propositions, often more clearly than they have, suggesting the logical consequences of their premises. Morrow carries with him a thick looseleaf notebook of case law—to let the judge and jury know the weightiness of his argument—but Rea is unperturbed, his drawl and country wit defusing Morrow's combustible passion.

Finally Morrow finishes. Bonsib answers his charges. The case they are going to unveil, he says, is a classic type of conspiracy. The audience listens up: finally, this isn't law, but the where, when, and how of the case. The prosecution, he says, will show bits and pieces that fit together to show a "commonality of players and circumstances." Evidence will prove that Tribble was conspiring to sell cocaine for a year; that Tribble was getting the dope from an unknown source; that Len Bias was a "courtesy middleman"; and that Tribble told Gregg and Long that the cocaine in the room came from Tribble's "stash" and that he was getting some more the next day.

"I hear a railroad behind me," starts Morrow in rebuttal. For five minutes he denies Bonsib's accusations, painstakingly painting in the grays of legal discriminations before exploding into the primary colors of his rhetoric, warning the judge that unless he rules in his favor, "That freight train is not going to be behind me, but riding right over me."

Rea is nonplussed. Morrow's performance pleases but doesn't convince him. Well, he says, he's going to let the prosecutors go on to see if they can prove their charge of conspiracy, warning them that if they fail they run the risk of having the proceeding declared a mistrial.

Then, with the anticlimactic matter-of-factness that haunts the proceedings, he tells Mr. Harding to begin.

~~~

It takes Harding seven minutes to outline the state's case. Bias came home "elated," he says. He and Tribble bought beer and cognac. When Long and Gregg entered the room, they asked Tribble where the cocaine came from and Tribble said, "From the bottom of the stash. I'm getting another kilo tomorrow." When Baxter interrupted the party, they hid the mound from the roommate's sight; after he left they started snorting. "We're going to show you Brian Tribble is a cocaine dealer," Harding says. "We're going to take you into the inside world of cocaine dealing."

Already smacking his lips, Morrow rises, his eyes alight with
~~~

worry and sincerity. This is his first public presentation to the jury. Like a chess player he must seize control of the center of the board and reject the prosecution's definition of the trial.

"This case is about evidence," he tells the jury. "Not the evidence of rumors and innuendo that the state will bring up about the character of my client, but the evidence the state will provide about the night of June 18." Relentlessly he reminds them of the defendant's rights. An indictment is not evidence. As he sits in the dock, Brian Tribble is cloaked in innocence; the state must prove its case beyond a "reasonable doubt" and to a "moral certainty."

And what are the facts? Grimacing and squinting, Morrow gives his version of the tragic night. There was "joy" at the party that night, he says, "there was"—the psychobabble sounds strange coming from this tough guy—"support from his friends." The cocaine, he implies, wasn't unusual, because cocaine is a fact of life in our society today. So the only real evidence presented will be the words of Gregg and Long, and if the two boys tell the truth—Bonsib objects, but Rea keeps to his laissez-faire attitude; he wants the jury to hear as much as possible—they won't say where the cocaine came from. "I want you to think about a shotgun when you hear the testimony of Long and Gregg," Morrow says, nodding to the prosecution. "A shotgun sitting right on this table pointing at Long and Gregg. And maybe if they don't give the right testimony"—his voice hardens, a second-rate British actor—"someone will pull the trigger on that shotgun and Gregg and Long will be charged with some of the charges Brian Tribble is."

Then, as a preamble to the actual testimony, the prosecution plays the tape of Tribble's call to 911. His blurred, slurred speech fills the silent courtroom with the by now familiar stammering directions to go past Hungry Herman's, the plea to come quickly, the insistence that it is Len Bias, man, Len Bias, he can't die.

The recording marks the start of the tragedy; what is now going to happen is the end. A mystery is an initiation, a gaining of secret knowledge, and, in drama at least—Christian or pagan—the knowledge revealed is the truth. At the heart of the fascination with Leonard's death are unanswered questions. What happened in that room? Who brought the drugs? Most important of all, who was the real Len Bias? The persistent attraction his death has for people is their ungratified desire for the truth. Now, finally, the mystery will be solved.

The first witnesses are perfunctory. Before going into the specifics of Tribble's culpability, Bonsib wants to establish facts: Leonard's death, that cocaine was found in the dumpsters and Leonard's car, that Tribble was present in the room. At the least this evidence proves possession.

A fireman who was part of the emergency squad describes the confusion and disbelief in the room on their arrival. "It's just a frenzy," he says, "when there is a working code, trying to do everything at once." He says Leonard never regained consciousness. The paramedic who follows the fireman confirms the story. "There was no electrical activity in his heart," he says as though Leonard's body were a dead engine the medics were trying to jumpstart.

Morrow is short with both. He limits his cross to a simple question: Did Gregg or Long tell either of them that Bias was taking cocaine? They answer no, and the point is made: Brian Tribble at least called 911, while Gregg's and Long's lies might have cost Bias his life.

The rest of the day remains undramatic. Bonsib drags out a huge green garbage bag filled with debris—beer bottles, empty pizza cartons, telephone messages. By the time he finishes cataloging the detritus his previously neat desk is a riot of junk. The physical evidence is unintentionally dismaying and pathetic. The scene of this tragedy was a real dorm room, the actors were kids whose biggest worry was whether to go for some more crabs or get a pizza—an environment in which the awful finality of death was wildly out of place. But Bonsib has no feel for this aspect of the case. He presents these items from a dorm party as though they were the remains of the St. Valentine's Day massacre.

The university cop named Schallhorn describes in detail his discovery of the cocaine. ("Jesus, is this guy stupid," comments one television journalist. "He came up and opened the car door.

The crew noticed the white powder on the floor. 'What's that?' he said. 'You think it could be drugs?' ")

A quartet of witnesses then traces Bias's last night.

Mr. Bias with broad, stooped shoulders and an expressionless face tells about his son's trip to Boston. Keith Gatlin, thin as a grasshopper, with large, alert eyes, describes Leonard as happy and calm—"same as always." He mentions a touching moment. He went to bed at eleven-thirty—not before telling Long, who was going to the store, that he wanted a hardball candy—and woke around three to the sound of laughter. One imagines him disoriented, rising in the dark room, maybe a little pissed at the noise, then sinking back into sleep with the relaxation that comes from knowing where you are, maybe now even enjoying the boisterous celebration of his roommates. God damn! Lenny had really made it! The next thing he remembers was being woken by the paramedics.

A young woman named Madelyn Woods—pert, intelligent, pretty, a junior executive at a local television station—testifies that Leonard called her from the dorm sometime around eleven; after leaving work, she spent fifteen minutes with him there. "His mood was very jovial," she says. "He was delighted to be drafted by the Celtics."

A lanky wiseguy who runs the Towne Hall, the local liquor store, fills in Leonard's last sure stop before going back to the dorm. Leonard came by at ten to one, he says, and bought a six-pack of malt liquor. A big fan, the store manager desisted from asking the star for his autograph. Leonard left and the store manager and his female coworkers argued whether Bias was wearing a European or American suit. Bias returned five or ten minutes later for some cognac. "I said, 'Well, you got some money now. Why don't you buy a big bottle.' And I thought, hell, I let him go the first time, I'm going to get him now." So after Bias paid for the cognac—"He had enough to pay for it without any trouble"—the manager got him to sign a picture. Did he still have the original? Bonsib asked. "Yes," he answers resentfully, "it's in the top right-hand drawer of your desk."

The afternoon ends with Baxter, Leonard's roommate. He leans forward, the attentive boy always ready to answer as he relates the long story of the morning, eager to be helpful. His testimony confuses everything: if he didn't see any cocaine when he rode in Bias's car, then where did the drug come from?

It has been a good day for Morrow, and more seems to follow. Back in Baltimore at his office he receives a note to call a friendly Washington lawyer. He connects and finds that his gamble of publishing Moore's name has paid off: the lawyer knows Moore as a professional snitch. Excited, Morrow takes notes as the lawyer fills him in on Moore's background and his informer testimony in other trials. But what about Moore's juvenile offenses, he asks the lawyer. What juvies? says his friend. There are no juvies. The guy's forty-five years old. It's the right kind of information; but it's about the wrong Moore.

The next morning, after the now obligatory argument between counsels at the bench, the first piece of Bonsib's conspiracy is put into place: Terrence Moore takes the stand.

The appearance is a matter of necessity, not planning. The night Moore's name became public, the kid was mugged. Wiseman and Bonsib were waiting to meet him for a final debriefing and were worried that their star witness was disappearing on them. When they finally located him in a hospital, they checked him out, securing him in a motel room. "We wanted to know he was going to be all right and that he was going to be available to testify the next morning," says Bonsib.

At first Bonsib thought the attack was related to the trial—it wasn't—but he was also worried that Moore would become frightened about "diming" on Tribble and try to flee. Moore evidently had already shown some disinclination to denounce Tribble. The night after the attack, Bonsib claims, Moore was scared to death. And if Moore vanished, so would Bonsib's case to prove Tribble was a player in the "inside world" of big-time drug dealing.

Limping into the witness box, Moore does look like an authority on that world. Slight, dark-skinned, with black eyes, high cheekbones, a small chin, and enormous eyelashes, he appears like a vision out of the urban nightmare—the big-city urchin washing windshields for small change, break-dancing, bopping down the street looking to do bad, a signature of our national life as identifiable as retired stockbrokers in duck-hunt-patterned ties.

Sitting back from the mike, seeming uncomfortable in the courtroom, Moore begins his tale.

In March 1986 he was attending Pathways, a local reform school. When the bus dropped him off he would return home and call or "beep"— the court mike suddenly shrieks and Moore jumps back. After Luckett fixes the machine, Moore taps it with a finger suspiciously, as though the instrument might bite him. He's a child afraid of the unknown. But he's a child from another world. To him the commonplaces of middle-class lives are the mysteries; his everyday existence of prisons, trials, probation officers, plea-bargaining, and dealing is impossible for everyone else in the audience to imagine.

Still keeping his distance from the mike he resumes his story. He would "beep" Mr. T., and Tribble would call him back. Moore's code number was 007. If he wanted Tribble to return the call in a hurry, he would use the code 911. He would ask Tribble if Tribble had product. If Tribble said yes, Moore would meet him around H Street or Montana Terrace. Moore himself had seldom gone there before. Tribble would give him the product—anywhere from fifty to one hundred two-inch-square ziplock bags. Moore would then sell the bags, charging from ten dollars—a low price used to hook a client—to fifty. After selling out, he would split his take with Tribble, keeping nine hundred for himself, and giving three thousand to Tribble. Sometimes his share would be less, depending on his losses.

After a while—Moore has no sense of years; his life is divided into his stays at different penal institutions—he was kicked out of Pathways and went underground. He met Tribble on Montana Avenue. Tribble asked if he needed anything. But Moore told him he was chilling out and—

Bonsib interrupts. So far Moore's testimony has been a study in interruptions. Morrow has been on his feet continuously, adding a "thank you" each time the judge overrules his objection. In addition, Moore speaks in an almost unintelligible mumble, still sitting far from the mike as though he doesn't want his words recorded so that they can be used against him. Besides, his language is such a peculiar mix of business and street argot—General Secord as Sportin' Life—that the jury loses track of what he's saying and asks the judge to get the witness to back up and explain.

Moore starts to speak again and the mike shrieks again—

"Mr. Luckett," the judge implores, "can't we do something with that mike?"

Luckett fiddles with the wires, adjusts the position, and assures his boss everything is all right now.

Judge Rea gives his country-boy smile. "All right, Mr. Moore, now you just talk up," he says, encouraging the witness, "just wrap your lips around that mike like Ella Fitzgerald in the Memorex commercial and answer loud and clear."

"What did you mean by 'chilling out'?" Bonsib asks again.

Checking out the area to see if it was safe because he didn't want any "brush back," Moore explains.

He tries to recite the schedule of his various incarcerations, but the dates escape him. ("Why should he be different from the president?" asks one reporter during a recess, referring to Reagan's just-announced confusion over when he might have first heard about the Iran-Contra plans.) But at some point he went to the Jobs Corp. While there he would meet Tribble. Tribble sold him "fish scales"—

Rea leans back farther in his seat, clearly enjoying the arcana, and asks for an explanation.

With his usual businessman's specificity, Moore explains that "fish scales" are flakes of very pure cocaine, as opposed to the powdery, cut—diluted, that is—street version of the drug. Presumably it was flakes like these that drifted down from under the glove compartment in Leonard's car. Anyway, Tribble told him the fish scales came from freaks who were holding—

Rea leans even farther back in his seat.

"A freak," Moore explains, "is a lady who doesn't have respect for herself."

"All right," Rea says, looking at Moore with a faint smile as though the witness were an anthropological exhibit.

Moore continues, the sixteen-year-old commanding the attention of the packed court. He never met Tribble's freaks, Tribble just told him the freaks were holding for him. Sometimes he and

Tribble went to Classics or another nightclub called Chapter III. Tribble drove either a jeep or a Mercedes. The first time they went he had to stay outside because he was too young to enter. He sat in the car in the parking lot. People would come up to Tribble and talk and ask him for drugs and sometimes Tribble would say yes and sometimes no. When Tribble went inside he would drink champagne or Dom Perignon, which Moore guessed "was a wine." Sometimes Tribble was accompanied by his cousin, who dressed in shorts and tank tops. He also saw Len Bias there.

Morrow offers another objection, occasioning a long argument at the bench. During the intermission, Moore sits stiffly in his chair, staring straight ahead.

Not ten feet from him, Tribble for once forgets Morrow's injunctions and stifles a series of yawns—from nervousness, not boredom. Moore's testimony has shaken him. "When Terrence Moore was testifying, Brian was in tears," Morrow recalls. "He said, 'What is this? This is supposed to be a trial, supposed to be the truth. I never saw this guy before in my life, and he's sitting there telling me that he's been buying drugs from me for the last two years? How can he do that? I never saw this guy before in my life! I never thought people were going to stand up and *lie*! I mean they might have come up and argued. They might have said, you know, this looks funny. But . . . I never expected them to produce a witness who was going to come up and say I'm a drug dealer!' "

Finally, Moore tells how he ended up in the courtroom. In January 1987 he was locked up; the police took his phonebook and xeroxed it. When they gave the book back to him, Moore tore it up. Currently, he explains, he is under indictment as an adult for three charges of breaking and entering. He doesn't know what the possible sentence might be, only "what the people on the street be saying." And he knows the state will make a recommendation if he told the truth in this trial and that's why he's done what he has.

Morrow is already set. His tasks are two: to discredit Moore's testimony and also to restore Brian's faith. Positioning himself between the witness and the jury, Morrow adopts a nasty, muted sneer, as though the person being addressed were too negligible even to warrant a full-voice anger.

"When's your birthday?"

"July first, sir." Whether it's due to coaching or street smarts, Moore never drops the acknowledgment of superiority.

"You take drugs today?" Morrow follows, the question coming out of the blue.

Moore answers no—always with the respectful "sir." Rea interrupts to ask if the boy had taken drugs that week, and Moore admits to smoking marijuana.

Morrow goes to work, trying to force the kid, who was afraid of a mike several moments ago, to admit he's scared to enter the adult prison population. Certainly his worry would be justifiable; if Moore isn't concerned about his survival in prison, he's the only one in the courtroom. But Moore answers coldly—and with his unstated desperation, movingly—that he has "no choice" about what prison will be his future address.

Morrow shifts his ground. "Do you have trouble with the English language?"

"To a certain extent."

"Did any doctor ever tell you that you have a mental problem?"

"To a certain extent."

"What?"

Moore refuses to be embarrassed by his weakness. "I'm quick-tempered."

Morrow begins his main line of attack: trying to prove that Moore invented his testimony to get out of jail—that Moore is a scared, frightened kid trying to act tough who will use his knowledge of the street to implicate Tribble by telling generic stories that could apply to any dealer. The dialogue becomes a baffling exchange about "preliminary hearings" and "waiver hearings" and other dates on the judicial calendar, the boy managing to thread his way through the labyrinth of appearances. His life is a blizzard of criminal offenses and courtroom appearances. At the age of ten, convicted of assault and battery. A stay in Boy's Village. How long? Moore doesn't recall. A 1984 arrest for assault and remandment to Montrose. How long? He doesn't recall.

"They all kind of blend together, don't they?" Morrow asks, his snide voice instructing the jury that the boy can't be trusted with anything.

Bonsib objects, of course. But notwithstanding Morrow's snide manner, the comment is perfectly true. The litany of charges—Morrow's recitation makes the boy's record seem proof of a profound sociopathy—is endless. No wonder the kid can't keep track of the seasons of his imprisonment.

"You say one of the burglary charges was at night," Morrow hounds him, trying to show the jury how many years the kid faced. "All of them were in the daytime. That's ten years."

"I didn't know that," Moore answers.

"You're charged with 'malicious destruction,' which is three years."

"I didn't know that, sir."

"Are you aware you are charged with assault and assault with intent to beat?"

"No sir."

"You're charged with breaking and entering at Day's Inn. You're charged with theft."

"That charge is dropped."

Along with everything else it turns out Moore has been arrested for indecent exposure. When Morrow comes upon the misdemeanor, Bonsib jumps to his feet.

"Your Honor," he protests, red-cheeked, concerned by now that the recitation of Moore's felonious record will jeopardize his testimony in the eyes of the jury, "I want the jury to know that he was taking a you-know-what in public and that he wasn't. . . ." His arms flail in the air as words fail him.

Rea helps him out. "You mean, opening his raincoat in public."

"Yes, your honor," Bonsib relaxes, "exactly, thank you."

When the questioning resumes, Morrow makes Moore go through his lurid tale about Tribble.

"Freaks," Moore explains when Morrow asks him once again what the word means. "Girls you just use. You just walk on them. They think one thing and you think another." He doesn't remember the names of Tribble's freaks.

But Moore does remember Bias. He met Bias on Columbia Road, a curving thoroughfare that serves to divide official Washington from the District. Moore didn't know him personally. He never talked to him, just passed words with him for three or four minutes at the most, like 'What's up, man? How you doing? You're shaking out?' He wasn't going to be having a conversation with him, he explains to Morrow testily, not with the police right there, he couldn't be talking to him and watching his back at the same time.

"It's your testimony that Len Bias would hang out there?" Morrow asks incredulously. After all the hassling over the dispositions of the case, he has managed to wring something out of Moore he believes will thoroughly discredit him with the jury.

"I saw him down there four or five times," Moore continues. "I didn't say he was there every day."

"What was he doing?" Morrow goes on.

"He was minding his business," Moore shoots back. "Like I was doing mine."

Sitting in the front row, Alan Goldstein is unimpressed. Moore's facts are colorful enough to show that he knows the life of dope-dealing, but they are generic: they could be used to describe any dealer. Nothing Moore has said convinces him that Moore knew Tribble or Bias. "He was a piece of crap," says Goldstein. "He came off as just absolute trash. . . . In fact, it was funny to me. I just said, who created this guy? This guy is like a creation of somebody's."

~~~

Goldstein is present in the courtroom because his clients, Long and Gregg, are going to testify next. They make up the next piece of Bonsib's puzzle.

Long takes the stand first. He's a large guy, tall and beefy, a football torso on a basketball's player's legs. He strikes one as immediately likable, a classic basketball type—the "big man" whose enormous size is matched by an easygoing, pleasure-loving spirit. Because of his academic difficulties and poor play on the court, Long has been stigmatized as a dullard; but on the stand, he is articulate, forthcoming, emotional.
~~~

"David Gregg and I went to dinner at the campus cafeteria. We would mess around. Do a bunch of nothing. Then Covington [Keeta Covington, a football player] suggested we get some crabs. So we thought that was a good idea. Lenny walked in around ten, ten-fifteen. He was excited and happy, carrying a basketball bag with a Celtic jersey and everything. He went back into his room and came out and said we were going to celebrate. We all said, okay, we were down. Madelyn Woods came in right after and went into his room and stayed a short time and then went out. He came back out and said he was going to drain his lizard and we all knew what he was saying because he hadn't been with a girl for three days. He called someone and left. We didn't know if he was going to see a girl or whether he was going to the liquor store. But he didn't come back. So we went down to the Seven-Eleven store and got some chips and stuff and went back and I went into my room."

Long fell asleep watching David Letterman. The next thing he knew Bias was waking him up.

"Lenny said, 'Wake the fuck up! We're going to celebrate!' " It was around two. I got some pants on. I didn't want to be sitting around in my shorts with a bunch of guys."

Bias knocked on Gregg's door. The star was carrying a medium-size brown paper bag. Bias entered Long's room, Tribble behind him. Bias said again they were going to celebrate—Long "knew what he was talking about"—and Long went to get a beer from the fridge, where he met David. When the two of them walked into the room there was a pile of cocaine on the mirror.

Interrupting the testimony, Bonsib takes out a mirror and a jar of coffee creamer and asks Long to show the amount of cocaine. As Harding approaches Long with the exhibit, Morrow considers doing a Columbo, tripping Harding accidentally on purpose and sending the Coffee-Mate (absurdly dignified by its presence in the courtroom) flying around the room. Grimacing, he restrains himself, figuring he's on thin enough ice with the judge already. Long pours a cupful onto the mirror and—as Mr. Luckett holds a ruler alongside the petite mound—Harding takes memorial Polaroids of the evidence.

Then comes the crucial testimony.

After Long and David entered the room, "Brian said something about they 'got it from the bottom of the stash' " and that " 'they were getting a new kilo tomorrow.' "

This is different from and considerably more ambiguous than what Harding has claimed Long will say. Does the "they" refer to Tribble and Bias or to some other third party?

But the prosecution doesn't ask this question. Instead the testimony is interrupted for another demonstration, as Judge Rea asks the ex-player to show how they would snort the chemical.

Taking out a University of Maryland ID card, Long separates the powdery coffee creamer into thin lines.

"Do you have to use a University of Maryland ID?" Rea asks.

Long explains any thin edge will do and that after separating the powder into lines, they would snort it up through a straw.

"You put the straw in your nostril?" Rea asks Long, peering over the edge of his high desk.

"Near it, Your Honor," Long answers.

Long returns to the events. They passed the coke around. Phil Nevins pounded on the door at one point, but they ignored him— "We told him to go to bed," Long explains with his usual candor. Later Baxter arrived. They kept him waiting outside while they stuck the coke in a desk drawer, and then let him in.

Baxter stayed with them for close to an hour. After he left, Tribble took out the coke and they passed it around. For three hours they snorted. Then Lenny got up to go to the bathroom, but "he was all fucked up."

"So we told him to sit back down and he dozed off and that was when he had the seizure. I recognized that he had a seizure because I had taken a course and Brian did because his sister has those problems. I held his tongue so he wouldn't bite it and David held him because he was shaking. Brian called his mother. I'm not sure what she said but I think she told him to put something in his mouth and call the paramedics. Brian called them. I was monitoring Lenny and giving him CPR. Brian came over after calling 911 and we knew they were on their way. I had mentioned to one of them to get the coke off the mirror. As I remember, David went out with the coke and I don't know what he did, but he took it out of the room. David placed the mirror in my closet in my dirty clothes bag."

When the paramedics took Bias to Leland Hospital, Long stayed behind, collecting the straws and beer bottles and tossing them with the trash into the dumpster behind the dorm. After the hospital he went back to his room where he met Jeff Atkins. Together they went to Cole Field House and from there to Driesell's, where he and David Gregg spoke to the coach for a half-hour.

But this isn't the most shocking testimony. When had he first started using cocaine, Bonsib asks.

"Len Bias introduced me to coke," he explains. "Lenny knew I had smoked marijuana before. One time he knocked on my door and he had a dollar bill and he said, 'Try this.' " Long says he never purchased coke, using it only in his dorm, except for once at Tribble's apartment after a game against North Carolina State. "Usually we would get something to eat. I went back to the room and Lenny called me and said we were going to Brian's. Lenny drove us in Brian's car—a brown Volvo. It took fifteen minutes to get to Tribble's apartment. Tribble was listening to music and watching television. We sat down and he offered us a beer and we started using coke." They stayed all night—he remembers Tribble's roommate getting up to go to work. But he had never seen so much coke as he did the night Lenny came back from Boston.

For Morrow—after the nightmare of Moore's testimony—Long's statements are relatively relieving. But he still wants to underline the crucial points of Long's answers to the jury. As he later explains: "It's very difficult for them to assimilate all the data. So . . . I want to make sure that I red-line those aspects of the data that I'm sure they want to remember, so I can thereafter use it on argument. And they may not remember it throughout the trial and they couldn't sit down and give you a concise synopsis of the important and salient facts in the trial, but when I go into closing argument, I can pull out these little words that I've red-lined: Do you remember? He didn't know who brought the drugs in the room. Remember? That's one technique of cross-examination. Can be dangerous. I've seen it backfire on people. . . . You say, 'If I understand your testimony correctly, you never saw Brian bring it in the room. Is that correct?' 'Well, actually I did.' That's the danger you have if you do that."

Taking his cue from Long's testimony, Morrow gets him to shift most of the blame from Tribble onto Bias. Long didn't know if Bias had the coke in the paper bag. Bias had supplied him with coke about five times previously and Tribble was only with him twice when they snorted. When he would ask Bias where the coke came from, Leonard would say, "Don't ask no questions."

"You testified that 'they' got it?" asks Morrow, getting to the nub of the defense. "Now you don't know who 'they' is, do you?"

"No, sir," says Long.

"When Mr. Baxter came by you told Tribble to put the coke away."

"Yes, sir."

Morrow repeats the point. "*You* told him to put it away?"

"Yes, sir."

"You passed it around as a matter of convenience, didn't you?"

"Yes, sir."

"But you were never charged with distribution of cocaine?"

"No, sir."

Finally, Morrow, to discredit Long, hammers at the player's not telling the emergency squad that Bias had been using drugs.

"I don't recall what I said," Long repeats.

"When the emergency medical team came you lied to them," Morrow goes on, trying to prove Long just told Marshall what the state attorney wanted to hear. "You lied to them," he harrows Long. "You lied to them because you didn't want to get into trouble, didn't you?"

"No," he answers with dignity and conviction. He is guilty—but not of the charge Morrow has leveled against him. "I lied because I didn't really believe Lenny would pass away and I didn't want to ruin his reputation."

That afternoon Morrow and Bonsib take their fight out of the courtroom.

"After the trial that day I went out and I wanted to get some other statement," remembers Morrow. "I can't even recall what it is at this point. But I went to the office. I said, 'Can you give it to me?' Bonsib said, 'Well, it's back there somewhere. If you want it, you're going to have to wait because my parents just came in from out of town, and I'm going to go out to dinner with them or something, and they've been waiting for me, so I'm not going to get it right now. You can come back if you want to.' And I said, 'Bob, let me be real straightforward with you. I don't really give a *fuck* if your parents came in from out of town. The fact is, I need this stuff. I'm in the middle of a trial, I want to get ready for the next day, get it for me!' He said, 'I'm not getting anything for you! You wait until I'm ready to get it, or you go on without it.' And I really thought at that point that I might just see what would happen if I grabbed him by the throat. But I restrained myself. So I left. Not getting what I came to get."

Bonsib's account more or less jibes.

"I don't want to speak bad of Tom," he says, "but on this particular day he came up at the close of the day, up in the lobby, and was hooting and hollering and ranting and raving about something, I don't remember what. . . . I said, 'I'm talking to my folks, they just got in town, give me five or ten minutes and I'll be with you.' And he didn't want to wait. He wanted to talk about something. I don't even remember what it was. And I asked him to give me a couple of minutes to say hello to my folks because they had come in the middle of the trial that day. I hadn't had a chance to even say 'Hi' to them, and I was right in the middle of a conversation with them. And he came busting up here, without an appointment, without any prearranged thing, and wanted to talk to me. Which was fine. All I did was to ask him to wait for a few minutes, and he didn't want to wait. So we got into it. Basically over nothing. But that consequence was, he left in a huff, and *I* left in a huff."

There is an additional consequence. At the end of that day's testimony, Bonsib has decided to call Driesell to the stand. But Morrow has not yet read Driesell's grand jury testimony. Bonsib claims he intended to give Morrow the document, but then, when they got into their argument, he forgot. Morrow doesn't accept this story.

Whatever the truth, the result is that when Morrow arrives at court the next morning, he finds the several-inches-thick testimony of Driesell on his desk and is greeted with the news from

Harding that the ex-coach will be taking the stand after David Gregg.

"I said, 'Why didn't you give it [the testimony] to me last night?' He said, 'I forgot.' . . . 'I was in your office last night and you forgot that Lefty was going to testify and that maybe I want the grand jury testimony? . . . That's bullshit.' For the first time in the trial I really started getting pissed. 'Well, how about I have an opportunity to read through this before we call Lefty?' He said, 'No, we're getting ready to go now.' So at that I went to the judge. I figured there's no point in even talking to Bonsib. I said, 'Judge, . . . I was supposed to have these transcripts in advance of the witness's testimony, and I just received this today and Mr. Bonsib did not give it to me last night when I was in his office asking for another piece of critical information because he was busy. I'd like to have an opportunity to read it before the witness gets on the stand.'

"The judge said, 'Well, Mr. Driesell is a very busy man. As you know, he's been kind enough to come down here to share his very limited time with us. I think it would be rude to make him sit around while you read that.'

"I said, 'Well, Your Honor, I surely don't want to be rude to Mr. Driesell, but my client's on trial here, facing twenty years. I think that a couple of technicalities like "due process" and so on would help if I had a chance to read the transcript.' And he said, 'Well, Mr. Bonsib, why don't you just tell us what Mr. Driesell is going to say? And, you know, maybe it's going to be short or something like that? And then we don't need that.' "

Bonsib answers that Driesell is being called essentially to confirm the testimony of Gregg and Long. He wants to dispel the idea that Long and Gregg were simply making up what Marshall wanted to hear. Morrow is satisfied, Rea is happy there's no cause for recess, and testimony begins.

Driesell is preceded by David Gregg on the stand. Colorlessly, monosyllabically, his long, hollowed face pointing down at the floor, he repeats Long's version of the events of June 18 and explains what happened to the coke.

After Leonard went into seizures Long told him to take the cocaine. He carried the mirror into his room and shook the powder into a bag—a "cookie bag or something," he says, demonstrating with the coffee creamer again. His hand had been shaking and at least half the powder spilled onto the dorm-room floor. He came back into the room and gave Tribble the bag—he doesn't say Tribble asked for it—and he never saw the coke again. Then, after the paramedics left he returned, spraying cleanser on the carpet and running the foam into the spilled coke. He says he had taken coke, since his freshman year, and confirms Long's account of the party after the North Carolina State game, adding that Tribble went to sleep while they tooted through the night. He insists his testimony is the truth, but indicates Marshall yelled and screamed a lot at him and Long when they lied to him at first.

Then Driesell enters, his large, beefy frame filling the witness box.

"You don't need a microphone, do you, Coach?" asks Judge Rea, joking with the living legend.

Driesell breaks into an easy smile and tells him no. He speaks in his low-keyed drawl, one leg crossed over the other, a log book in his hand. It is the first time he has talked about the events of that night under oath in public testimony; everyone in the courtroom waits to hear what he has to say about himself—not his testimony about Tribble.

"They were very emotional," he says about Long and Gregg when they met with him in the basement of his house. "David kept saying, 'Terry, tell coach what happened!' Long said Bias came in real late and he and Brian came in together or maybe Brian came later and that Brian brought in coke and that Leonard took it and that Brian said, 'Don't put your head back when you snort, you'll get a header,' but Leonard said, 'I'm tough,' and threw his head back and he had a seizure and then it happened again and Long administered CPR and they called the paramedics."

For all the reporters in the room of course, this testimony is news. Driesell's statement contradicts his previous denials of knowing anything about drugs; the next day every paper calls attention to the discrepancy.

But for Morrow Driesell's description has another significance.

"It was obvious to me that that was the one piece of evidence that had been missing in the case from the beginning. Someone who would say that Brian Tribble brought the coke in. They didn't have that before. Long and Gregg didn't give that to them. But now Lefty's trying to give it to them through something Long and Gregg said. Not only was it not prior consistent testimony, it was prior testimony inconsistent with what they testified in court."

At first Morrow believes Bonsib too has been surprised by Driesell's testimony. "I . . . felt that, well, nobody with the reputation of Bob Bonsib is going to pull a trick like that. . . . So I dutifully made my motion for a mistrial and then the judge predictably denied it. [Then] at lunchtime [I] read the [grand jury] transcript. Much to my surprise, at three separate points in the transcript Lefty says the same thing: Long and Gregg told him Brian brought it into the room. So my new perspective is that it *wasn't* a mistake, it *wasn't* inadvertent on Lefty's part, Bonsib *wasn't* surprised by that particular testimony. My only rational conclusion is that he knew *exactly* what he was doing, and my only conclusion from the facts is, that he deliberately misled me.

"Then Harding comes up . . . after I get done reading the transcript. And he says, 'Are we all squared away? Are you ready to go?' I launched into him and Ava Lias launched into him. I had never seen her so exercised. She said, 'I can't understand how you can walk in here, after what you just pulled.' He said, 'What are you talking about?' She said, 'We just read the transcript.' She was beside herself, she was so upset. I was afraid I was going to smack him. . . . I was afraid that if I started talking I was going to get more and more angry, and I didn't want to do anything that I would later regret. . . . Then we went down to court . . . I made my tirade about having been misled, it was the most blatant instance of prosecutorial misconduct that I had ever witnessed. . . . At that point . . . I felt that there were no longer any parameters of trying to play the game by the rules and be real fair. I [thought] I had been ambushed intentionally, and I felt that that was a classic example of proving to me that the prosecution was determined to get my client, whatever the price."

After the judge instructs the jury to disregard Driesell's testimony concerning Tribble, the prosecution concludes its case with two witnesses.

Gail Diamond, Julie Walker's roommate, a large woman wearing big, round glasses and carrying a Judith Krantz novel, stares at Bonsib with a look of quizzical disbelief as she tells the little she has already reported to the grand jury about Brian's safe.

The last to testify is a muscular, black PGC police officer named Ray Evans. He is decked out in thick gold rings and bracelets, the sort of gaudy show Leonard himself was attracted to. An undercover cop, he says he worked at Classics as a bouncer as a part-time job. There he saw Bias about once a month. He saw Tribble more frequently. Tribble used to come on the nights when customers dressed casually. He would arrive around eleven and leave around one. He would be treated differently from other customers; he seemed well known and never had a problem getting a seat. When he entered he would talk to lots of people, shake lots of hands, and drink lots of champagne—there was always a bottle of champagne on his table, sometimes Dom Perignon. The people he talked to were special too: they usually made trips outside or went to the bathroom. The trips to the bathroom lasted five minutes—and sometimes they would be to the same stall. Sometimes the females would take something from the males and go into the bathroom by themselves. From the behavior he observed it appeared to him possible that narcotics transactions were taking place.

"Do you go to Classics?" Morrow starts, after a denunciation of Evans's testimony as something from the Salem witch trials and a routine motion for mistrial.

"Yes," Evans answers in an annoyed mumble.

"Are you a dope dealer?"

"No," the police officer answers. "That's ludicrous."

Morrow pesters him, asking whether Evans is familiar with a series of drug tests. Evans says no—which seems suspicious for a cop experienced in narcotics work, except Morrow is mixing false test names with real ones, hoping to show the man's a liar.

"As a police officer aren't you obligated to stop a misdemeanor or felony?" he asks.

"I have to take a break sometime," Evans replies.

"You watch a lot of people in the bathroom?"
"I watch people pretty much doing anything."
"You spend a lot of time in the bathroom."
"A fair amount of time."
"If I shook the hand of the foreman of the jury you wouldn't think we were engaged in a dope deal."
"I'd have to observc further."

~~~

The next day is a holiday. Rea declares the court recessed until next Monday at twelve o'clock, when he can return from his daughter's high-school graduation. Bonsib leaves, desperately annoyed at himself. In a long trial it's the little things that can kill your case; the judge has already instructed the jury to disregard Driesell's testimony about Tribble. If Rea admonishes him and Harding for prosecutorial misconduct when the trial resumes, the jury might be convinced that their case is bogus.

"I went that night to a Bar meeting. And I was telling people that I know and that I respect in the Bar, that I screwed up that thing, because I really felt like we made a judgment call that was bad. That we should have given it to him the night before, and it bothered me. But in the heat of a battle, and this was a hard-fought trial, sometimes you make mistakes. And we made a mistake. . . . He should have had it the night before so he had the evening to read it. And if there's *anything* I could change in that whole trial, I would change that. Really, that's the only thing that I would change in the whole trial. But we didn't and we made the judgment and we made a mistake, and I have to live with that. And I do. We paid the price during the trial for it. There's no question."

The mistake harms Bonsib's case in another way. He and Harding have always wanted Tribble to testify. Thcy believe if Tribble takes the stand they will be able to destroy his credibility. "We had a fair amount of ammunition on him. . . . Why did he have a safe at somebody else's apartment? Why was he over there first thing in the morning after his friend had just died? Why did he leave the hospital so quickly, when all of Bias's other friends stayed
~~~

around? Why did he go back in the car? What did he do with that cocaine, after he's alleged to have taken it out of the room? Why did he stuff it under the dashboard? Why did he even take it from the room? Why didn't he flush it down the toilet? Was it because it was worth so much money and he wasn't going to flush it? I mean all of these are questions that could have been asked."

But now—because of the flap over Driesell—Morrow takes advantage of his client's constitutional right not to testify and denies the prosecution the chance of questioning Tribble.

"I thought Brian would make a good witness," Morrow says. "And I still think he would have made a good witness. . . . But . . . the state had made it clear to me that they were going to do anything they had to do to get him. And I figured that would apply to his testimony in cross-examination. The judge had indicated that [he] wasn't going to be a filter. The judge was letting lots of stuff in . . . and I figured the same thing was going to happen when [Tribble] took the stand. . . . They were going to bring out every rumor, every bit of gossip . . . and just totally destroy his character on the basis of the fact that if they couldn't prove he was guilty, they could at least prove that he was a scumbag and hopefully the jury would find him guilty on that basis. So I just decided that I wasn't going to subject him or his family to that."

Without Tribble, the defense is minimal. After still more motions for mistrial—Ava Lias presents them this time, Judge Rea coaxing her along with his pleased smile—Morrow presents three witnesses.

The first stuns the court. Sherrie Hersey is a striking, long-legged young woman with dyed red and blonde hair that falls in cornrows down one side and is gathered into a crowd of wild curls on the other. To the amazement of the courtroom observers, she announces that she works at the post office. But everything she says after that is anticlimactic. She is the mystery woman reported to have been with Tribble the night of Leonard's death. She testifies she was with Tribble at his apartment when Leonard arrived;

while waiting in the living room for Tribble to get dressed, she accidentally sat on Bias's carrycase and Leonard told her to get off of his pouch. Then Bias drove her and Tribble to her house in Washington.

Next Johnny Walker recounts the story of searching the car.

Finally, Julie Walker reclaims Tribble's character. He never drank champagne at Classics, never drank Dom Perignon—she had never even known what the "wine" was until she read it in the newspaper. Tribble had offered her the use of his safe. She doubts he opened it regularly, since the safe was in her closet and she never noticed her clothes or luggage disturbed. Brian had a beeper because his parents needed to contact him during a period of Priscilla's sickness. Tribble didn't mingle with people anymore than anybody else in Classics.

More telling than any of her testimony is her appearance. The "freak" Terrence Moore referred to is a woman of enormous self-possession. Her schedule would do Benjamin Franklin proud: work from eight to five-thirty in the afternoon, followed by three hours of school. Bonsib tries to damage her during his cross, barraging her with questions about the safe and Tribble's friends. But she remains unscathed. When she rises from the combat and leaves the witness chair, she gives Mrs. Tribble a large, open wink, and it is impossible not to think that Tribble's mother is wondering when her son is going to get smart and marry the girl.

The only thing left is a mistrial motion.

The jury is excused and the arguing begins. Morrow issues a double challenge, asking the judge to drop or sever once again the conspiracy charge and also to declare a mistrial on the basis of prosecutorial misconduct regarding the Driesell testimony. Looking up at the judge, his face twisted with disdain, as though simply being part of this process is distasteful, he tells Rea the business with Driesell's testimony is the worst case of prosecutorial abuse he has ever witnessed.

Rea listens in his usual posture, leaning back reflectively. Well, he asks, doesn't Morrow think that a curative instruction to the jury would be sufficient to compensate?

Normally he couldn't agree with the judge more, Morrow says, but the inflammation in this case is too high—

Bonsib enters the duel and the two attorneys fence, a dry run of the final arguments that will start this afternoon. Morrow and Mrs. Tribble were the only people guilty of pretrial publicity, says Bonsib. No one can find an instance when the state said something about the evidence. 'Neither have I,' answers Morrow, 'I haven't *begun* commenting on the evidence in this case.'

After lunch Judge Rea makes up his mind for the last time. In his sleepy drone, rubbing his eyes, he declares the state is guilty of misconduct, but that the grievance is insufficient to declare a mistrial. The case will go to jury.

For a good hour before the final arguments the judge instructs the jury.

His voice wandering in and out of the thick woods of legal paragraphs, Rea reads what laws pertain to the case and how the jury should interpret them. The defendant is presumed innocent. The state has the burden of proving its case to a moral certainty. A reasonable doubt is a doubt founded on reason, not caprice or whimsy. In making their decision the jurors must consider the evidence. In evaluating the evidence they must consider their own experience and common sense. His monotone parses each charge. Conspiracy is a crime distinct from other crimes. Possession may be actual or constructive. By now three jurors are catnapping, the long-hair rousing Morrow's polyester gamble out of his sleep with a couple of gentle nudges. Yet the moment is impressive. Rea's voice trails and sometimes he stumbles over himself as he enters into the specifics of each charge, but inexorably the moral and social gravity of the undertaking emerges. For one moment the jurors will remove themselves from all the distractions that cloud everyday judgment and determine what is true and what is just. Who ever thought a dope trial could possess such dignity?

When Judge Rea is finished Bonsib goes into his argument. In his opening statement Morrow referred to the anniversary of the

Constitution. Now Bonsib reminds the jury of the coming bicentennial. This trial, he continues, wanting to answer any accusations of misconduct by the government, honors the tradition about to be celebrated. The trial represents the ideal way of bringing a defendant to the bar of justice. No one can claim Mr. Tribble has not enjoyed every chance of a fair trial. He is going to review the evidence in the trial and if he forgets some evidence it's only because there is so much. He speaks with a reasonable, calm tone, arms crossed in his favorite position, a teacher laying out to his students how they should approach a problem. Quickly he gets to the heart of his argument. Was Len Bias bad? No. He was a role model. A hero. But heroes have weaknesses. He liked cocaine. And Mr. Tribble took advantage of that weakness, fed that weakness and eventually let that weakness destroy Mr. Bias. So he is not going to hold anything back about Mr. Bias. Bias was a technical distributor of drugs. But he was not a drug dealer. And now the jury should wipe him out of their mind because there is only one real issue here: Is Mr. Tribble a drug dealer?

Pointing to two charts made on construction paper, Bonsib shows the dimension of Tribble's crime. On the first chart are added up the various amounts of coke found in the dorm and car. A minimum of one ounce, he announces after his dramatic addition of one gram to another. Eighteen hundred to twenty-four hundred dollars worth of cocaine. That's a lot of cocaine, ladies and gentleman.

The second chart could come from the Wharton School: it consists of a series of circles showing the hierarchy of Tribble's supposed drug network. At the top is a circle with an X representing Mr. Big, the unknown source. Under him is Tribble. Fanning out from Tribble's circle are spheres representing Moore and Bias and other runners Moore implied worked for Tribble.

Then he launches his attack on Tribble. Mr. Morrow has made a lot of Gregg and Long's not informing the emergency crew about Bias's using cocaine. But Mr. Tribble never said anything either—and Mister Tribble was his best friend! If Bias had cocaine himself, why did he go with Tribble? When Gregg asked where the coke came from Bias didn't speak, Tribble did. And on the night after the North Carolina game, Bias didn't have the cocaine; he and Gregg and Long went to Tribble's house.

He's halfway through his argument, but the jury already looks bored and skeptical. One woman juror stares out the window, clearly not interested in what he's saying. Bonsib realizes he's in trouble, but he plows ahead. Mr. Tribble wanted to attach himself to the rising star of Mr. Bias—goodness knows where Tribble could have gone after that! And if the coke in the bag wasn't Tribble's then why didn't Tribble get rid of it? Because Tribble isn't a fool: he wasn't going to throw a thousand dollars of his product away on a whim. He even blames Moore's troubles on Tribble—Moore may be a juvenile delinquent, but Mr. Tribble was partly responsible for making him that way. "This is the case of a drug dealer, neither more nor less. We are asking nothing more than fair verdict."

Morrow starts with an apology. He's sorry he's been emotional, but he can't hide his feelings. Arguing a case like this is a tough thing: Is he asking the right questions? Is he asking enough questions? Is he asking too many questions? He's sorry about something else too. He doesn't have any props . . . except one—this young man here. He puts his hand on Tribble's shoulder and leads him over to the jury, the young man whose future, he reminds them, will soon be commended to their judgment.

Morrow goes on for over an hour. He is in his favorite mode, full attack.

Mr. Harding promised you Long and Gregg were going to say the coke came from Tribble, he tells them. I told you I didn't think so. I kept my promise, Mr. Harding didn't. Mr. Bonsib says this is a fair trial. Then why aren't Gregg and Long on trial? Mr. Bonsib talks about physical evidence. But what is the physical evidence? Reasonable doubt, ladies and gentlemen of the jury. Reasonable doubt. One way of thinking of reasonable doubt is as light through a curtain. When something is missing, when something doesn't make sense that's a reasonable doubt. And everything in the case seems to admit some reasonable doubt. Why would a big-time dealer worry about a thousand-dollar bag of coke? That's a reasonable doubt. And what about the bag that presumably Gregg said he put the coke in. Gregg said the present container "was similar" to the bag. What about Moore? The jury saw the "freaks" he talked about? Were Julie Walker and Gail Diamond "freaks?" What about the telephone number that was in Moore's book? Well, over the weekend he checked the number. The number doesn't relate to Tribble at all. The number is for the Prince George's County Department of Aging—and not just that number. He's called every possible variation of the digits and none of them have any possible relation to Tribble. Reasonable doubt, ladies and gentleman—and I suggest that's not light coming through the curtain, it's the noonday sun!

Unlike Bonsib, Morrow pumps himself up as he argues. The jurors listen attentively. His energy is communicating itself as truth to them.

In his seat, Bonsib realizes he has made a mistake—not of fact, he is certain, but of temperament. Somehow he has misgauged the nature of the trial. He has viewed it as a dope-dealing case; now it becomes clear to him the case is much more complicated than that—it is a judgment of a community and a hero.

And Morrow is still just warming up. The state's attempt to drag Lenny Bias's name through the mud is shameful and embarrassing, he tells the jury. Officer Evans. How do you confront evidence like that produced by Ray Evans? People shaking hands, going to the bathroom, walking out to the parking lot. His scorn is palpable. That's the evidence the state produced for me that I was to attack, ladies and gentlemen—I might as well try to tack Jell-O to the wall as attack that sort of evidence.

And why has the state allowed itself to do this, to put on this shameful episode? Because it wants to protect Arthur Marshall and the University of Maryland.

"These two gentleman here have referred to themselves throughout this trial as the State of Maryland. The State of Maryland—like they sit on some big chair somewhere overlooking the rest of us while they're the State of Maryland and they decide what the law of the State of Maryland is and they decide what the violations of the law of the State of Maryland are and they decide who is going to pay the price. Well, let me suggest something to you, ladies and gentleman. These two people are not the State of Maryland. They're two attorneys. That's all. You—each and every one of you as you perform your duty and evaluate this evidence—you're the State of Maryland. . . . So don't answer to anybody.

. . . Answer to no one but yourselves. . . . Ladies and gentleman, if Len Bias were here today, he would be ashamed—ashamed of the State of Maryland for attempting to make a scapegoat of his best friend. . . . And if you're going to make yourselves a party to making Brian Tribble a scapegoat, then we have got nothing on Iran or South Africa or Russia. . . . I pray that that doesn't happen in the State of Maryland in 1987, because if Brian Tribble is convicted on the evidence that has been produced before you in this case, may God have mercy on every one of us."

Watching Morrow, Bonsib considers how best to refute the defense's arguments.

"It [Morrow's closing] was, I thought, an attempt on his part to try to throw as many possible things for the jury to hang their hat on us, as he could. Number one, the prosecution's being unfair. Number two, this is a racial thing, without saying it. Number three, there's no evidence that my client brought it in. Number four, they're attacking Bias here—how can they attack a dead man, who can't defend himself? Number five, my client didn't bring it in. Therefore, without saying it, Bias must have brought it in. I mean he was able, on one hand, to say they're smearing Bias by calling him a dope dealer, yet at the same time he is inferring that since his client didn't bring it in, that somebody else *had* to, and the only other person that the evidence showed could have brought it in, was Bias. And he put it together very, very effectively. So I thought he did just a superb job in his closing argument. . . . I knew that he was scoring points, and I was having some question about how to come back and deal with the various moves. Morrow had lived through this case from Day One, and I could see right then that he had a better sense of the emotional undercurrents of the case than I did. I was up in Baltimore all that time. . . . I didn't plan on a closing argument that was going to deal with the emotion and the jury's collective sense of what this whole thing was about. I was focusing strictly on the evidence. . . . I tried to come back, and to argue some of the facts. I also tried to come back with some emotion . . . to let [the jury] know that we take offence at being accused of unfairly prosecuting this guy, that we believe this man is a dope dealer, and if he's a dope dealer, he's not a nice person. And that they ought to convict him."

Before Morrow sits, Bonsib springs up, cheeks flushed with fury.

"Ladies and gentleman," he shouts, voice quivering, "I am not Bud Marshall's man! I was hired by Alex Williams to clean up this community. I don't have to listen to Mr. Morrow's rantings and ravings to save his dope-dealing client. I don't care if this man is acquitted or convicted, I'll still get my paycheck. But"—he crosses over to Morrow's table—"look at him!" "Look at him!" he repeats, taking full advantage of the freedom permitted in closing arguments. He points to Tribble. His rage is insuppressible. "This man is a dope dealer!"

Sitting next to Tribble, Morrow makes a note to motion yet again for a mistrial because of Bonsib's abuse of the client.

At ten to two the jury recesses. Morrow refuses to speculate. "I never attempt to predict what the jury's going to do or how long it will stay out. I'm too deeply enmeshed in the case. The only thing I'm sure of is that whatever I say I'll be wrong."

While the jury deliberates there is the time to review everything, to ask the question that every reporter, every observer is thinking: How would you vote? "I don't know what I'd do," says one local courtroom buff. "I listen to one side and I'm persuaded and I listen to the other and I go the other way." Morrow has clearly won on the legalities of the case; and Bonsib's tantrum at the end was embarrassing. So surely one would vote not guilty on all the serious counts. Maybe enter a guilty verdict on possession—though how are Long and Gregg less culpable of this criminal act than Tribble?

Still, the hypothetical verdict is unsatisfactory. Too much has been left unanswered. Indeed, as the reporters review and re-review the trial—at six or so the jury is still out and Judge Rea, ever vigilant, commands them to order box dinners and take a little walk before resuming their work—the common opinion is that the trial has posed more questions than it has answered. Why didn't Baxter see the powder if it was in the car? Why didn't Tribble throw the coke away? Both Long and Gregg went to get beers separately when they woke up—what a coincidence! What the hell was the safe doing at Julie Walker's? Morrow has always dismissed the safe as another instance of Tribble's bad judgment, a kid trying to be a bigshot. But not a lot of twenty-four-year-olds have private safes they keep in their best friend's house. While it is impossible to imagine that Tribble arranged the robbery at Walker's, the coincidence of the theft and Bias's death is remarkable. Yet the state offered no substantial proof Tribble was a dealer. After a year of extensive investigating the only person they could dig up to testify against him was a mean, scared kid facing years and years in prison—and they didn't discover him until a month before the trial began! It's impossible to believe Tribble is a mastermind drug dealer; it's equally difficult to accept the notion he's an innocent, unknown in Montana Terrace. Morrow makes fun of Moore's testimony about Bias. But Leonard is the kid who would do anything for a few extra bucks, the guy who sold T-shirts of himself down in North Carolina, autographed pictures for a couple of bucks; one night he went with Tribble to clean an office, liking the heavy, manual work, liking the hundred bucks he got at the end. Everyone always said about him that he always needed money, he always had money. So one day he sells something. It's not unimaginable.

At seven the jury finishes dinner. "Well they've been fed and walked now, so they can work the rest of the night," says Judge Rea, as though the tribe of twelve is a thoroughbred in his stables. He and Morrow and some reporters trade PGC stories. Morrow tells about his walk-on role in the film *And Justice For All.* "I didn't see you in that," says Judge Rea. "That's because Pacino was so worried about my thespian abilities he had all my scenes cut," answers Morrow.

Shortly after nine, word comes that the jury has decided. There is the rush for the seats. Even at this last moment, the guards at the door check the reporters for possible guns and knives. But no one can keep order. The reporters fling the contents of their pockets on the desk and hurry into the courtroom. They cram the front seats, the squad from the *Washington Post* arranging between themselves who will cover which attorney, who will interview the family.

The rest of the assemblage enters: Tribble, flanked by Morrow and Ava Lias; Bonsib and Harding; Mrs. Tribble and her children, daughter on one side and stern-eyed Junior on the other. Mr. Tribble is home with Priscilla.

For the last time, Mr. Luckett—he gives Mrs. Tribble an encouraging smile—adopts his stern face and tells the court: "All rise! All rise! The superior court is now in session. Honorable Justice Rea presiding."

Sleepy-eyed and skeptical, Rea mounts the stage and tells Mr. Luckett he can let the jurors in.

The familiar twelve troop in, one laughing before walking through the door.

The court clerk announces the historical call: "Harken to the members of the jury. Do you all agree?"

The foreman rises, a white-haired engineer who spent most of the time listening to the testimony with an impassive, studious face.

"How do you find?"

In the front-row bench Mrs. Tribble stiffens and grasps the arm of her daughter for the comfort of flesh.

"We find the defendant Brian Tribble—"

She gasps—as though she can breathe for the first time since last summer. If there won't be truth, there will at least be mercy: the jury declares Brian Tribble innocent.

EPILOGUE

A month after Tribble's acquittal, James Bias filed a civil suit charging Leonard's life-insurance company, the Fidelity Security Life Insurance Company, Reebok International, and Advantage International with breach of fiduciary duty and breach of contract, negligence, fraud, and negligent misrepresentation. After more than a year, the judge dismissed charges: the Biases are pursuing the case on appeal.

Advantage, Lee Fentress's firm, remained unaffected by Leonard's death. The following year they signed David Robinson, an upstanding Navy midshipman who was touted to be the next decade's dominating center. Fentress refused to discuss Leonard's death, his press secretary and attorney saying he wanted to put the tragedy behind him and look to the future.

Driesell refused to admit his court testimony contradicted his previous statements. "I didn't know that drugs had killed him," he told the press after his appearance in Upper Marlboro, "and I wasn't going to say that unless I was positive." In the spring, around the second anniversary of Leonard's death, he announced he was accepting an offer from James Madison University in western Virginia, a school eager to gain recognition through its sports program. Looking for some gimmick to announce his return, Driesell held a twelve-midnight practice on the first day allowed by NCAA. The old salesman was back: Driesell's unorthodox, headline-stealing scrimmage made the front page of the *New York Times* Sunday sports section.

Chancellor John Slaughter also left the University of Maryland, becoming president of Occidental College in Los Angeles, a prestigious liberal arts school. Robert Wade, the man he appointed to take Driesell's place, coached Maryland into the NCAA playoffs his second year, but was criticized for being too hard a taskmaster. The following winter the NCAA announced it was investigating violations in the Terrapin basketball program. In the spring of 1989, Wade resigned, according to his public statement, "for the best interests of family, the basketball team, and the university community." His resignation agreement included receipt of 60 percent of his salary, the sale of his house at fair market value, and $5,000 for moving expenses. Three years after Leonard's death, the university announced a new national search for a basketball coach. Dick Dull remained unemployed for at least a year.

The night of the Tribble victory, Morrow went to a bar with some reporters.

"We stopped someplace, and I felt that, Christ, I would walk in there and there'd be lights and cameras everywhere I went. Instead the bar was dark and nobody knew who I was. Here I am with these newsguys who want to talk to me, and I walked in and said, 'Hey! Everybody recognize me?' It was the first opportunity for any celebrity I've ever had, and I was surprised how quickly it was forgotten. Reality is a harsh mistress." A short time later, he left Weinberg and Green to open his own practice. In one recent case, he argued that his client, accused of murder, was a cocaine addict made crazy by his dependency and therefore could not be held responsible for his actions. "They laughed it out of court."

Bob Bonsib second-guessed his trial strategy for a few weeks after the verdict. But he remained committed to his judgment about what occurred on the night of June 18. "There were factors other than simply strict evaluation of the evidence that might have gone into the verdict. Twelve people. Maybe they're right. Maybe they're wrong. I certainly respect their verdict and by their verdict they found not guilty, so he was not proven [guilty] beyond a reasonable doubt. And, again, I'm not accusing Tribble of now being a dealer, because that wouldn't be fair. He's been acquitted and he should be presumed to be innocent. But if you're asking for my subjective, personal opinion as to whether we put on a case, and whether I would put on the same case today, and whether I felt comfortable that what we were putting on were the facts as we thought them to be, the answer is yes, and there's been no change in that."

Terrence Moore went to jail.

Congress passed a new drug bill in the fall of 1988 that for the first time committed significant money to treatment and drug education. Upon taking power, the Bush administration showed that it saw drugs solely as a law-and-order issue. In January Bush named William Bennett, the ex-Secretary of Education, his new drug czar. Shortly after, the administration tried to capitalize on public horror at the use of semi-automatic weapons by the crack gangs. He called for the National Guard to patrol Washington, D.C., to stop the escalating violence of the crack wars in the nation's capital. Although the impact of the new drug bill had yet to be felt, the future was not particularly hopeful. In 1988, on average, more than one murder had been committed per day in D.C., a record-breaking statistic; the next year threatened to set an even higher record. Other indicators signaled that perhaps the crack tide was receding, but only after having created a level of public tolerance for drug use that would have been unthinkable even in the sixties.

Terry Long disappeared into Richmond, his hometown, out of reach of the members of the press who bothered him, the coaches who let him down, the attorney who saved him.

David Gregg worked with Bob Wagner to get into another school. When a writer asked to interview him, his hardworking stepfather, who had raised him, demanded some payment. In the age of television and movies, he believed everyone was profiting off the calamity of his son.

"I loved Leonard Bias," Brian Tribble said the night he was freed. "I always have. I always will." For a while after his acquittal he enjoyed celebrity. He hosted a nightclub—Brian Tribble night—and entertained the idea of becoming an actor or model. An agent contacted him; Tribble flew out to the Midwest to speak to a writer who would coauthor a book with him, but the deal seemed to cost him money rather than earn it, and he lost interest. In the spring, his older brother, Junior, was busted by the police on a number of drug and drug-related charges. He pled guilty to two counts and was sentenced to six months with five years' probation. The word in prison, said one longtime PGC lawyer, was that one guy the police would pay anything for was Tribble: if you had something that would nail him, you could name your price.

The secret of Leonard's lost hours that final night, the subject of so much energy and speculation, remain Tribble's privileged possession. It is doubtful he will ever share that information with the world and it is doubtful that what he has to say would provide the simple explanation people want. More likely the final clue would only lead to new mysteries. After all, it was not Tribble but Leonard who started the lies. Son, lover, player, and the other variations on these themes, Christian, stud, meal ticket—in whose presence did Leonard ever present these separate pieces as one whole, seamless self? Fragmentation was a circumstance of his life.

After Leonard died there was of course the possibility of seeing him whole. But people didn't want to and no hero emerged to challenge their reluctance and insist on the truth. Leonard's death was the worst crime a society can commit against itself: the destruction of one of its own children. But this tragedy was followed only by another: the refusal to confront what had happened.

Yet it would be violating Leonard's own spirit to end his story on a note of defeat. Despair is not what you hear when you talk to those who knew him; you hear the voices of people in love. With all his limitations, Leonard possessed one transcendent gift: the gift of appetite. For those who shared his life, it was his passion—his desire, curiosity, daring, his unique mix of grace and aggression—that made him a star, not his scoring average or future wealth. He represented for them the sense of infinite possibility, the raw quick of life that is embodied in the image of youth. His loss is our diminution; the memory of his abiding promise is our hope.

About the Author

Lewis Cole has published two previous books on basketball, *A Loose Game* and *Dream Team.* He has written for *Rolling Stone*, *Manhattan Inc.*, and other magazines, and teaches screenwriting at Columbia University. He lives in New York with his wife and son.